Building Theory in Political Communication

JOURNALISM AND POLITICAL COMMUNICATION UNBOUND

Series editors: Daniel Kreiss, University of North Carolina at Chapel Hill, and Nikki Usher, University of Illinois at Urbana-Champaign

Journalism and Political Communication Unbound seeks to be a high- profile book series that reaches far beyond the academy to an interested public of policymakers, journalists, public intellectuals, and citizens eager to make sense of contemporary politics and media. "Unbound" in the series title has multiple meanings: It refers to the unbinding of borders between the fields of communication, political communication, and journalism, as well as related disciplines such as political science, sociology, and science and technology studies; it highlights the ways traditional frameworks for scholarship have disintegrated in the wake of changing digital technologies and new social, political, economic, and cultural dynamics; and it reflects the unbinding of media in a hybrid world of flows across mediums.

Other books in the series:

Building Theory in Political Communication

The Politics-Media-Politics Approach

GADI WOLFSFELD,

TAMIR SHEAFER,

and

SCOTT ALTHAUS

OXFORD
UNIVERSITY PRESS

OXFORD
UNIVERSITY PRESS

Oxford University Press is a department of the University of Oxford. It furthers
the University's objective of excellence in research, scholarship, and education
by publishing worldwide. Oxford is a registered trade mark of Oxford University
Press in the UK and certain other countries.

Published in the United States of America by Oxford University Press
198 Madison Avenue, New York, NY 10016, United States of America.

Library of Congress Cataloging-in-Publication Data
Names: Wolfsfeld, Gadi, author. | Sheafer, Tamir, author. | Althaus, Scott L., 1966– author.
Title: Building theory in political communication : the politics-media-politics approach /
Gadi Wolfsfeld, Tamir Sheafer, Scott Althaus.
Description: New York, NY : Oxford University Press, 2022. |
Series: Journalism and political communication |
Includes bibliographical references and index.
Identifiers: LCCN 2022020179 (print) | LCCN 2022020180 (ebook) |
ISBN 9780197634998 (hardback) | ISBN 9780197635001 (paperback) |
ISBN 9780197635025 (epub)
Subjects: LCSH: Communication in politics. |
Mass media—Political aspects. | Press and politics.
Classification: LCC JA85 .W649 2022 (print) | LCC JA85 (ebook) |
DDC 320.01/4—dc23/eng/20220622
LC record available at https://lccn.loc.gov/2022020179
LC ebook record available at https://lccn.loc.gov/2022020180

DOI: 10.1093/oso/9780197634998.001.0001

1 3 5 7 9 8 6 4 2

Paperback printed by Lakeside Book Company, United States of America
Hardback printed by Bridgeport National Bindery, Inc., United States of America

This book is dedicated to my ever-growing family: Lauren, Noa, Dana, Eli, Shay, Shakked, Matan, Adva, and Ram.
—Gadi Wolfsfeld

To Alona, Ido, Shaked, and Nitzan.
—Tamir Sheafer

To Colin, Kyra, and Curtis.
—Scott Althaus

Contents

Acknowledgments

This book project started in 2013 when Tamir and Gadi drafted a coauthored paper for the American Political Science Association conference that proposed using the PMP approach as an organizing principle to help scholars adopt a more comprehensive approach to thinking about political communication. An extended email conversation about that paper with Scott resulted in a rough outline for a coauthored book that was shared among the three of us in October 2013. It's taken eight years since then to organize our thoughts, reorganize them, scrap them, reorganize them again, wait for Scott to scramble the mix still further, and then sort it all out into some semblance of chapter drafts. We had some of the best arguments with one another in writing this book, as well as some of the most satisfying brainstorming sessions any of the three of us can remember. Laughter frequently ensued, frustrations emerged and resolved as conceptual differences were clarified, and the book made slow but steady progress toward its current form.

In many ways, this book remains a work in progress, because our hope in publishing it is to expand this fruitful conversation beyond the three of us to include scholarly colleagues around the world and across many disciplines. And we never would have made it this far were it not for the generosity of colleagues and students to provide feedback and reactions that sharpened our thinking and enlarged our theoretical horizons to imagine the political communication field from a much higher and also more granular vantage point than we ever had when the project started.

The faults and weaknesses of the arguments presented here are ours alone, but the innovations and strengths often originated in feedback we received from many generous colleagues along the way. We are grateful to Eran Amsalem, Christian Baden, Meital Balmas, Amber Boydstun, Dan Hallin, Ben Miller, Lilach Nir, Eike Rinke, Julie Sevenans, Shaul Shenhav, Knut De Swert, Rens Vliegenthart, Stefaan Walgrave, Hartmut Wessler, and Alon Zoizner, along with participants at the 2018 Deliberative Quality of Communication Conference at the Mannheimer Zentrum für Europäische Sozialforschung (Germany), participants at the 2019 Political Communication Pre-Conference for the American Association for Political

Science annual meeting, and students in Scott's 2019 graduate seminar on political communication for stimulating us to produce a better final product than ever would have been possible without their constructive feedback and encouragement.

We are especially indebted to Lance Bennett, Michael Delli Carpini, Regina Lawrence, Moran Yarchi, and Barbara Pfetsch for detailed comments on several draft chapters that greatly sharpened our thinking, and to Peter van Aelst and Andreas Jungherr, whose extensive comments on the entire manuscript helped us to improve the final book in several key respects.

We also owe a special thanks to our extremely helpful editor at Oxford, Angela Chnapko, the series editors Daniel Kreiss and Nikki Usher, the production team at Oxford, and our copyeditor James Morrison.

1

The Politics-Media-Politics Approach

The field of political communication has come a long way in a short time. Thirty years ago, the field had no dedicated journal. Few researchers identified primarily as political communication scholars. Most of the field's published research originated from and focused on a single country—the United States.

Today we have two specialty journals devoted solely to political communication research. Political communication studies appear regularly in leading journals across several disciplines. Doctoral programs are bursting with young researchers who identify primarily as political communication scholars, and cross-national comparative research is such a vibrant subfield that it has spawned its own handbook industry.

The times are good for political communication research, and yet the field is also straining under the weight of its own successes. Against the ever-growing variety and scale of empirical studies, the theoretical moorings of political communication research are increasingly overextended and underexamined. The opportunities to conduct innovative research on a wide range of political communication phenomena using diverse and nuanced data sources have never been more promising, and yet our ability to synthesize insights across research literature and to make collective sense of what we are finding has never been more wanting.

This gradual dimming of theoretical vision—and along with it, our capacity to grasp the whole from the parts of what we study—has many sources. New communication technologies have produced ever-more-complex divisions of labor between professional news organizations and, in Jay Rosen's memorable phrase, "the people formerly known as the audience" (Rosen, 2006, para 1). Yet many of the field's still-reigning theoretical touchstones, such as agenda setting and indexing, seem to assume a largely unidirectional flow of content from elites to masses. Another source is the pressure to narrow our theoretical scope in order to develop core competence. Few of the key challenges in political communication research can be solved without holistic and interdisciplinary thinking, and yet the mastering

Building Theory in Political Communication. Gadi Wolfsfeld, Tamir Sheafer, and Scott Althaus, Oxford University Press.
© Oxford University Press 2022. DOI: 10.1093/oso/9780197634998.003.0001

of any part of the field's rapidly expanding and increasingly narrow research literature demands subject-matter specialization and deep methodological expertise that necessarily constricts theoretical horizons. There are other origins as well, most stemming from recent developments in the field (Bennett & Pfetsch, 2018).

Three deeper tensions within political communication research that exacerbate theoretical disorientation have roots that go back to the earliest years of our field. First, although media independence from political power is widely celebrated as a necessary condition for the effective functioning of political communication systems, this type of media independence remains hazily conceived, is rarely operationalized in ways that could admit empirical investigation, and is itself a major factor in degrading effective communication between citizens and governments. Instead of clearly describing this key quality of theoretical significance, or what benefit it is supposed to safeguard, the literature tends to offer directional critiques that fault media performance as being insufficiently independent from government power without ever defining what *sufficiently independent* might look like (at least, so says Althaus 2003, 2012). Yet this very literature so desiring of more independent media tends schizophrenically to neglect the longstanding observation that media independence from political power can create perverse incentives to undersupply the informational needs of democratic citizens.

Walter Lippmann in the 1920s (Lippmann, 1922) and the Hutchins Commission in the 1940s (Commission on the Freedom of the Press, 1947) described fundamental tensions in political communication systems that arise when the basis of media power in economic markets is misaligned with the basis of political power in free and fair elections. When the need to attract advertising revenue influences the kinds and amount of political information within easy reach of citizens, then increasing media independence can impair citizens' ability to safeguard their interests. Yet while this foundational insight—which explains why market-driven news tends to undersupply the kinds of high-quality reporting that could benefit informed citizens—remains universally acknowledged, it also remains chronically neglected as a topic of sustained inquiry in political communication research today.

Second, most of the places our field has studied for empirical insights are "WEIRD": Western, educated, industrialized, rich, and democratic (Henrich, Heine, & Norenzayan, 2010). Most scholars of political communication are so-called WEIRDos, too—just ask their students. But most of the world is not. So while we know (or think we know) a great deal about how political communication works in the advanced democracies of Western Europe and North America, we know far less about how any of this applies to anywhere else in the world. Few political communication researchers have much to say about political communication in autocratic regimes, or in the developing world, or in emerging democracies. And while it is clear to many observers that our standard insights may not apply very well to those cases, the field as a whole seems unaware that its most significant debates address matters that hardly concern most of the world at all. This book will not solve these problems, but later chapters will make some tentative steps in what we see as the right direction.

Third, the field of political communication has aspired for decades to accumulate empirical insights relevant for the practice of democracy without quite managing ever to get around to building theory—at least, not the kind of theory that could potentially be falsified. Instead, we are good at building interpretive frameworks that pose as theories. All three coauthors writing these words stand as guilty as the rest and just as proud of the contributions we are criticizing. Interpretive frameworks are necessary steps in theory construction, and there is no shame in building them. But they are intermediary steps. To realize their potential, they must then give birth to claims taking the form of predictions—claims that can be tested and potentially falsified by others. But instead of going the next step to generate falsifiable hypotheses, our field's interpretive frameworks have tended to bloat outward to absorb any exceptions and anomalies that fail to confirm initial intuitions. Like the Blob of science fiction fame, these ever-distending interpretive frameworks smother as they stretch. Their ability to ingest voraciously any evidence contrary to original expectations reveals their limited theoretical utility far more than their potential explanatory power. Hypothesis generation is needed before hypothesis testing can proceed, and for that we need a larger theoretical map on which to orient specific empirical tests.

So we have a gradual dimming of theoretical vision with many causes, of which five seem especially clear: new technologies moving up the expiration date of old theoretical perspectives; required specialization stemming from an abundance of new data, methods, and literatures to master; a difficulty defining media independence from governmental control; a focus on WEIRD cases; and a struggle to gain the theoretical elevation needed to generate testable hypotheses. Yet this bill of particulars is no indictment. It is an opportunity, one that this book hopes to press forward into theoretical momentum for our field.

Gaining this momentum requires a few elements that this book aims to supply. First, we need common points of conceptual reference to better align disparate literatures in ways that cumulate, integrate, and synthesize knowledge across specialty areas. Second, we need a clear focus on the larger systems and dynamic processes in which specific political communication phenomena are situated, so we can better see the connections between seemingly unrelated topics. Third, we need clearly defined evaluative criteria for assessing the performance of media and political activity to replace familiar expressions of knowing disappointment when media systems fail to live up to vaunted expectations. Fourth, we need these evaluative criteria to be useful across regime types (not just advanced democracies of the Northern Hemisphere). Fifth, we need new theoretical vistas for understanding systems of political communication that can move the field past interpretive frameworks and toward development of testable hypotheses.

This book aims to start a larger conversation that will gradually supply these needed elements. We sketch a generalizable conceptual map with broad utility across multiple subfields, which provides some guidelines for moving beyond WEIRD cases, is agnostic to communication technologies, is capable of stimulating development of testable hypotheses, and holds potential for enduring value to the field. The book's chapters aim to illustrate this concept map's basic components, demonstrate how to apply it, and showcase its usefulness.

Our Goals

The ultimate goal of this volume is to contribute to the joint effort for building cumulative knowledge in the field of political communication. We do so by adapting, refining, and extending the Politics Media Politics (PMP) principle (Rahat & Sheafer, 2007; Wolfsfeld, 2004, 2011; Wolfsfeld, Segev, & Sheafer, 2013). It is best to think of PMP as an intentionally broad *conceptual map* that we hope will be adopted and adapted by other researchers working in the field. The PMP conceptual map provides a basis for building cumulative knowledge in a number of ways. First, as more researchers consciously use the map, it will allow them to locate and integrate their studies within the more general body of work in the field. This should prove especially important for researchers working on topics that are not normally theoretically linked. Examples would include those studying the role of the media in election campaigns and those examining the role of the media in terrorism, wars, and other crises. In addition, as with the digital maps that we all use today for getting from here to there, the PMP map allows us to zoom in and out for the purposes of obtaining a variety of conceptual perspectives. This function is critical for thinking about issues such as the level of analysis that one is studying. Finally, a detailed map tells us where we've been and how to get where we want to go.

The second major goal of PMP is to propose two core propositions that serve as critical reference points for everything that follows. The first proposition is entitled the "politics first" proposition and the second is called the "media selection and transformation" proposition. These propositions will be detailed below and will serve as major threads that tie all of the chapters together.

The book's chapters aim to illustrate this concept map's basic components, demonstrate how to apply it, and showcase its usefulness. Taken together, the book's chapters serve to provide:

1. A general conceptual framework for synthesizing and integrating research findings across disparate strands of the political communication literature;
2. That can be applied cross-nationally and over time;
3. To assess how media performance might usefully contribute to successful political performance;
4. Across a wide range of regime types and information systems;
5. With the purpose of cumulating knowledge across diverse and specialized research communities;
6. To increase the efficiency, relevance, and practical importance of scholarly research on the practices of political communication around the world.

In developing this general framework, this book also aims to enlarge and refine the concept of media independence to clarify what it means, why it is politically important, what it looks like in practice, how it is constrained or enlarged, and when it is likely to have important implications for political performance.

The Politics-Media-Politics Principle

The PMP principle can be best understood by first presenting the overall approach and then breaking it down into the two separate propositions raised above. The overall approach states: *The role of all forms of media in politics can be understood as a process in which variations in political ecosystems have a major impact on media systems, values, practices, and resources, which can then have dependent, independent, and conditional effects on political processes.*[1] The reason for starting with this overall principle is to introduce both of our major propositions in one statement. It is important to stress that "all forms of media" include traditional media, digital media, and entertainment media (Chadwick, 2013; Williams & Delli Carpini, 2011).[2]

We start by considering the key dependent variable: political processes. A political process refers to any and all significant phenomena and developments that can be linked to contests and policies which affect who has power over others and how that power is exercised. Most important political processes take time. This is certainly true of the political processes that are of central interest to us in this book: significant changes in public opinions and policies, electoral campaigns, violent conflicts, and attempts to bring peace. There are, however, other political processes that can develop over a much shorter period of time. Examples would include political events that are set in motion by a natural disaster such as an earthquake or a major flood, assassinations of political leaders, and major terrorist attacks. Indeed, as further developed below, in the digital age these sudden disruptions may have become more significant than in the past.

One of the key elements in building our conceptual map is to employ the term *ecosystems*. These are elaborate and interconnected systems that emerge from competitive environments in which resource scarcities provide incentives and impose constraints. We use the term *ecosystem* to encompass the combined influence of structures and incentives operating together to dynamically (and differentially) affect the performance of all political actors and modalities of communication. Throughout the book we shall focus our attention on political ecosystems and communication ecosystems. We will discuss these terms more in detail below and will break them down into three dimensions of analysis: structural, cultural, and situational.

Next, we need to explain what is meant by stating that media can have "dependent, independent, and conditional effects" on political processes. A dependent effect refers to those situations in which media mainly reflect and amplify what is happening in the surrounding political environment. One example will suffice. Consider a situation in which the government has a broad level of elite and public support for a certain policy and, due to a lack of any serious opposition, little dissent emerges through news organizations or social media systems. In such a case, the impact of the media system will be limited to deciding whether to cover or ignore the policy, and if the former, how prominent the coverage should be. We would consider this a dependent effect.

The notion of an independent impact refers to those situations in which various forms of media discuss political issues or events in a particular fashion because of factors that are better attributed to the logic, incentives, and constraints of the communication ecosystems in which they are embedded. One of the best examples of this has to do with the extent to which citizens and journalists in a particular country have easy access to the internet. Such variations in access to the internet can have a significant impact on the role that digital media play in political processes (Chadwick, 2013; Williams & Carpini, 2011). While some might argue that these technological variations can be traced back to political variations, it makes more sense to think of them as independent factors that comprise what we will be calling the communication ecosystem. Nearly all aspects of communication ecosystems will have roots in political processes (e.g., free speech protections enshrined in constitutions or reflecting long-standing social mores and cultural norms), and we agree that political ecosystems often serve as the "first mover" in the development of communication ecosystems. Yet simply stating that "it's politics all the time" would lead to some incorrect inferences about the communication ecosystems' power to affect political processes. As further detailed below, some developments in communication ecosystems do "have a life of their own."

A conditional effect refers to those instances where the effect of different forms of media on a political process varies among different political contexts. Not surprisingly, we deal more with this type of effect in the chapter that deals with comparative political communication (Chapter 5). Thus, the effect of what is known as "strategic media framing" on people's cynicism depends on the country's political culture (Schuck, Boomgaarden, & de Vreese, 2013).

It is also important to emphasize that we want to limit ourselves to talking about those situations in which communication has a significant impact on political processes. We have little interest in minor political changes.

There are many cases when the role of media attention is either minor or insignificant.

In the next part of the discussion, we break down our overall principle into the two specific propositions: The "politics first" proposition and the "media selection and transformation" proposition.

The Politics-First Proposition

The politics-first proposition states: *The role of all forms of media in politics can best be understood as one in which variations in political ecosystems are the most important factors leading to variations in communication systems, values, practices, and resources.*

Politics is said to come first both empirically and analytically. The more empirical and testable part of the argument is that media almost always react to changes in the political world, rather than initiating them. This is especially obvious when discussing political events. When it comes to traditional media, editors assign journalists to certain "beats," and then journalists "report" what happens. The reason for the quotation marks around the word *report* is to remind us that professional journalists, as well as users who generate content, all distribute political information in ways that select and interpret political events (which is detailed in the second proposition). Nevertheless, apart from a few exceptions discussed throughout this book, politics always comes first.

The idea that politics comes first is supported by previous theoretical and empirical work on the topic. Three of the most important are statements by Bennett (1990) and Entman (2003), as well as Gamson and Modigliani (1989). Bennett's early work on what became known as the indexing hypothesis was based on the idea that the media agenda, as well as the range of debate on issues appearing in news coverage, was keyed to what was being discussed by elected officials (see also Bennett, Lawrence, & Livingston 2008; Livingston & Bennett, 2003; and Bennett, Lawrence & Livingston, 2006). Entman's (2003) cascading activation model can also be seen as a politics-first approach. His causal chain of political influence on frames begins with the US administration, which mostly includes the White House, the State Department, and the Defense Department. Gamson and Modigliani's (1989) seminal work on changing media coverage concerning nuclear energy also makes a politics-first argument. The authors' basic claim is that, although it took years, political activists in the anti-nuclear movement were able to introduce competing frames into media discourse about the issue. As a result, many citizens and decision-makers began to better understand the dangers associated with building nuclear plants.

It is worth taking note of an important difference between the first two theories (indexing and the cascading activation model) and Gamson and Modigliani's (1989) work on nuclear energy. The first two (Bennett, 1990; Entman, 2003) are clearly top-down models that emphasize the ability of those in power to have a major influence on media performance. Gamson and Modigliani (1989), on the other hand, emphasize that change in the way media cover public issues can also come from political activists, which is a more bottom-up approach. We believe that changes in the political ecosystem can come from a variety of directions, and although it is important to attempt to track the direction of influence, the most important issue for us is to understand what has changed in the political ecosystem and how any such changes affect the communication ecosystem.

The Political Ecosystem

The *political ecosystem* refers to all institutions, values, actions, practices, and events that jointly influence how political actors compete for influence and control in a particular time and place. It encompasses the opportunity space that shapes how political actors go about choosing and pursuing goals, including the types and societal distribution of resources for acquiring and exercising political power. The political ecosystem can be thought of as the political context that helps shape how political processes unfold. But this is all fairly abstract. In order to better envision the concept, we propose thinking about the political ecosystem in reference to three analytical dimensions: structural, cultural, and situational. We shall also employ these three dimensions when talking about the communication ecosystem. We present an outline of the discussion that follows in Table 1.1.

The structural dimension has to do with institutional structures that define the system and performance of government within a particular time and place. One of the more important things about structural factors is that they normally remain in place for a considerable amount of time, so their impact on media systems, values, practices, and resources will be relatively long term. The most obvious example is whether a political system

Table 1.1 Analyzing the Political Ecosystem

Analytical Dimension	Definition	Usual Time Frame	Important Examples
Structural	The institutional structures that define the system and performance of government within a particular time and place	Long term	Level of democratization Electoral system Institutional dispersion of power
Cultural	The aggregate of individual and collective values, beliefs, norms, and actions among political actors concerning political matters within a particular time and place	Medium term	Level of political consensus among elites in support of policy or overall legitimacy Level of political extremism and violence
Situational	Major events or circumstances that have an impact on the political agenda within a particular time and place	Short term	Terrorist attacks Election results Assassinations Authorities' level of control over particular events and flow of information about issues/policies

tends toward autocracy, democracy, or some other distribution of sovereign power. Thinking broadly about this dimension allows us to move beyond the WEIRD countries we discussed earlier. Also included within the structural dimension of analysis is the institutional dispersion of political power in a particular time and place. If there is one hypothesis that political communication researchers around the world have found useful, it is the relationship between political power and access to the media (Bennett, Lawrence, & Livingston, 2008; Entman, 2003; Harcup & O'Neill, 2001; Williams & Delli Carpini, 2011; Wolfsfeld, 1997, 2022). Those with the most power have routine access to professionally generated media attention, while those without power have little choice but to come in through the "back door" by carrying out some form of deviant behavior (Wolfsfeld, 2022). To put it succulently: if you are not politically important, you had better be interesting. This general rule also applies to the digital media. While political elites and celebrities easily generate attention in various social media and political blogs, those who lack such status and resources have to produce something especially interesting if they have any hopes of "going viral."

The cultural dimension of the political ecosystem refers to the aggregate of individual and collective values, beliefs, norms, and actions among political actors concerning political matters within a particular time and place. We are using the term "political actors" in a very general sense, meaning any individual or group who has at least a minimal interest in politics. In this sense, even citizens who occasionally discuss political matters would be considered political actors. It is macro concept referring to the political zeitgeist writ large, which echoes what Iyengar and Kinder (1988) called "the tenor of the times" (p. 81). Factors associated with the cultural dimension should be seen as intermediate-term variables when it comes to their rate of change. Thus, public beliefs and discourse about major social issues certainly change over the course of years, but significant variations are unlikely to occur over weeks or months.

There is one aspect of the cultural dimension that has proven especially important in political communication research and will come up frequently in this book: the level of political consensus among domestic elites (Bennett, 1990; Bennett, Lawrence, & Livingston, 2008; Hallin, 1989; Wolfsfeld, 1997, 2022). In general, when governments enjoy a high level of consensus among elites about certain policies, most professionally produced media coverage tends to reflect and reinforce this support. The most obvious examples of this phenomenon take place during the early stages of wars, when those in the opposition are reluctant to exhibit any dissent for fear of being seen as traitors (Groeling & Baum, 2008). When wars drag on and the government's policies become more controversial, this too is reflected in media coverage. As Hallin (1989, p. 116) has put it, the topic moves from the "sphere of consensus" to the "sphere of legitimate controversy." The same can be said about what happens when elites and publics come to alter their beliefs concerning major social issues such as civil rights and the death penalty, as will be discussed in Chapter 4.

The cultural dimension of analysis is also extremely helpful when looking at how media coverage of social issues varies cross-nationally. The issue of LGBTQ rights provides a perfect example. The political contexts surrounding this issue in Russia, India, and Western Europe, for example, will differ greatly, and this is reflected in the news frames employed in each country to cover the issue. An analysis using the PMP principle examining these differences would be similar to what one would find looking at changes that took place over time in the United States and Western Europe. Whether one is looking at such issues across time or across cultures, the focus should be on how variations in political ecosystems lead to variations in how all forms of media deal with such issues. We will return to the cross-cultural perspective in Chapter 5.

Another important variable which is considered part of the cultural dimension of analysis is the level of extremism and political violence in a particular time and place. The question here is not about one particular case of violence (which is covered in the situational dimension of analysis), but rather concerns an ongoing problem within a particular society over a particular period of time. All forms of media—especially sensationalist media—feed on extremism, violence, and conflict, which is more than likely to lead to even more extremism and violence. If this becomes the norm rather than the exception, it will clearly have an impact on the ability of leaders to maintain control over policies and events and will make it difficult for decision-makers to put forward and implement policies in other areas of concern. Having a relatively calm political ecosystem is especially important for those who hope to use the media to promote peace (Wolfsfeld, 2004). We will return to this issue in Chapter 3.

The situational dimension of the political ecosystem refers to major events that have an impact on the political agenda within a particular time and place. One aspect of the situational dimension that has become especially important in the digital age concerns the ability to control the flow of information about major events (Wolfsfeld, 1997, 2017, 2022; Wolfsfeld & Tsfroni, 2018). Just the fact that citizens are now able to record and upload video of events as they happen creates serious challenges for the authorities (Wolfsfeld & Tsfroni, 2018). Videos of Black Americans being killed by police would be just one example of this changing dynamic (Carney, 2016; Lawrence, 2000; Taylor, 2016). In addition, the difficulties that authorities in many countries face in maintaining secrecy is another important example of how changing political ecosystems can have an effect on the ability of the media to gather information, which then can have an impact on a political process. Recent examples include embarrassing information coming from WikiLeaks (Chadwick, 2013; Sifry, 2011), the Snowden affair (Gurnow, 2014), and the Panama Papers (Obermayer & Obermaier, 2016).

What we learn from these examples is that in the digital age the situational dimension of analysis may have become even more important than in the past. Turning to a non-WEIRD example of how a single event can have a major impact on the political process, it is worth considering the suicide of Tarek el-Tayeb Mohamed Bouazizi in Tunisia on December 17, 2010. The story is by now well-known. Bouazizi was infuriated after being slapped by a policewoman and ignored by the authorities in a confrontation over a fine he was given for having an illegal vegetable stand. He then committed suicide in protest by setting himself on fire. The story went viral and led to massive protests throughout the country (Howard & Hussein, 2011). Remarkably, a mere 10 days later, the president of Tunisia, Zine el Abidine Ben Ali, resigned. We will have much more to say about the role of social media in the Arab Spring later in this volume (see also Wolfsfeld, Segev, & Sheafer, 2013). For now, we simply want to point out that this incident is an excellent example of why the situational dimension of analysis should be considered an essential element when thinking about how sudden variations in political ecosystems can have a major impact on all forms of media, which in turn can have a significant impact on politics.

This brief overview of the three analytical dimensions within the political ecosystem is suggestive only. We offer no comprehensive inventory of relevant considerations or variables within each dimension; just the idea that thinking of the political ecosystem in terms of these three dimensions can be a productive start toward generating testable hypotheses about political communication phenomena.

The Communication Ecosystem

The next step is to detail what we mean by the term *communication ecosystem*, which in our view encompasses both communication environments and all forms of media systems. The latter is defined by De Vreese, Esser, and Hopmann (2017, p. 5) as encompassing market competition, market commercialization, and journalistic professionalization. Van Aelst et al. (2017, p. 4) define a political information environment as:

> [t]he supply and demand of political news and political information within a certain society. The supply side encompasses the quantity and quality as well as the structure of political news and information available through various old and new media. The demand side encompasses how various segments within a society make use of political news and information and the quality of that information.

Hallin and Mancini (2004) present three models of media systems differentiated on the basis of four variables: the development of media markets, the degree and forms of political parallelism, journalistic professionalism, and the role of the state. Another useful definition is Williams and Delli Carpini's (2011) "media regimes" as "a historically specific, relatively stable, set of institutions, norms, processes, and actors that shape the expectations and practices of media producers and consumers" (p. 16).

Based on the above, we define *communication ecosystems* as encompassing all of the resources, practices, and actions taken by individuals, groups, and institutions in collecting, processing, transforming, and distributing information, images, messages, and stories to others. This definition is intentionally broad and includes all forms of media, including traditional news media, digital media, and entertainment media. While it is clear that not all (or even most) media content is political, for the purposes of this book we will focus on content which has at least some link to the world of politics.

It is important to point out that we will not go into too much detail in this book about the norms, routines, and constraints of every major type of communication system. Our focus is quite explicitly and consistently on drawing scholarly vision up to the "30,000 foot level" of enduring concepts that are not specific to any particular channel, mode, or platform of communication. Although we certainly deal with it, those looking for a great deal of specification about the digital media may be especially frustrated. One reason is that any attempt to summarize the "state of the literature" about this dynamic body of work will soon be rendered obsolete as both the technologies and the scholarship in this field continue to develop. To avoid being overly time-bound in our references, we therefore paint with broad brushstrokes and vague generalities when discussing the digital forms of communication that are so rapidly evolving at the time of this writing.

In addition, we understand that questions of what exactly is or is not considered political can be open for debate. It is also clear that there will be a certain amount of overlap between the political and communication ecosystems. We intend to argue below, however, that this does not present any insurmountable difficulties for those who choose to adopt these analytical categories.

When talking about traditional news media, we have in mind every stage in the production of news, including decisions about which reporters to send to which locations, what types of information and images journalists are expected to gather, who are likely to be their most important sources, how much space and/or time should be devoted to covering the story, what is the most newsworthy part of the story that receives special prominence, how the story is framed, and how the story is circulated or made available to the public. It also includes the economic incentives that structure particular media markets, as well as the available resources of journalistic professionalism and of audience attention, advertising revenue, and access to newsworthy sources that form the raw material over which information suppliers compete.

When it comes to digital media, researchers will be asked to consider a similar set of factors. What types of individuals or groups are constructing the stories that are being told and shared? What do we know about the organizational structure, political affiliation, technological infrastructure, and financial resources of those involved in producing the content? What types of routines do they use for gathering the information and images they are putting online? How much "traffic" do they generate, and what can we learn about the size and characteristics of their audience? While this is admittedly a rather large (and nevertheless incomplete) set of questions to ask, it hopefully provides some direction for those who hope to better understand how digital media transform political information and events into messages and stories.

A variety of nontraditional media have also become an important part of communication ecosystems in many countries. We agree with Chadwick (2017) that an excellent way to approach this topic is to talk about "hybrid media systems." Here is the way Chadwick describes his view of the modern system:

> The hybrid media system is built upon interactions among older and newer media logics—where logics are defined as technologies, genres, norms, behaviors, and organizational forms—in the reflexively connected fields of media and politics. Actors in this system are articulated by complex and ever-evolving relationships based upon adaptation and interdependence and simultaneous concentrations and diffusions of power. Actors create, tap, or steer information flows in ways that suit their goals and in ways that modify, enable, or disable others' agency, across and between a range of older and newer media settings. (2017, p. 4)

In general, it can be said that we see the emergence of these newer forms of communication as easily integrated into the PMP conceptual map. We make three claims in this regard. The first argument is that we see the various features of the emerging digital ecology as mostly variables to be studied when thinking about different communication ecosystems. Thus, there will be some ecosystems where the digital media have become more dominant, and others where their influence is more limited. Second, it makes sense to look at much of the digital media as *critical tools* for political partisans to spread their messages. This includes what Benkler, Farris, and Roberts (2018) refer to as "network propaganda" where "the architecture of a media ecosystem makes it more or less susceptible to disseminating . . . manipulations and lies" (p. 24). For reasons detailed below, this is a somewhat different approach than that taken by proponents of "mediatization" (Decon & Stanyer, 2014; Mazzoleni & Schulz, 1999; Meyen, Thieroff, & Strenger, 2014; Strömbäck & Esser, 2014). Finally, we will argue that it makes no sense to attempt to understand the roles that digital media play in politics without first considering the political context in which they are operating. The actual role of digital media in any particular time and place is also rooted, first and foremost, in the surrounding political ecosystem.

The Media Selection and Transformation Proposition

The second underlying claim for the PMP principle states: *All forms of media do not* merely *reflect the nature of the political ecosystem; they can also have an independent effect on political processes by selecting and transforming political events and issues into stories.* The best way to understand this point is to think about variations in communication ecosystems. As noted above, we define communication ecosystems as encompassing all of the resources, practices, and actions taken by individuals and institutions in collecting, processing, and distributing political information to others.

The underlying logic of this second claim is that the power of any form of media comes from its ability to transform political events into *stories.* Our choice of the word *stories* rather than *news* is based on the need to include the ways digital forms of media, as well as entertainment media, transform these events into communicable information. Here we adopt the Williams and Delli Carpini (2011) approach in which they talk about "hyperreality." The authors emphasize that it is difficult to distinguish between the events themselves and the stories people are being told about an event. Naturally, not everyone is being told the *same* stories, and this has become even truer in the digital age. Nevertheless, while the variance among stories is worthy of study, one can often identify certain narratives that dominate public discourse, and they can have major influences on political processes. These stories can be found in traditional news media, digital media, and sometimes in entertainment media. Any serious analysis will attempt to assess which stories appear to have greatest impact on political leaders and the public, regardless of whether these stories are formally constructed by professional journalists or informally discussed among social media users.

There are other forms of political content, besides stories, that can be found in both traditional and digital media. This would include some forms of what some have referred to as "data journalism" that makes databases searchable, interactive, and informative for the public and do not necessarily rest on turning data into stories (Coddington, 2015; Fink & Anderson, 2015; Lewis, 2015). We would argue, however, that, although there are no doubt exceptions, all forms of political information sharing become more powerful when they tell stories, especially when many different forms of media are telling similar stories about political issues and events.[3]

We are not claiming that the "media selection and transformation" proposition is a completely original idea, quite the contrary. Many have studied the many ways different forms of media can alter political realities. Nevertheless, when this proposition is *combined* with the "politics first" proposition, it should lead to a more nuanced approach to the topic. The linkages between the two ecosystems are critical because they force researchers to think about the three distinct types of "media effects" discussed above: dependent, independent, and conditional.

Three Dimensions of Communication Ecosystems

As with the political ecosystem, it is useful to employ the same dimensions of analysis to better understand how various aspects of the communication ecosystem can influence political processes: the structural, the cultural, and the situational. We provide an outline of the next part of this discussion in Table 1.2.

The *structural dimension of analysis* refers to institutional structures that define the systems and influence the performance of all forms of media in a particular time and place. As was the case with regard to this component of the political ecosystem, such structures do not change quickly or easily. One of the obvious but important ramifications of this is that political leaders will find it exceedingly difficult to have a major impact on those media practices that are rooted in long-standing structural arrangements.

Three types of structural variables are especially relevant for understanding variations in the ways media can influence political processes: the extent of official and unofficial control over various forms of media, the economic base of a media system, and the technological infrastructure available for transmitting political information and stories.

There is little need to elaborate on the first variable concerning the amount of official and unofficial control over the media. The greater the level of press freedom, the more the public will be exposed to a variety of political opinions, and this has a direct impact on the political process. In addition, when governments have a greater level of control over traditional media, it will increase the importance of digital, harder-to-control media as channels for dissent (Wolfsfeld, 1997, 2022, 2017; Wolfsfeld & Tsfroni, 2018).

A second structural variable that is especially important is the underlying economic base of the traditional and digital media. Communicating political information entails costs of various kinds, both to gather information and to disseminate it to dispersed populations. The amount of money available to fund media operations, audience demand for certain types of information, and the difficulty of serving different audience groups with particular kinds of content through various channels all contribute to structuring opportunity costs that motivate information providers to participate in political communication flows. As a result, economic factors that provide constraints and incentives to political information providers are among the most important

Table 1.2 Analyzing the Communication Ecosystem

Analytical Dimension	Definition	Usual Time Frame	Important Examples
Structural	The institutional structures that define the systems and influence the performance of all forms of media within a particular time and place	Long term	Level of press freedom Economic base of all media Technological infrastructure
Cultural	The aggregate of individual and collective values, beliefs, norms, and actions among content producers concerning the collection, construction, transmission, and veracity of political stories within a particular time and place	Medium term	Sensationalism (tabloidization) Reverence toward officials Culture of investigative reporting Level of hate, racist, violent, and false rhetoric in the social and partisan news media
Situational	Major events or circumstances that can influence how content producers collect, construct, transmit, and validate political information within a particular time and place	Short term	Lack of access to relevant events Professional scandals Public attacks by political leaders on journalists Major spike in social media discourse around a particular event

influences on journalistic behavior around the world (Hanitzsch & Mellado, 2011; Baker, 2002).

While the types of constraints and incentives that have an influence on non-journalistic forms of media are different, they too can have significant effects on how the digital media function. As pointed out by Poch and Martin (2015), there are both intrinsic and extrinsic forms of motivation that can influence those producing user-generated content. Altruism and a sense of political efficacy would be good examples of intrinsic motivations, while economic rewards (e.g., YouTube payments) would be considered extrinsic motivations. Political activists using digital media are looking to reach the widest possible audience, and they also have limited resources with which to do so. Those who study media economics have little choice but to look at all forms of media and how they both compete and cooperate with one another in hopes of achieving communicative goals (Cunningham, Flew, & Swift, 2015; Hoskins, McFadyen, & Finn, 2004).

A third example of a structural variable that helps define the communication ecosystem is the *technological infrastructure* available for collecting, constructing, and transmitting political stories in a particular time and place. As with the other factors, this variable is important for understanding changes both over time and cross-culturally. When thinking about historical changes, one would naturally point to the invention of radio, television, and the internet. The introduction of television, for instance, dramatically cut newspaper circulation in the United States (Robinson & Martin, 2009), while the burgeoning number of entertainment options available to television viewers following the advent of cable reduced the overall amount of television news viewing (Prior, 2007). More recently, the introduction of social media platforms and other digital technologies dramatically cut the amount of revenue available to the newspaper industry.

If one were to do a cross-cultural analysis in the digital age, it would be critical to understand how many citizens had access not only to the internet but also to more traditional forms of media. In interviews with political leaders in the Democratic Republic of the Congo and Burundi, it became clear that the most important struggle for political influence centered on an ongoing competition over radio broadcasts.[4] An important study by Pierskalla and Hollenbach (2013) found that cell phones were a major asset in Africa for collective action. One of the most significant technological changes in the Arab world was the introduction of the Arab satellite news channels, especially Al Jazeera (Lynch, 2010; Miles, 2010; Samuel-Azran, 2010). For the first time, millions of Arab citizens were given access to a dramatically different type of news, and this made it more difficult for Arab dictators to maintain control over the flow of political information in their countries.

One particular set of structures that have become major elements in many communication ecosystems are digital media platforms. This group would include such well-known businesses as Google (which owns YouTube), Facebook (which owns Instagram and WhatsApp), and Twitter. A better understanding of how these various businesses are financed and designed would help us assess why some political stories go viral, as well as the effects such variables have on how these stories are being told and disseminated.

Perhaps the most obvious examples would be examining the institutional algorithms that are used to regulate and shape the content that reaches participants in digital networks. The study of such algorithms would fall within the structural dimension of analysis. Consider, for example, a study by Schmitt, Rieger, Rutkowski, and Ernst (2018) that looked at the attempts by some social media platforms to place "counter messages" as an antidote to extremist content. The researchers found that these algorithms may have had exactly the opposite effect by directing more people toward extremist content.

There are also studies that attempt to look at the ever-changing interactions between social media platforms and more traditional media. An important example is provided by Nielson and Ganter (2018). They argue that the traditional media are becoming "dependent upon new digital intermediaries that structure the media environment in ways that not only individual citizens but also large, resource-rich, powerful organizations have to adapt to" (p. 1600). While platform research is only getting started, it is clear that it focuses on an important set of questions for political communication researchers to consider.

All of these changes in technology are critical in understanding both how various types of media turn information, images, and events into political stories and to whom those stories are then distributed. As we shall emphasize throughout this book, this is one of the central areas in which we can expect to find independent influences on political processes. Governments can certainly restrict people's access to these technologies, but a look at the overall historical trend shows that technological differences across both time and cultures have had major effects on the role of communication in politics.

This brings us to the *cultural dimension of analysis* for the communication ecosystem, defined as the aggregate of individual and collective values, beliefs, norms, and actions among content producers concerning the collection, construction, transmission, and veracity of political stories within a particular time and place. The term *content producers* refers to both professional journalists and nonprofessionals who create political content. However, as discussed later in this volume, when nonprofessionals generate political content with the specific goal of having an influence on political processes, they become political activists as much as movement leaders. Then their activities would be better placed within the rubric of the political ecosystem.

A good example of this dimension has to do with the extent to which different communication ecosystems tend to privilege sensationalism (or tabloidization) in journalistic reporting. Sensationalism refers to the extent to which a premium is put on drama, and this can influence every stage of the news production process. Although every communication ecosystem has some media channels that are more sensational than others, the most important question is often whether or not political actors feel the need to adopt more dramatic rhetoric and behavior in order to compete for headlines (Wolfsfeld, 2004).

Wolfsfeld (2004), for example, found that the level of sensationalism in the communication ecosystem was a critical factor in comparing the role of the media in the Northern Ireland peace process to its role in the Israeli peace process with the Palestinians. The fact that the Israeli press was more sensationalist led to near hysterical coverage of Palestinian terrorist attacks and put pressure on those opposed to the Oslo Accords to employ extremist actions to remain in the headlines. While the less emotional tone taken by the Northern Ireland media was certainly not the major reason for the relative success of that process, the resulting news stories were much less likely to be destructive than those in Israel. We return to this example in Chapter 3 when exploring the role of media in violent conflict and peace processes.

Another cultural variable influencing communication ecosystems comes from the demand side of the equation, rather than from what content providers supply. The information-seeking habits of media consumers are key factors in shaping cultures of information provision. The availability of larger overall potential audiences, as well as the tastes and preferences that structure consumer demand for different types of information, will all influence the opportunity costs of market entry and content provision in communication ecosystems. Likewise, desirable alternative information sources or entertainment options can simultaneously draw audiences away from more traditional news outlets, while also enhancing the possibilities for exposure to certain types of news (Baum, 2002; Prior, 2007; Bright, 2016).

This brings us to the *situational dimension of analysis*, referring to changes in the communication ecosystem stemming from major events or circumstances that can influence how content producers collect, construct, transmit, and validate political information within a particular time and place. As before, we are referring here to specific events and circumstances that usually take place in a relatively short period of time, which can have a significant effect on the opportunity structure for journalists and nonprofessionals to produce particular kinds of political stories.

The first set of circumstances has to do with those factors that prevent journalists and others from gaining physical access in their attempts to cover events. These types of situations are especially likely to happen in the midst of violent conflicts. Journalists' access can be restricted either through formal regulations put into place by the military, or because it is simply too dangerous for reporters to travel in the area. Thus, very few Western journalists were willing to cover the 2011 revolution in Libya because the risks of being killed were simply too great. In such circumstances, story selection and construction might be more heavily influenced by nongovernmental organizations such as Médecins Sans Frontières/Doctors Without Borders (Meyer, Sanger, & Michaels, 2017) or citizen-based groups such as Bellingcat that find their own way of producing political stories and detecting fake news.[5]

There are also events that can change the way journalists and others produce political stories and how they are received by the public. The eruption of the #MeToo movement that broke out in 2017 after sexual abuse allegations surfaced against Hollywood producer Harvey Weinstein is a perfect example of this phenomenon.[6] The massive response by women around the world led both professional journalists and social media users to pay a great deal of attention to the continual abuse of women.

The 2016 election of Donald Trump as US president also had a major impact on journalism, especially in the United States. The constant attacks by Trump and others on the integrity of professionally produced media content clearly put the American media on the defensive. While the election itself should be considered part of the political ecosystem, any reactions by the various forms of media would be considered changes in the communication ecosystem. There may have also been some unintended consequences, such as the "Trump bump": an increased growth of online readership for mainstream news outlets like the *New York Times* and the *Washington Post*.[7] Although each attack on the media can be considered a separate event, their cumulative impact can be significant. Surveys show that right before the 2016 presidential election, Americans' trust in the news media had reached the lowest levels recorded since Gallup first began asking about this topic in 1972.[8]

Many situational factors influence communication ecosystems by attracting popular interest or shaping editorial decisions about the newsworthiness of particular topics, persons, or events. For example, once a critical mass of news outlets in a competitive market decides to publish a story, it can be very difficult for other competitors to ignore it (Boczkowski, 2009). And once a story rises to prominence, it can remain the center of media attention if it retains sufficient interest to audiences or sufficient importance to content providers (Boydstun, Hardy, & Walgrave, 2014).

The 2016 "Pizzagate" hoax is a good example: several right-wing media sites in the United States began reporting on a WikiLeaks dump of emails from then-candidate Hillary Clinton's campaign manager, John Podesta, that supposedly indicated Clinton supporters were running a child trafficking ring out of a family-run pizzeria in Washington, DC. The story was false, but it led an armed man to drive hundreds of miles to fire three shots inside the pizzeria in an effort to get to the bottom of what he believed was a political cover-up. That event moved the story from the right-wing fringe into the mainstream media, where it received significant airtime for a number of days.[9]

Separating the Two Ecosystems

One challenge with the PMP approach is whether it is possible any longer to make a clear distinction between the political and communication ecosystems. There is no denying that there is always going to be a certain amount of overlap between these two ecosystems. The more obvious examples would include political activists who create their own blogs and Facebook pages to promote their ideologies, and journalists who actively promote their views about policies or leaders and in doing so become, in every meaningful sense, political actors.

Nevertheless, we do believe that political communication researchers can distinguish between the two ecosystems, both analytically and methodologically. We return to our definitions of each realm in order to better understand the boundaries. The political ecosystem was defined in a way that centers on the ongoing competition over influence and power that are central to the world of politics. From a methodological point of view, we would be attempting to find a way of assessing the actors and events that are participating in that competition. This means that researchers studying the political ecosystem should do everything they can to collect empirical data that come from sources other than media reports. Wherever possible, these researchers should attempt to measure political ecosystem variables based on what is happening in what used to be called the "real world," whatever that is anymore.

The communication ecosystem was defined to focus on all individuals and organizations involved in producing, distributing, and validating all of these different forms of information. Methodologically, the target would be on those who see themselves as intermediaries attempting to communicate information to others. An interesting issue has to do with how to classify user-generated content in terms of our two ecosystems. Should attempts by political leaders and activists to exploit the digital media be considered part of the political or the communication ecosystem? Perhaps a real-life example could be instructive. Former President Trump was a voracious Tweeter. Sending his messages out on Twitter was an extremely effective way of bypassing the traditional news media, which he viewed as hostile (Ott, 2016). These tweets were part of a communication strategy to leverage the communication ecosystem for advantage in the political ecosystem. When Twitter (as well as other social media platforms) made a policy decision in early 2021 to ban Trump because his content was no longer acceptable for the platform's standards, this substantially degraded Trump's ability to shape information flows and also changed the political storylines about Trump (in line with the PMP's "selection and transformation" proposition). We freely admit that in a case like this, trying to draw sharp lines around which actions were political and which were communicative becomes nearly impossible.

We nonetheless argue that although there will inevitably be overlaps and points of ambiguity between the two ecosystems, there are still significant analytical and conceptual advantages in considering them to be separate realms, as this book aims to demonstrate. Those working in the field of political communication—and especially those adopting the PMP approach—should be mindful of these overlaps, but there is no reason to believe that this in any way undermines the utility of our approach.

How PMP Builds on Previous Models

As suggested earlier, the PMP approach intentionally builds upon the important work done by other scholars in the field of political communication. In keeping with our overall goal of laying a strong foundation for cumulating knowledge, it is helpful to say a few words about how we see our own approach in relation to others.

Two approaches that were mentioned earlier were Bennett's indexing hypothesis (Bennett, 1990; Bennett, Lawrence, & Livingston, 2008; Livingston & Bennett, 2003) and Entman's (2003) theory of cascading activation. Although there are important differences between the two approaches, we have suggested that both can be considered "politics first" theories. The major thrust of their argument is how those with power are able to both set the media agenda and limit the range of views being presented in the media.

There are two things we want to say here about differences between the PMP approach and these two conceptual approaches. The first is that we believe important changes in the political ecosystem can come from a variety of directions. They can certainly come from "above" when governments, members of the opposition, or major figures in the military plan or execute policies or actions that have an impact on the political world. Changes can also come from "below," both through the collective actions of political movements and from dramatic events that are caught on cameras as they occur. This idea was suggested quite some time ago by Lawrence (2000) and was referred to as "event-driven journalism" (see also Bennett, Lawrence, & Livingston, 2008; Livingston & Bennett, 2003). As noted, the difficulties those in power faced in gaining control over stories have grown even greater in the digital age.

When one thinks about the situational dimension of analysis, one also realizes that some major shocks to the political ecosystem come from "out of nowhere" in that they don't come from above *or* below. We would put in this category such events as natural disasters, pandemics, and some forms of attacks (including cyberattacks) from other countries. So, in contrast to indexing and cascading activation, the PMP approach assumes that significant changes in the political ecosystem can come from a wide variety of sources and directions.

A second major difference between these two approaches and PMP is that previous theories did not go into much detail about how variations in communication ecosystems can also have an important impact on political processes. To put it differently, by overemphasizing the dependence of (traditional) media content on officials, these approaches did not give enough weight to the many ways in which all forms of media can have their own independent impact on politics. This is why our "media selection and transformation" proposition is an integral element of the PMP approach. It is true that Entman's (2003) cascading activation model does give some credit to independent inputs from the traditional media and some cyclical influences, but we believe the PMP approach goes into more detail about how *variations* in media ecosystems (including the digital media) must also be considered.[10]

This brings us to the competing approach referred to as *mediatization*. The extensive literature on mediatization emphasizes how the internal logic of media systems shapes and constrains the ways that political actors prioritize and describe policy issues (Decon & Stanyer, 2014; Mazzoleni & Schulz, 1999; Meyen, Thieroff, & Strenger, 2014; Strömbäck & Esser, 2014). From this theoretical perspective, the news values of media systems appear to drive political action in ways that undermine the autonomy and authority of political institutions. Since those who believe in indexing and cascading activation argue to the contrary that political institutions exercise inappropriate amounts of control over the topical agenda and framing of seemingly independent news organizations, mediatization and indexing would appear to be directly contradicting one another, and it would seem that one must be right and the other wrong.

We disagree. Using the conceptual map developed in this book, we argue that they're both right, as far as they go. They only seem to be contradicting one another because they're focusing on different parts of a larger process. Until now we haven't had a good conceptual framework for describing the elements of that larger process addressed by these literatures. Within our framework, indexing and cascading activation both address the PM component of a larger dynamic process, the stage where politics affects media coverage. In contrast, mediatization addresses the MP component, the stage where media coverage influences political action. Both of these stages are component parts of a larger PMP process.

But simply describing the PMP dynamic isn't enough. There are dimensions of analysis to bring to the fore that will also help us connect these literatures and the disparate claims they're making, so that political communication scholars can begin developing testable hypotheses about when we might expect something resembling mediatization or indexing to be the more likely outcome of larger confluence of factors shaping both the political and communication ecosystems.

PMP: The Exceptions That Prove the Rule

The PMP principle can be used as a conceptual map to organize a broad range of research findings. While we hope that this book will demonstrate that it can usefully be applied to a wide variety of research questions, there is no doubt that there will be important exceptions to our rules. Most of these exceptions will have to do with those cases that contradict the "politics first" proposition. Two types of circumstances come readily to mind. One is when some form of media is responsible for *initiating* a political process and political actors find themselves *reacting* to what is coming out in the media. The second set of exceptions happens when the *independent* impact of the media is far more important than the actions of political actors or the surrounding political environment. While this issue will be raised throughout the volume, a brief discussion of each of these exceptions is in order.

The most likely cases in which the media can be seen as the primary in-itiator in a political process have to do with cases of investigative reporting (Aucoin, 2007; De Burgh, 2008; Houston, 2010). Journalists' ability to un-cover political corruption remains an important incentive for journalists and non-journalists working in a variety of political environments. When ana-lyzing such cases, it would be helpful to ascertain how much the major discov-eries were the result of reporters' hard work and how much can be attributed to political actors initiating stories in order to damage their opponents. It is worth remembering that even in the case of Watergate, Woodward and Bernstein were extremely dependent on anonymous governmental sources for many of their leads about the scandal (Carlson, 2010; Woodward, 2005; Woodward & Bernstein, 2012). Nevertheless, in this and many other cases, hard-working journalists should be given the bulk of the credit for exposing political corruption.[11]

A second class of exceptions would be where media communications take a relatively minor political event and blow it out of proportion. An excellent example of this from 2010 is when Terry Jones, a Florida pastor, threatened to burn a copy of the Koran.[12] The threat received a dispro-portionate amount of media attention leading, among other things, to reactions by US Secretary of State Hillary Clinton and US Secretary of

Defense Robert Gates, who claimed that such an act would "put U.S. troops in harm's way."[13] The point is that on any given day there are thousands of citizens threatening to carry out extremist acts in a large number of countries, and editorial decisions by traditional journalists, partisan journalists, and digital media users to exaggerate the importance of this type of threat can become self-fulfilling prophesies.

It has to be admitted that making a clear and hard-and-fast distinction between these exceptions and the more significant events that fall into our situational dimension of analysis is not a simple task. This becomes especially difficult when significant political actors either stage what Boorstin (2012) called "pseudo-events" or when actors exploit "media storms" that can emerge from incidental events (Boydston, Hardy, & Walgrave, 2014) in order to promote their agenda and preferred frames. It perhaps makes the most sense to think about such events along a continuum where one end is characterized by clearly significant political events such as assassinations and the other end contains "nonsignificant" events that are either commonplace or do not appear to have any intrinsic political importance.[14]

What to "Do" with PMP and the Question of Falsification

There are two final issues that need to be addressed. The first has to with questions about how we expect researchers to utilize PMP. The second has to do with whether it is possible to put PMP to an empirical test that can falsify its claims. There is certainly a risk that by trying to include everything, we risk explaining nothing.

The first goal of this book is to provide a conceptual map, designed to contribute to the building of cumulative knowledge. It should accomplish this goal by persuading researchers specializing in different topics of interest to integrate their work using a common starting point. What these researchers have in common is that they are all attempting to say something about the role of media in a large variety of political processes. The PMP approach is designed to facilitate cross-fertilization of ideas across lines of specialization by serving as a (hopefully powerful) heuristic.

Given the way it is formulated for this purpose, it may be difficult to falsify the core propositions of the PMP approach as a whole (which serve merely as an interpretive framework, rather than anything like a developed theory). What *can* be tested and falsified, we claim, are the more specific research questions that are *rooted* in PMP. We give numerous examples of such questions throughout the book. Hopefully, as empirical studies employing the PMP approach begin feeding back and sharpening the general model, they will provide us with a more comprehensive and dynamic theory for understanding the role of all forms of communication in a myriad of political processes. Few of the studies we cite throughout the book explicitly mention PMP in their work. Nevertheless, we hope to convince the reader that each of these works provides evidence that both our general approach and our two propositions are useful.

A useful parallel to what we are trying to accomplish would be for readers to think about social constructivism (Andrews, 2012; Burr, 2015; Lock & Strong, 2010; Sheafer & Wolfsfeld, 2004). The central argument being made by those who support this approach is that the meanings that societies attach to objects, norms, and institutions are the result of unspoken agreements and shared conventions. This general approach—some might even consider it a theory—would also be virtually impossible to falsify. It has nevertheless proven to be extremely useful in a wide variety of studies, many of which involved testable hypotheses. The real question that needs to be asked about social constructivism, and about PMP, is whether other approaches can be found that are more useful in helping to provide better and more complete answers to the research questions we are asking.

Our second goal with the PMP approach was to propose two theoretical propositions that *can* be tested and falsified. The "politics first" proposition claims that in almost all cases, politics drives media rather than the other way around. The argument is that politics comes first both analytically and chronologically. While the analytical aspect does seem difficult to falsify, the chronological argument can be tested. Indeed, this is exactly what was done in a study of the role of the social media in the Arab Spring (Wolfsfeld, Segev, & Sheafer, 2006). There are various ways to empirically examine those cases in which media appear to be driving politics, rather than the other way around. This includes the exceptions we discussed above.

It is must be admitted that constructing an empirical test for the "media selecting and transformation" proposition will be a bit more difficult. The reason is that the underlying assumption has become virtually a truism in the field of communication. This does not mean that more specific hypotheses that are rooted in this general assumption (e.g., the effects of news frames on individuals) cannot be tested and falsified. But it would be difficult for any serious researcher to deny that the ways in which various forms of media select and transform political events into stories are not an important factor in what happens in everything from election campaigns to wars.

There is one way, we would argue, to undermine the "selection and transformation" proposition. The first would be to find multiple cases where the media failed to play any role in the final political outcome in question. Studies that demonstrate that media played neither an independent nor intervening role in political processes could provide an important modification to this proposition. One is reminded here of those who once argued for the "minimal effects hypothesis" (Klapper, 1960), as well as those who propose a new version of that idea (Bennet & Iyenger, 2008; Chaffee & Metzger, 2001).

Plan of the Book

The plan for the book is as follows. In Chapter 2 we will provide details about how the PMP principle can be used to explain the long-discussed role of media coverage in election campaigns. One of the important goals of Chapter 2 is to show how the six dimensions of analysis (three from the political ecosystem and three from the communication ecosystem) can be employed to better understand the ultimate role of the media in politics. Chapter 3 will move to dealing with the role of various forms of media in violent conflicts and peace processes. This will be one of the first efforts to deal with these two topics using the same conceptual framework. In Chapter 4, we will provide details about how the PMP principle can be used to explain the role of media in historical changes such as the success of the civil rights movement in the United States. Chapter 5 is devoted to showing how the PMP principle can help us better understand cross-cultural differences in the effects media can have on political processes. In this chapter we make an especially concerted effort to move beyond the usual focus on (what we have called) WEIRD countries. In Chapter 6, the final substantive chapter, we go in a completely different direction by attempting to say something meaningful about the normative implications of the principles we have developed. The idea is to apply some of the lessons we learn to better clarify the roles that various forms of media can play in supporting political representation in both democratic and authoritarian regimes. We end the volume with a short Conclusion that both summarizes the major arguments and puts forth some suggestions for future research.

2

PMP and Election Campaigns

It is not surprising that the role of the media in election campaigns is a central topic in the field of political communication. There are a number of reasons for this emphasis. The conventional wisdom is that the ability of candidates and parties to exploit all forms of media to promote themselves is a major factor in determining the likelihood of victory. This also explains why modern election campaigns spend so much money hiring experts, staging newsworthy events, hiring a digital team to manage social media, and paying for advertising. The competition over all forms of media is seen as critical to victory. Indeed, it would not be too far a stretch to argue that in many democracies the competition over media is what most people are thinking about as "the campaign." The goal of this chapter is to demonstrate how the Politics-Media-Politics (PMP) approach can help us better understand the roles that different forms of media play in election campaigns.

One of the advantages for researchers who study the role of media in election campaigns when compared to other topics is that the task of defining and quantifying the major dependent variables is, for the most part, pretty straightforward. We are talking about a contest over all forms of media and voters with a definite deadline (election day). It is true that we are not only thinking about who wins. Research about such topics as the overall public images of candidates and parties, how different people come to their decision about how or if to vote, and the extent to which citizens take an interest in the campaign are all legitimate research topics where many types of media are likely to play an important role.

The discussion will be divided into three sections. In the first section we will discuss certain aspects of the political ecosystem which are likely to be important. This part is meant to demonstrate how and why the "politics first" proposition is useful. The second section talks about some variables that can be considered part of the communication ecosystem. This part of the discussion is mostly linked to the "media selection and transformation" proposition. The third and final substantive section talks about what we are calling the "second P." To clarify, this term refers to the second P of the PMP

Building Theory in Political Communication. Gadi Wolfsfeld, Tamir Sheafer, and Scott Althaus, Oxford University Press.
© Oxford University Press 2022. DOI: 10.1093/oso/9780197634998.003.0002

principle: the political processes that can be influenced (at least in part) by the political and communication ecosystems. In this particular chapter on election campaigns, we will relate to four "media effects" variables that have received considerable attention in the literature: agenda setting, priming, framing, and electoral victory.

There are three major goals we hope to achieve in this chapter. First, we hope to convince readers that using the PMP approach to this topic provides a much broader and nuanced understanding of those factors that influence what role various forms of media can play in election campaigns. Second, by filling in some important elements in our conceptual map, we hope to provide those working in this field with some ideas about how they can use the framework as well as contribute additional elements to the map. Finally, we believe that we are providing the conceptual groundwork for those working on the topic of political campaigns to have a more productive dialogue with those working in other fields in political communication. This point should become abundantly clear as we apply the PMP approach to the other topics in the chapters that follow.

In order to help guide the reader through the argument, we present an overview (Table 2.1) that provides details of our claims. It deals with our six dimensions of analysis and examples of the "second P" that are likely to be especially relevant when studying the role of various forms of media in election campaigns. We recommend referring back to the table as you read through the chapter.

The Political Ecosystem Surrounding Election Campaigns

We will deal here with two variables from the political ecosystem that can have a major impact on media (P > M): the competition over the electoral agenda and the ability of candidates and political parties to promote their preferred frames to the various forms of media. The conceptual map is designed to allow future researchers to add components to this list. In this chapter our goal is relatively modest: to demonstrate the utility of the PMP approach to studies of the roles played by media in electoral campaigns. We will focus our attention on three major forums where this competition takes place: in traditional media, in social media, and in political advertising. Political advertising is the battleground that receives understandably less attention between elections.

Table 2.1 PMP and Election Campaigns: An Overview Table

Dimension	Political Ecosystem	Communication Ecosystem	"Second P"
Structural	Electoral system	Level of formal, informal, and financial control over various forms of media	Agenda Setting
	Election campaign laws and regulations	Communication infrastructure	
	Existing distribution of political power	Rules and regulations about political advertising	Priming
Cultural	Relative success of competitors in political mobilization	Strategic framing of campaign in traditional and newer media	Framing
		Norms for viralworthy content	
		Popularity of entertainment programs dealing with election campaigns	
Situational	Erupting political scandals	Media storms	
	Major security or economic events	Attacks on journalists	Electoral Success

The Structural Dimension of Analysis

As a reminder, the structural dimension of analysis refers to *institutional structures that define the system and performance of government within a particular time and place.* What interests us in this part of the discussion are the institutional structures that provide advantages and disadvantages to candidates and political parties competing over all forms of media.

While there are many institutional structures, rules, and regulations that can have an influence on these competitions, we will focus our attention on three sets of factors that have received a good deal of attention in research in this field. As can be seen in our overview table, we will deal with the nature of the electoral system, election campaign laws and regulations, and the existing distribution of political power when the election campaign begins. Our argument is that each of these political variables has an important impact on what happens in various forms of media during an election campaign, and this explains why the analysis begins here.

The electoral system clearly has an important impact on media coverage of campaigns as well as digital discourse. Electoral systems might be proportional (or parliamentarian), majoritarian (or presidential), or a combination of both. Proportional systems usually result in a multiparty system, while majoritarian systems in a two-party system. Esser and Strömbäck (2012), for example, argue that majoritarian systems provide a greater incentive for running strategic campaigns that rely heavily on money and media, compared with proportional systems. Campaigns in majoritarian systems tend also to be more confrontational than in proportional systems (Esser & Strömbäck, 2012), and less issue-centered (Strömbäck & Kaid, 2008). We will elaborate on the various roles of political and electoral systems in Chapter 5, which adopts a comparative approach to the topic. This is because we can only fully understand the impact of differences in electoral systems by looking at the issue cross-culturally.

Let us take a moment, however, to consider what happens to those who run for office in a multiparty system, in which a number of parties have a chance to be elected to the Parliament, as opposed to the two-party system of the United States. Technically, of course, the United States has more than two parties that field candidates. In the 2016 presidential election, for example, thirty-one people were on the ballot in at least one state.[1] But, given the "winner-take-all" electoral system, it is perfectly reasonable to consider the US system to be a two-party system. It is not surprising, therefore, that apart from a few exceptions, only the Democrat and Republican candidates receive any significant attention from the different forms of media. While some "third-party" candidates may be "fortunate" enough to generate some publicity by being considered "spoilers," this is the exception rather than the rule.

In multiparty systems, the competition over the media during election campaigns is very different. This would include such countries as Germany (Cox & Schoppa, 2002; James, 2017), Israel (Rahat & Hazan, 2001), and Italy (Cox & Schoppa, 2002). The fact that many parties have a realistic chance of being elected to the legislatures and the fact that many already have representatives in positions of power have important implications for what happens in the media. Not only are the traditional media more likely to grant coverage and even legitimacy to a wider variety of parties, but it also ensures a more varied number of mentions in social media (Samuel-Azran, Yarchi, & Wolfsfeld, 2015; Yarchi, Wolfsfeld, Samuel-Azran, & Segev, 2016). As discussed further below, "major" parties are still considered more newsworthy than those that are considered "minor" parties, but a multiparty system does provide some exposure for a much larger number of candidates and parties in the various forms of media.

The second set of variables in the political ecosystem are the election campaign laws and regulations. Here we will focus on just one such set of regulations which clearly has a strong connection to the competition over the various forms of media: those having to do with campaign financing. The amount of financial resources a political party or candidate has at their disposal is a critical component in determining their ability to compete within all of the different media. The list of campaign advantages money can buy is quite long. It would include the ability to hire professional advisors and workers, to carry out campaign research, to stage newsworthy and (what can be called) "viralworthy" events, to carry out research on voters, and to purchase time and space for their advertisements. Although it is true that a campaign that places a major effort on user-generated content will be less expensive than one that depends primarily on paid advertising, hiring a sophisticated social media team that can work 24/7 also costs serious money.

Many Americans are aware of the major change that took place in campaign financing as a result of the 2010 Supreme Court ruling in *Citizens United v. FEC* (Epstein, 2011; Levitt, 2010). This controversial decision allowed contributions to political candidates and parties by corporations and Super PACs. This change provided a massive increase in the ability of those running for office to raise money for their election campaigns. Given the advantages of having money in terms of influencing traditional and social media, it would be difficult to underestimate the extent to which this decision changed the way American election campaigns are dominated by money.

The major point to remember here is that the rules governing campaign financing vary greatly over time (as happened in the US) and country (Norris & Van Es, 2016). There are countries, such as the United States, where there is almost no limit on the amount of money that political parties can raise from both the wealthy and ordinary citizens. Similarly, in India, Sahoo and Tiwari (2019) have taken note of the dramatic increase in corporate financing of the various political parties and argue that this has had a dramatic impact on the elections. In Malaysia the system is set up so that the parties have "grossly unequal access to funds" (Gomez, 2012, p. 1370). Norris and Van Es (2016) provide the most comprehensive analysis of these cross-cultural variations.

The third and final structural factor to be considered is the distribution of political power in a particular time and place. This brings us back to the more general relationship between political and media power discussed in Chapter 1. Those who hold office enjoy a wealth of advantages when it comes to dominating political discourse in both the traditional and social media. First, those in power are always inherently more newsworthy because of their political status (Bennett, Lawrence, & Livingston, 2008; Entman, 2009; Vos & Van Aelst, 2017; Wolfsfeld, 1997, 2022). Almost everything a president or prime minster does or says is considered newsworthy, as it can affect the entire country.

Perhaps even more importantly, the ability of heads of state to implement major policies during election campaigns is almost always going to generate headlines, and this in turn can have an influence on the electoral agenda. It is worth noting in this regard that presidents and prime ministers appoint a long list of other officials, including cabinet ministers, who can also make news by either making post-election promises or carrying out crowd-pleasing policies. In most countries, those in power also employ thousands of workers who can contribute to this effort either directly or indirectly.

This is often referred to in the literature as the "incumbency bonus" (Boas & Hidaglo, 2011; Green-Penderson, Mortensen, & Thesen, 2011; Prior, 2006; Smith, 2013; Tresch, 2009). The relationship between level of power and access to the media can also be applied to a multiparty system in which the size of the party in the outgoing legislature can be translated into the amount of exposure the party receives in the media (Hopmann, Van Aelst, & Lganante, 2012; Rahat & Sheafer, 2007; Strömbäck & Kaid, 2009).

An excellent study on this topic was published by Hopmann, de Vreese, and Albæk (2011), which deals with the incumbency bias in five national elections in Denmark. One of their main conclusions was that "the more unevenly political power is distributed, the more visible the government is" (p. 264). It is important to note that this study also talked about variables having to do with the communication ecosystem, although they concluded that "changes in news coverage seem to be more driven by changes in the political system than changes in the media market" (p. 264).

All of this is not meant to suggest that those in power can either easily or automatically control electoral agendas or media frames. In fact, there may be good reason to believe that some of the advantages that incumbents enjoy between elections are *less* pronounced during campaigns. Logic suggests that those in the opposition become more newsworthy as stories focus on the election. In a study entitled "The Incumbency Bias Revisited," Green-Pedersen, Mortensen, and Thesen (2015) found that challengers increase their presence in the traditional media during an election campaign as journalists make a concerted effort to construct more balanced coverage. It is also worth noting that in the United Kingdom, there are laws in place that ensure that those in the opposition get more coverage at that time, even when they are not considered particularly newsworthy (Hoppman, Van Aelst, & Lganante, 2011; Strömbäck & Kaid, 2009).

In spite of this, it is almost always better to be in power when running for election than to be in the opposition. And in those regimes that have partial or complete control over various forms of media, the advantages of having political power are far greater.

The Cultural Dimension of Analysis

When we talk about the cultural dimension of the political ecosystem, we refer to *the aggregate of individual and collective values, beliefs, norms, and actions concerning political matters within a particular time and place.* In some ways, it can be said that while the structural dimension of analysis provides us with a fairly accurate understanding of the starting position of the various runners, it is the cultural and situational dimensions that can determine who wins. For those who have a passion for politics, this is where the magic happens.

We shall focus our attention here on just one of many possible variables that could be considered important: the relative success of competitors in political mobilization. The notion of political mobilization refers to the ability of candidates and parties during an election campaign to increase their overall level of passive and active support among potential voters. In the end, journalists and social media users are constantly attempting to figure out who has the best chance of winning, and based on those evaluations, they grant coverage and increased digital traffic. There is a more general point we will be making here that will come up again in later chapters: political success leads to media success. The relationship between successful mobilization and media success will also come up when we talk about social movements in Chapter 4, which deals with the role of media in historic change.

It is helpful to start by thinking about indicators of successful political mobilization in the United States. One would want to look at doing well in early and late polls, the ability to raise money to run the campaign, mobilizing relatively large crowds at election rallies, and winning (or at least doing well) in primaries. It is fairly obvious that accomplishing all of these goals will lead to more media attention and, in many cases, legitimacy. It is equally clear that those who fail in most or all of these areas will receive much less media attention, and this could lead to more problems and even defeat.

Thinking about the effect of successful political mobilization on all forms of media provides a perfect example of why the "second P" is rarely the "final P." Successful political mobilization in an election campaign will almost always lead to more and often better media coverage, and as the number of supporters grows, it will also lead to more social media traffic. In most cases, this will lead to even more successful mobilization and more media coverage. On the other side of the coin, those candidates and parties who are less successful may be framed as "losers" long before the election is over. It should also be remembered that in a parliamentary system there is a certain threshold that parties have to pass in order to get a single seat. If the polls published in the media suggest they will not pass that threshold, voters will be reluctant to "throw their vote away."

Perhaps the best indicator that can be used in cross-cultural research on this topic is achieving success in opinion polls. This is considered the clearest indication of the potential electability of candidates and parties. The media's enormous interest in such polls is part of what is meant by the term "horse-race" coverage (DeVreese & Semetko, 2002; Strömbäck & Kaid, 2009; Wolfsfeld, 2022). As Australian researcher Jackman (2005) has put it: "Polls are the lifeblood of media coverage and punditry during an election campaign" (p. 499). For a relatively recent review of this topic, see Lavrakas, Traugott, and Miller (2019).

We are purposely leaving out of the discussion the many variables that are linked to successful political mobilization. These would include such variables as the number of voters who identify with the party, public opinion about incumbents' performance, the relative charisma of various candidates, how well their messages resonate with voters, their organizational skills, and the strategies they develop for both competing over media and winning the election. These and related variables will continue to be studied as scholars attempt to better understand both the competition over the various forms of media and who wins elections. In terms of those who would consider adopting a PMP approach to this issue, our suggestion would be to consider all such variables to be part of the cultural dimension of the political ecosystem.

The Situational Dimension

In almost every election campaign, "big" stories erupt that can have a clear influence on the political ecosystem surrounding the campaign. We will intentionally leave aside the question of the veracity of such stories (e.g., "Pizzagate") but rather will focus on the extent to which they receive attention in the various forms of media as well as the effect they have on the electoral agenda and on the relative popularity of the candidates or parties (M > P).

It should be remembered that sometimes changes in the political "situation" can be based on actions initiated by political actors. Thus, in January 2019, in the midst of a (third) election campaign in Israel, Trump announced his "deal of the century" whereby Israel would be allowed to formally annex major parts of the occupied territories, supposedly as a first step toward peace with the Palestinians. This was considered a gracious gift to Benyamin Netanyahu's attempts to be re-elected.

It has to be admitted that it is not always easy to make a distinction between those situational changes that are best attributed to something erupting in the political ecosystem and those that are initiated in the media. It is especially difficult in the digital age to make this distinction when many bloggers and social media users have become, for all intents and purposes, political activists. Our argument would be that when such users do become successful political activists, this should be seen in the same light as what happens when social movements have an impact on the political environment.

We will provide three examples of important specific events that had a major impact on all forms of media and on election campaigns. Two are from the United States and one is from India.

The first example from the United States takes us back to the presidential election of 2008, when Senator Barack Obama ran against Senator John McCain. Obama was extremely fortunate that the economy was entering into what would later be labeled the "Great Recession" (Singer, 2011; McCarty, Poole, & Rosenthal, 2013). While McCain was not technically the incumbent, he was closely identified with President George W. Bush, who was leaving office after two terms. If one had to pinpoint one particular event, it took place in September 29, 2008, when the Dow Jones Industrial Average dropped over 777 points (Scotto et al., 2010). Given how close this date was to the November elections, it is hard to find a better example for an event that dominated the electoral agenda and likely had a major impact on the results.

The second US example has to do with the 2016 election race between former secretary of state Hillary Clinton and Donald Trump. Most readers might assume that this would be the place to talk about the infamous story of Trump bragging about grabbing women's genitals (Blumell & Hummer, 2017; Griffin, 2017). However, for reasons details below, we consider the origins of that particular scandal to be better regulated to the communication ecosystem because it was initiated by the entertainment, traditional, and digital media.

Here, however, we want to remind readers about the Hillary email scandal, and specifically the decision by FBI director James Comey, who on October 28 (11 days before the election) notified Congress that the FBI had started examining more emails (Comey, 2018). The email scandal was found to generate more coverage in the traditional media than any other story (Watts & Rothschild, 2017). It also led, unsurprisingly, to a large spike in Twitter traffic (Darwish, Magdy, & Zanouda, 2017). The reason why we place this scandal within the rubric of the political ecosystem is because the FBI became a major political actor (even if unintentionally) and the Trump campaign was extremely successful in exploiting the event in all forms of media. Their creation of the term "Crooked Hillary" was especially memorable.

In keeping with our pledge to also apply our PMP model to non-WEIRD countries, we turn to the 2019 election campaign in India. On February 14 of that year, a suicide bomber killed 40 people in Indian-controlled Kashmir. As one commentator put it: "With general elections just weeks away, the conflict gives Modi and the Bharatiya Janata Party a clear advantage.... Modi's calling card is projecting strength, decisive leadership, and nationalism. This crisis allows him to tap into all three."[2] Terrorist attacks during any election campaign are almost guaranteed to provide advantages to one of the candidates in both the competition over the electoral agenda and their chance of winning.

In sum, this discussion has hopefully demonstrated to the reader the advantages of always starting any analysis of the role of the media in election campaigns by examining the structural, cultural, and situational factors that are likely to have a major impact on all forms of communication. For those who accept our "politics first" proposition, it makes little sense to think about the role of the media in elections without first considering the surrounding political environment.[3]

The Communication Ecosystem in Election Campaigns

Variables associated with the communication ecosystem return us back to the "media selection and transformation" proposition. We are interested in understanding how the various forms of media select messages and events taking place during an election campaign and transform them into stories. Here, too, we are especially interested in factors that are likely to have an impact on the electoral agenda and the way candidates and parties are being framed.

It is fair to say that in the field of political communication, questions about and criticisms of how the traditional media cover political campaigns have been one of the cornerstones of research (Iyengar, 2018). As could be expected, more recent work has dealt with the role of the social media and other internet-based forms of political communication (Iyengar, 2018; Jungherr, 2016; Katz & Mays, 2019). Once again, we believe that using our three dimensions of analysis will provide researchers a more complete picture and will serve as a catalyst for a more productive dialogue among those working on this topic and those working on other topics in the field.

The Structural Dimension

The first structural factor in the communication ecosystem has to do with the amount of formal, informal, and financial control the authorities have over the various forms of media. Simply put, the more control those in power have over the various forms of media in a particular time and place, the less the competition over the media during an election campaign is likely to be fair and open. This refers to control over both the traditional media and all forms of digital media.

The discussion on this aspect will be intentionally brief because we go into much more detail in Chapter 5, which deals with comparative political communication. The reason is that the amount of formal, informal, and financial control that the authorities exercise over the various forms of media is just as important, or perhaps even more important, between election campaigns. The major point we want to make here is simply that the more the authorities in any time and place are able to exercise control over the various forms of media, the more likely they are to both dictate the electoral agenda and promote their interpretive frames to the media in order to get themselves re-elected. We will provide just two examples, one from a non-WEIRD country.

The first example is Turkey, which has become what Esen and Gumuscu (2016) refer to as a "competitive authoritarian regime." The major evidence comes from their study of the Justice and Development Party, led by President Recep Tayyip Erdoğan, and its control over the Turkish media during the 2015 election in that country. As they put it, they found that:

> . . . the party abused its control over the state-owned media and regulatory agencies; used legal actions to harass critics and reward supporters in the media and civil society; employed large-scale repression of opposition groups through the securitization of dissent; and relied on widespread use of public resources and abuse of public-policy instruments to gain access to greater private finance for the party. (p. 1582)

When thinking about informal and financial control during election campaigns, we need to also talk about the rise of partisan television, radio, and internet sites in the United States and other countries. In the United States, the fact that Fox News has the largest audience of all national news programs is an important element in thinking about the American communication ecosystem both during and between election campaigns.[4]

One of the more important questions in political communication in recent years has to do with the ways in which the two major ideological camps have created "echo chambers" where partisans can ensure a steady flow of agreeable news and information (Flaxman, Goel, & Rao, 2016; Garrett, 2009; Hayat

& Samuel-Azran, 2017; Jamieson & Cappella, 2008; Jasny, Waggle, & Fisher, 2015). For PMP, these studies raise critical questions about how the creation of different communication channels over time and place affects how citizens follow election campaigns. Thus, studying this issue falls squarely into the structural dimension of the communication ecosystem during and between election campaigns. The extent and impact of these echo champers are important to study, but we would again want to remind those working in this area to also look at political forces and contexts as critical factors in when and how such echo chambers become relevant.

Our second set of variables in the structural dimension has been labeled "communication infrastructure." The intentionally broad term refers to the availability of various communication technologies in a particular time and place, their levels of penetration among the general population, and the extent which they are vulnerable to sabotage. As noted earlier, this is an area where we would expect to find the greatest evidence of media having *independent* effects on political processes. As also discussed earlier, this does not negate the idea that some changes in "media regimes" are rooted in political influences (Williams & Delli-Carpini, 2011). Indeed, one of the more interesting challenges in this field is to assess how much weight to give to the underlying political, social, and economic forces in shaping the technology of election campaigns, and how much "the medium is the message" (McLuhan, 1964). Nevertheless, as Williams and Delli-Carpini (2011) point out: "once in place a media regime determines the gates through which information about culture, politics, and economics passes, thus shaping the discursive environment in which such topics are discussed, understood, and acted on" (pp. 16–17).

In any case, when we consider either historical changes (see Chapter 4) or cross-cultural differences (see Chapter 5), it is hard for even the most skeptical theorists to deny the importance of technological variations. Here we will focus specifically on the impact they have on the competition over various forms of media during an election campaign.

Certain candidates and parties have an especially good "fit" with particular media. One of the commentators who was able to best summarize this idea is Gabler (2016): "What FDR was to radio and JFK to television, Trump is to Twitter."[5] In each case we are talking about presidential candidates who, due to both their inherent traits and their keen sense of how best to exploit each medium, were able to maximize their advantages in dominating electoral discourse (see also Ott, 2017).

It is well known that the introduction of digital media has had an impact on election campaigns in the Western democracies (Iyengar, 2018; Jungherr, 2016; Katz & Mays, 2019).[6] Rather than attempt to review this mountain of research, it will suffice to say that the advent of the digital age has provided political candidates and parties with four major advantages that were unavailable in the past. First—and former president Trump is the best example of this—it allows candidates to bypass the traditional media and communicate their messages in a variety of formats directly to voters. Second, it provides them with a relatively easy means for generating newsworthy stories in the traditional media. Use of digital media as a stimulus for grabbing headlines is considered an essential element of campaign strategy both for influencing the electoral agenda and for promoting preferred frames. Third, digital media allow candidates to motivate citizens to get actively involved in the campaigns by spreading messages to others. Finally, digital media allow candidates and parties to collect massive amounts of data about voters that can be used to better shape messages and to get the vote out on election day.

Then there is the more sinister side of the technological sword. Persily (2017) provides an excellent summary of major changes in his aptly titled article: "The 2016 US Election: Can Democracy Survive the Internet?" Persily begins his detailed analysis of the 2016 campaign with the following summary:

> Whereas the stories of the last two campaigns focused on the use of new tools, most of the 2016 story revolves around the online explosion of campaign-relevant communication from all corners of cyberspace. Fake news, social-media bots (automated accounts that can exist on all types of platforms), and propaganda from inside and outside the United States—alongside revolutionary uses of new media by the winning campaign—combined to upset established paradigms of how to run for president (p. 63).

In terms of PMP, these dramatic changes in the communication ecosystem can lead and have led to various forms of media having independent (or semi-independent) effects on election campaigns and perhaps even on their outcomes. As noted, we also believe that, as with any new technology, some candidates and parties will be more successful than others in exploiting these new tools for both good and evil.[7]

Research questions for those studying the effects of technological changes on election campaigns in non-WEIRD countries can sometimes center on different technologies. One of the more fascinating issues in these studies is the increasingly important role of mobile phones in such campaigns (Frère, 2010; Karan, Gimeno, & Tandoc, 2009; Smyth & Best, 2013; Wasserman, 2011). Here, too, the specific role of mobile phones in election campaigns varies, partly because of how much the technology is available at a particular time and place and due to differences in the surrounding political ecosystem.

We shall take note of just two studies to illustrate such variations. The first was carried out by Karan, Gimeno, and Tandoc (2009) and examined the attempts by the Gabriela Woman's Party to influence voters in the 2007 Philippine elections. The party's lack of funds prohibited almost all mainstream advertising, so campaigners turned to the internet and mobile phone communication. The results of the study revealed that although the party was not very successful in exploiting the newer media, exploiting mobile phone technology proved especially helpful. In what was considered a success, the party won two legislative seats, and many of their votes came from absentee ballots.

Another study is by Alikah (2018) concerning the role of satellite television in Iran. It is interesting that this particular technological innovation has received far less scholarly attention than digital media. Alikah argues that although the Iranian government has done all in its power to block these channels, they have created more "media pluralism" in that country.

The third structural factor has to do with political advertising. There are major differences among countries about how advertising time and space are distributed among the political parties (Kaid, 2004). We have labeled this set of variables as "rules and regulations for political advertising." In the United Kingdom and Ireland, for example, paid advertisements on some forms of media are forbidden. Some European Union countries have specific time slots when advertising may be aired. In Japan, parties are allowed to pay for advertising but cannot mention specific candidates (Tak, 2006). In Iran, all political content is heavily censored, and a law passed in 2007 established significant restrictions on political advertising, including the internet (Sreberny & Khiabany, 2010). All of these variations have a clear impact on the relative ability of candidates and parties to compete.

This part of the discussion was meant to demonstrate why it is helpful to think about the formal and informal ways in which the communication ecosystem surrounding elections can have an impact on the competition over the electoral agenda and the framing process. These three sets of variables are important examples that should be studied further; we hope that other researchers will add to this list.

If we want to return to the competing runners metaphor, we can put it like this. If the institutional structures of the political ecosystem establish where the runners begin the competition over various forms of media, the communication ecosystem helps determine the rules for running the race. Some runners are given a shorter lane for running the race, while others may find themselves competing with heavy weights attached to their ankles. As researchers, our job is to examine both the political *and* the communication ecosystems in order to understand who is most likely to succeed in competing over and exploiting various forms of media to win.

The Cultural Dimension of Analysis

It is fair to say that the cultural dimension has received the greatest level of attention in the field of political communication. As a reminder, we are referring here to *the aggregate of individual and collective values, beliefs, norms, and actions among content producers concerning the collection, construction, transmission, and veracity of political stories within a particular time and place.* Almost every introductory political communication class deals with questions and criticisms about the norms and routines that the traditional media employ to cover election campaigns.

Probably the best-known claim in this field of research has to do with the previously discussed "horse-race coverage" or "strategic framing" (DeVreese & Semetko, 2002; Banducci and Hanretty, 2014). This line of research refers to the tendency of professional journalists to focus on the contest that is taking place during an election campaign, rather than on substance. Thus, a typical content analysis would show how the majority of stories look at candidate strategies and polling results, rather than where the candidates or parties stand on major issues. Some of these studies also look at the "second P," which would include variables such as a decline in political trust or suppressing voter turnout (Elenbass & DeVreese, 2008; Jackson, 2011; Norris, 2011). As will be detailed in our comparative chapter (Chapter 5), both the extent to which various media adopt this mode of reporting and the impact it has on voters greatly vary among different countries.

A newer set of research questions in the field concerns why some election campaign stories go viral and others do not. This clearly falls into the cultural dimension of the communication ecosystem. The underlying rationale for including this here is an attempt to understand the norms and routines of digital media that influence how users select and transform political events into stories. The question of what stories are and are not viralworthy is not the only way to confront this issue, but it is an important phenomenon.[8] It can have a major impact on both the election agenda and the most salient frames of candidates and parties.

Here are two examples of serious research that focused specifically on this issue. Darwish, Magdy, and Zanouda (2017) examined the ongoing contest on Twitter between Hillary Clinton and Donald Trump during the 2016 election. The bottom line was that in this particular realm, Trump destroyed Hillary Clinton. They analyzed 3,450 of the most viral tweets and retweets, showing that about 62% of the tweets were favorable to Trump, and about 33% were supportive of Hillary. Perhaps one of the most telling findings in this regard was that hashtags of Trump's campaign slogans (e.g., #Make America Great Again) were *200* times more likely to appear than Clinton's campaign slogans (#IAmWithHer and #Stronger Together). Unfortunately, the authors did not attempt to explain why the Trump social media strategy was so much more successful than that of the Hillary campaign. Nevertheless, these findings must be considered in any attempt to understand Trump's surprising electoral victory (see also: Buccoliero, Bellio, Crestini, & Arkoudas, 2020).

When one considers what is viralworthy in election campaigns, it is impossible to ignore the major importance of fake news (Alcott & Gentzkow, 2017; Tandoc, Lim, & Ling, 2018). We choose not to go into detail about this phenomenon, other than to say that it is hard to underestimate how easy it is to construct and spread these stories and how difficult it is for voters to distinguish between fact and fiction (Burkhardt, 2017; Shu, Wang, and Liu, 2018). Here, too, the empirical evidence tells us that fake news in support of Trump was far more likely to be spread than false stories that would have aided Hillary Clinton's campaign. In a major study of the issue, Alcott and Gentzkow (2017) found the following: "Our database contains 115 pro-Trump fake stories that were shared on Facebook a total of 30 million times, and 41 pro-Clinton fake stories shared a total of 7.6 million times" (p. 212). Thus, not only did Trump do far better than Clinton on Twitter, his supporters were also far more successful in promoting fake stories about his opponent on other social media.

The second example by Bene (2017) looked at the 2014 elections in Hungary. He looked specifically at which election stories went viral on Facebook. For those who have seen which campaign stories seem to catch on, his results ring true. He found that "citizens are highly reactive to negative emotion-filled, text-using, personal, and activity-demanding posts. Virality is especially facilitated by memes, videos, negative contents and mobilizing posts, and posts containing a call for sharing" (p. 513).

It would seem that those who hoped that the role of digital media in election campaigns would help solve the problems associated with traditional media coverage are likely to be disappointed. It makes sense that drama, which often means the story is negative, is still an important criterion for being considered viralworthy. Nevertheless, there may be some areas where the role of digital media may represent an improvement on what took place in the past. One example would be the fact that digital media are more likely than traditional media to provide citizens with the ability to be actively involved in an election campaign. The fact that Bene's (2017) Hungarian study found that "activity-demanding" posts were more likely to go viral supports this hypothesis.

It would not make much sense to talk about the communication ecosystem surrounding election campaigns without relating to a topic that has received a considerable amount of attention in recent years: the world of entertainment. We have labeled this variable "popularity of political entertainment programs dealing with election campaigns." Many scholars who have focused on election campaigns have devoted time and resources in their attempts to understand the ways in which the entertainment world can have an impact on elections (examples include: Balmas, 2014; Baumgartner & Morris, 2006; Day, 2011; Fox, Koloen, & Glory, 2007; Xenos & Becker, 2009). From our perspective, this is simply one additional form of media that has its own norms and routines for selecting and transforming events into stories. Not surprisingly, the role of entertainment media in politics becomes especially interesting during election campaigns. Two examples will suffice: one from the United States, the other from India.

A fascinating study on this topic was carried out by Gabriel, Paravati, Green, and Flomsbee (2018) that looked at people's exposure to Trump on the reality TV show *The Apprentice* and other media. It is perhaps helpful to know that the study appeared in a journal in the field of social psychology. Their conclusions certainly suggest that this type of exposure provides another explanation for Trump's surprising victory in the 2016 election:

Results suggested that exposure to Trump though The Apprentice and through other media predicted the formation of parasocial bonds with Trump. These parasocial bonds with Trump predicted believing Trump's promises, disregarding his unpopular statements, and having generally more positive evaluations of him. Parasocial bonds with Trump were also a significant predictor of self-reported voting behavior, even when examined concurrently with other likely predictors. This research suggests that parasocial bonds played an important role in the election of Donald Trump to President of the United States (p. 299).

The Indian study was carried out by Punathambekar (2015) and relates to what he argues was the critical role of satire in the 2014 elections in that country. He argued that one of the reasons for the rise in popularity of these formats was the declining trust in more traditional media. The author claimed that "satirical video became part of an intricate, networked, yet comprehensible intertextual field that linked the 2014 elections to long-standing political issues and debates around caste, class, gender and sexuality, and religious nationalism" (p. 394).

Thus, although we have given entertainment media scant attention in this volume, we hope that those working in this field will also consider using a PMP approach to the topic. It should be clear that in order to fully understand the role of political entertainment, one must again consider the more general political and communication ecosystems in which it operates.

The Situational Dimension

The situational dimension refers to *major events or circumstances that can influence how content producers collect, construct, transmit, and validate political information within a particular time and place*. During an election campaign, there are many circumstances that can influence, even for a short time, the ability of professional journalists and nonprofessionals to collect and distribute information about the campaign.

The first variable we want to mention are what have been called "media storms" (Boydstun, Hardy, & Walgrave, 2014; Walgrave et al., 2017; Wolfsfeld & Sheafer, 2006). Boydstun, Hardy, and Walgrave (2014) define a media storm as "a sudden surge in news coverage of an item, producing high attention for a sustained period" (p. 509). During election campaigns, these are the "big" stories that erupt and all forms of media react by giving them enormous amounts of space and time. As discussed earlier, they may originate in the political ecosystem, especially political scandals such as the Hillary Clinton email scandal that was discussed earlier. Nevertheless, when media decide to provide round-the-clock attention to such events, they serve, at the very least, as giant amplifiers that force the candidates and parties to respond. One would also want to investigate differences among media (e.g., Fox News versus CNBC), both in terms of the amount of attention they allocate to the story and the various media frames they use in interpreting the events.

In addition, despite our claim that politics comes first, some election stories are initiated by journalists or come from user-generated content. This is in keeping with our discussion in Chapter 1 that sees investigating journalism as an important exception to the "politics first" proposition. Thus, the major story of about then candidate Donald Trump bragging about grabbing women's genitals was first published in the *Washington Post* and was based on a recording from an episode of the TV show *Access Hollywood* (Harp, 2018). Many assumed that this particular media storm would have doomed Donald Trump to defeat (Blumell & Hummer, 2017; Griffin, 2017). The reasons why it didn't are far beyond the scope of this volume. For our purposes, the important reason for mentioning this event was because this media storm appears to have been initiated by people working for the entertainment media and was given a major boost by both the traditional and digital media. We therefore consider it an excellent example of how media can have an independent influence on political processes.

A second important variable that falls into the situational dimension of analysis refers to the attempts by leaders and others to restrict, intimidate, arrest, or even kill those attempting to report about the election campaign. Russia provides an excellent example of such efforts. Thus, before the 2008 elections, the authorities carried out a systematic "cleansing" of the Russian media (Azhgikhina, 2007). The acts included closing various institutions that were involved in journalistic analysis and a dramatic increase in the level of violence directed at journalists, especially in Moscow. A similar style of intimidation of journalists was carried out before the 2004 elections in Ukraine (D'Anieri, 2005).

Less extreme forms of intimidation can also occur in Western democracies. Attacking the media has become a fairly common thread for those running a more populist campaign. President Trump and Prime Minister

Netanyahu from Israel are well known for adopting this strategy. We might refer to this as the "hostile media exploitation" strategy, whereby candidates attempt to leverage negative media coverage to their advantage. Trump's ongoing charges of "fake news" and referring to the press as "enemies of the people" are an important part of the current communication ecosystem in the United States (Kalb, 2018).

It may be difficult to distinguish between the ongoing attacks on the media and what happens in the election campaign itself, but there can be little doubt that leaders are especially likely to attack the media during an election campaign. It is worth citing a quote by A. G. Sulzberger, chairman of the *New York Times*: "As I have repeatedly told President Trump face to face, there are mounting signs that this incendiary rhetoric is encouraging threats and violence against journalists at home and abroad" (Grynbaum & Sullivan, 2019, n.p.). Journalists attending President Trump's rallies were fully aware that they might have been verbally or even physically attacked.[9]

When major events erupt during an election campaign, the event itself will more often than not be thought of as belonging to the political ecosystem. Nevertheless, in keeping with the "media selection and transformation" proposition, it would be a mistake to ignore how the communication ecosystem adjusts itself to breaking news. Decisions about how to cover and how much to cover particular events are often motivated by commercial interests. There will always be legitimate debates during any election campaign about how much attention "the media" are giving to certain events, and how those events are being framed. Professional journalists and nonprofessionals are constantly making editorial decisions about these matters, and this can certainly have important effects on the electoral agenda and on media frames.

A final note about the situational dimension of analysis as it relates to the communication ecosystem is in order: We are fully aware that there will always be some overlap between attempting to understand the impact of a specific case (e.g., a crackdown on reporters covering an election) and factors that are considered more long lasting (e.g., a semi-authoritarian regime that continually censors the press). Our suggestion to researchers is to acknowledge such overlaps and to attempt to make a distinction among the various dimensions. This would mean giving some thought to those structural and cultural factors that are ongoing and those events that appear to represent a significant deviation from those more long-term patterns. It is also worth bearing in mind that it makes perfect sense to think about particular situational "shocks" being rooted in the other two dimensions.

A Brief Discussion of the "Second P"

We conclude this discussion by returning to the second P in the PMP cycle. As a reminder, the "second P" refers to those political processes that are likely to be affected by the variables discussed with regard to the political and communication ecosystem. It is also helpful to reiterate that we do not believe the *second* P is necessarily the *final* P. There are circumstances where the impact of various forms of media on political processes constitutes a significant change in the political ecosystem, and then the PMP cycle begins again. This is certainly likely when talking about the results of an election campaign. When someone is elected to political office, especially if that person becomes the leader in a particular country, it will inevitably lead to a significant change in the political ecosystem of that country and may also have international repercussions.

In the first part of this chapter, and in the overview table, we talked about four major topics in media effects research that could benefit from adopting the PMP approach: agenda setting, priming, framing, and electoral victory. We hope that the reader is now convinced that taking a step back to look at the broader picture we've outlined provides critical insights about the ways in which various forms of media in election campaigns can have an impact on all four of these dependent variables.

There is no need to go into detail about these four dependent variables because scholars in the field of political communication are already familiar with most of them. Rather, we shall highlight why we feel that the PMP approach can contribute to a more productive line of research in these areas.

We start with the topic of agenda setting, which is one of the most studied topics in the field (relatively recent articles include: Conway, Kenski, & Wang, 2015; McCombs, Shaw, & Weaver, 2014; Neuman, Guggenheim, Mo Jang, & Bae, 2014). The central argument of these studies is that even if the media do not tell you how to think, they do tell you what to think about. The typical study looks at the news stories that are highlighted in various forms of media and show that this is correlated with what many citizens think are the most important topics facing the country.

By adopting the PMP approach to this issue, researchers will be providing a much more complete understanding to this topic. The reason is that it makes little sense to ignore the political and communication ecosystems that have clear and powerful impacts *on* the media agenda. It is true that some scholars in this field have attempted a partial solution to this lacuna by talking about "agenda building" (for a review, see Denham, 2010), but this is a far from sufficient.[10] One could also argue that adopting a PMP approach to agenda setting could allow researchers in this field to better deal with cross-cultural differences and with the ways in which we need to develop new ways of thinking of this topic in the hybrid media environment of today (Neuman et al., 2014).

A similar argument can be made about the topic of priming (a relatively recent review of research on priming can be found in Tesler, 2015). One way to think about the difference between this topic and agenda setting is to claim that "when the media tells us what to think about, it also tells us how to think." As Balmas and Sheafer (2010) put it: "According to priming, issues that are most salient in the public's mind become the criteria for candidate evaluation. . . . Likewise, candidate attributes (e.g. leadership, morality) that are most salient in the public's mind become the criteria for candidate evaluation" (p. 5).

Adopting the PMP approach to priming once again will encourage those working in this field to take a step back and think about which factors in the political and communication ecosystems have an impact on this process. The fact that an issue such as the state of the economy or morality comes to be an important criterion in voting choices is firmly rooted in what is happening in the political world during an election campaign. Candidates and parties will also choose to place an emphasis on those issues (e.g., healthcare) that resonate with what voters, especially undecided voters, think about. In addition, the ability of various forms of media to help shape such criteria is related to the accessibility and popularity of various media in a particular time and place and the homogeneity of the agenda being promoted by the various media.

We admit that it is unreasonable to demand that every study in priming or any other media effect deal with so many variables. What would be reasonable, however, is for researchers working in these fields to acknowledge their relevance. We would also hope that scholars could incrementally add to the PMP conceptual map by studying some of the central variables associated with the political and communication ecosystems that are likely to have an impact on the priming process.

The same can be said about studies of audience frames and the influence they have on voters (Bennett & Pfetsch, 2018; Matthes, 2012; Schemer, Wirth, & Matthes, 2012; Slothuus & De Vreese, 2010). It would be difficult to accept the idea that the construction of media frames about the candidates, parties, and issues and their adoption by certain sets of voters are not heavily influenced by the surrounding political and communication ecosystems. So here, too, we are asking researchers working on this topic to help us better understand where different frames originate in the political ecosystem, how they are expressed in different media, and the political and communication factors that help us understand the successes and failures political candidates have in promoting those frames through media to various publics.

This brings us to the ultimate prize: winning an election. In some ways, we believe that it is here that the advantages of the PMP approach should be the clearest. Our reasoning is that researchers attempting to make a serious effort to understand electoral success need to consider *both* political and media factors (see, for example: Balmas & Sheafer, 2014; Erkel, Van Aelst, & Thijssen, 2018). If one thinks about any recent election campaign, PMP provides an excellent approach for understanding electoral victory.

Political factors, such as the state of the economy and the ability of the various candidates and parties to mobilize support, are clearly important. But how much various candidates received attention and legitimacy in both the traditional and digital media must also be considered. The research cited above about then-candidate Trump's major success in the realm of the digital media is an excellent example. It would be difficult to think of any political advisor working on an election campaign who would not be thinking about both the political and communication environments when attempting to develop a winning strategy. The same could be said about professional journalists and users posting on social media who try to predict which candidate is going to win. It is our firm belief that adopting the PMP conceptual map can make a significant contribution to those working on this topic.

There are also other important outcomes that can be studied using the PMP approach. These would include the overall voter turnout, varying levels of trust about the electoral process, public attitudes and frames about the various candidates and parties, and the decision-making process involved when deciding how to vote. One could, of course, come up with other outcomes to study, but this list of dependent variables should keep us sufficiently busy for many years to come.

3

PMP, Violent Conflicts, and
Peace Processes

The role of the media in violent conflicts, especially wars, has received a considerable amount of research in the field of political communication.[1] This
is not surprising because one could easily argue that the vast majority of traditional news media focus on conflicts. We should add that researchers are
similar to journalists because we find it difficult to resist the drama associated with violent conflict (Wolfsfeld, 2004). A more cynical, but probably accurate, claim is that professional journals and book publishers may be more
likely to publish work that can be linked to newsworthy events like violent
protests, armed rebellions, terrorism, and war.

A similar logic would provide a reasonable explanation for why there has
been much less research on the role of media in attempts at conflict resolution, including formal and informal peace processes. Peace is more desirable
than conflict, but not nearly as exciting. Even efforts to achieve peace are, for
the most part, pretty boring affairs. Add to that the fact that secrecy is often
an essential element in any peace process and one begins to understand why
attempts at conflict resolution rarely grab headlines (Wolfsfeld, 2004).

Here, too, because there is so much more research on media and violent
conflicts than on peace, the first topic will receive more attention in this
chapter. Nevertheless, this will be one of the first attempts to treat these topics
within the same theoretical framework. We will argue that that PMP conceptual map highlights why it is helpful to think of these issues as two sides of the
same coin.

In fact, many, if not most, of the points we plan to make here can also be
applied to attempts by governments to implement any policy over an extended period of time. This would include economic policies, educational
policies, as well as policies in the areas of social welfare, human rights, and
the environment. Perhaps we will be accused of overreaching, but it is our
firm belief that the PMP perspective can serve as a useful analytical tool for
better understanding the role that media play in all of these policy debates.

Building Theory in Political Communication. Gadi Wolfsfeld, Tamir Sheafer, and Scott Althaus, Oxford University Press.
© Oxford University Press 2022. DOI: 10.1093/oso/9780197634998.003.0003

Here, too, we believe that this is one of the ways our approach contributes to the field.

Our overall approach is to see these contests over the various forms of communication as part of a more general struggle for political influence that takes place within a particular political and communication context. The PMP approach does not restrict itself to the government perspective, but rather looks at the ongoing competition over policies between those in charge and those who oppose them. It is also designed to better understand the role of the many channels for communication in more internationalized conflicts. This approach is rooted in theoretical work by the first author, which was called "the political contest model" (Wolfsfeld 1997).

The basic theme of this chapter remains consistent with our previous discussions. If one wants to understand the role that various forms of communication play in conflicts and peace processes, it is critical to begin by considering the surrounding political ecosystem (the "politics first" proposition). Only then should researchers move on to consider how the nature of the communication ecosystem translates what is happening on "the ground" into stories (the "media selection and transformation" proposition). After that, we need to think about the "second P": the impact that all this has on how conflicts and peace processes develop. This "second P," such as a change in the amount of support for a war or a peace, is almost never the "final P."

The Politics First Proposition

The first point to understand is that when antagonists decide to initiate some form of violent conflict or a peace process, it is always a *political* decision. This does not mean that politics is the only consideration, but any government, formal opposition, or movement leader has to consider the political consequences of their actions. Decisions about whether or not to go to war, to carry out a terrorist attack, to begin or continue with a peace process, or to organize a series of protests or other forms of opposition require thinking about how elites and various publics will react. When it comes to major policies in the areas of conflict and peace, the reputation and the political or even physical survival of leaders will often depend on how other actors react to those policies. The implementation of such policies often takes time, and thus questions about whether to press forward or change directions are also based, at least in part, on political considerations.

Our approach assumes that antagonists see all channels of communication as tools for achieving their political goals. Decisions on how to best exploit each type of media channel involve both tactical and, in many cases, strategic thinking. Nevertheless, this approach also assumes that leaders *react* to what is being covered and discussed in the various forms of media. How and how much they react will also be based, in the end, on political (and other) considerations.

This is why we need to start this discussion by focusing on the structural, cultural, and situational dimensions of analysis concerning the political ecosystem with regards to issues of conflict and peace. The overview table for this chapter can be found in Table 3.1.

The Structural Dimension of Analysis

As can be seen, the first variable we list has to do with the level of "government control over media." This refers to the extent of the control, both formal and informal, that governments exert over all forms of media access and content. One could also think about the ability of certain guerrilla groups and terrorist organizations to take control over various channels of communication. Clearly the question of the authorities taking control is related to the level of democracy at a particular time and place. Democracy as a variable will be discussed in more depth in Chapter 5, which looks at how PMP can be applied to comparative political communication. Nevertheless, it is already important to remind scholars that they should always view the level of democracy on a continuum, rather than as a dichotomy of democracies and dictatorships.

With regard to control over the various forms of media, we will be mostly interested in how much those who oppose the authorities can be heard. Even if the government has formal control over traditional media, those in the opposition can sometime use digital media to get their message out (Abbot, 2012; Christensen, 2011; Reuter & Szakonyi, 2015; Wolfsfeld & Tsfroni, 2018). The amount of oppositional access to digital media can also change over time. Thus, during times of crisis, those in charge can simply shut down the internet in hopes of suppressing dissent (Aouragh & Alexander, 2011; Chowdly, 2008; Howard & Hussain, 2011; Williams, 2011).

A second structural factor to considered would be the overall level of control over relevant events (Wolfsfeld, 2022, 1997). We are referring here

Table 3.1 PMP, Violent Conflict, and Peace: An Overview Table

Dimension	Political Ecosystem	Communication Ecosystem	"Second P"
Structural	Government control over media	Communication infrastructure	Level of support for conflict/peace processes
	Government control over relevant events	Extent of shared media	
	Government control over flow of information		
Cultural	Level of elite and public consensus supporting conflict/peace policies	Level of sensationalism in journalistic coverage	Extent of internal violence
	Level of overall political discontent among the public	Norms and routines for conflict and peace discourse on digital media	
Situational	Major disruptive events	Disruptive stories in traditional and newer media	Political, military, and diplomatic success
		Violent attacks on journalists or bloggers	

to what happens "on the ground." In a war, the goal of the government and the military is to achieve a quick victory with as few casualties as possible. The question is the extent to which the war goes according to plan. When attempting to execute a peace process, control refers mostly to two major developments: how much the antagonists are able to move the negotiations forward, and how much they are able to prevent the eruption of violence from those opposed to the peace process. The reason for considering this a structural factor is that it refers to the successes or failures of institutions (mostly governments and militaries) as they attempt to execute their policies. We include the term "overall" because it is important to separate between more long-term trends and specific events that are considered part of the situational dimension of analysis.

Consider, for example the difference between the traditional press coverage of the Gulf War in 1991 (Bennett & Paletz, 1994; Entman & Page, 1994; MacArthur, 2004; Wolfsfeld, 1997) and the coverage of the Iraq War that began in 2003 (Aday, Livingston, & Hebert, 2005; Bennett, 2003; Bennett, Lawrence & Livingston, 2007; Horten, 2011; Kellner, 2004; Kull, Ramsey, & Lewis, 2003). During the Gulf War, President George H. W. Bush and General Norman Schwarzkopf were considered heroes as they quickly and effectively managed to expel the Iraqi forces from Kuwait with relatively few Allied casualties (Wolfsfeld, 1997). The American and Western press were enthusiastically supportive of the campaign. In contrast, the Iraq War dragged on for years, arguably even after it officially ended in 2013. After an initial level of success, the American forces were dragged into an ongoing guerrilla war in Iraq, and there can be little doubt that the increasingly negative portrayal of the war effort had an impact on publics and elites (Berinsky & Druckman, 2007; Holsti, 2011). This was perhaps even more the case in the United Kingdom, where public sentiment became increasingly disenchanted with Tony Blair's rationale for the British loss of life (Lewis, 2004).

A similar point can be made about the overall level of control over relevant events in a peace process. Wolfsfeld (2004) made this point when discussing the role of the traditional media in three different peace processes: the Oslo peace process between Israel and the Palestinians (that began in 1993), the peace process between Israel and Jordan (which led to an agreement in 1994), and the peace process in Northern Ireland (which led to the "Good Friday Agreement" being signed in 1998).

Neither Prime Minister Rabin nor Prime Minister Peres was able to take control over the violent protests against the Oslo peace process, which began in 1993 and came to a violent end with the eruption of the Second Intifada in September 2000. Similarly, Palestinian Chairman Yasser Arafat was unable (some would claim unwilling) to halt the terrorist attacks carried out by Hamas and the Islamic Jihad. As further detailed below, the media coverage of the violence was apparently a contributing factor to the ultimate failure of this peace process. It makes perfect journalistic sense to focus on the violence associated with the process, rather than the ongoing (and usually secret) negotiations (Wolfsfeld, 2004). But the PMP approach reminds us that the lack of control over the conflict events was the key change in the political ecosystem that then had a major impact on media coverage.

For younger readers, it is worth mentioning that there were no relevant social media in play in these years. There is not enough empirical research at this point to say something definitive about how the advent of the digital age might have an effect of the ultimate role of the media in peace processes. However, based on what we know about the ways in which the digital media make it easier for hate groups to spread their venom, there is little room for optimism.[2]

The leaders involved in the Northern Ireland peace process and the Jordanian peace processes were much more successful in taking control over the relevant events. The Northern Ireland peace process can be said to have begun in earnest with the Irish Republican Army (IRA) ceasefire in 1994 and was successfully completed with the signing of the Good Friday Agreement in 1998 in Belfast. Former US Senator George Mitchell played a key role in the negotiations between the Protestants and the Catholics (Mitchell, 2000). One of his key conditions for any who participated in the talks was that they refrain from any acts of violence. As pointed out by Wolfsfeld (2004), having a calm political environment was critical to convincing both journalists and the public that the seemingly intractable conflict could be resolved.

Leaders involved in the Israel and Jordan peace process were also able to take a high level of control over the peace process (Wolfsfeld, 2004). There were very few protests in either country against the agreements and no terrorism all. The negotiations went well, were completed in nine months and, as noted, the peace agreement was signed in October 1994. Taking control over relevant events is just as important in the course of a peace process as it is in a war.[3]

The final structural factor linked to the political ecosystem is one that has already come up in our previous discussions: control over the flow of information. The point being made here is similar to that made earlier concerning the amount of success on the battlefield. The ability of leaders to maintain control over the flow of information has a critical impact on how much access journalists, bloggers, and other creators of user-generated content have to competing frames of conflict. It is therefore no surprise that the ability of governmental authorities to formally censor information that is being sent from combat areas to domestic audiences has played a major role in managing the flow of information about a conflict (Carruthers, 2011; Knightley, 2004). Here, too, we see control as a structural factor because it refers to what is happening in the political ecosystem and reflects the level of institutional success. Nevertheless, as discussed further below, the challenges leaders face in achieving informational control are also directly linked to the nature of the communication ecosystem. This is especially true today given the technological developments in the digital age. Keeping official secrets in this period is infinitely more difficult than it was in the past (Schneier, 2011).

Wolfsfeld (1997) provided a graphic demonstration of the importance of this variable when he compared the role of the media in two violent conflicts. The first case was the Allied effort in the 1991 Gulf War. The level of Allied control over the flow of information was almost complete. Journalists found it almost impossible to gain access to war zones, in part because the vast majority of the war was fought from the air. Once the combat started, Saddam Hussein was unable to launch an informational counterattack.[4]

Other factors were critical to the ability of the Americans and their allies to dominate the informational environment. The first was the extremely high level of international support of the war effort, as President George H. W. Bush was able to mobilize a total of 39 countries into his coalition. This meant that official sources from all of these countries were more likely to provide supportive information to the domestic and international press. This again demonstrates important overlaps between the cultural and structural dimensions of analysis.

Wolfsfeld (1987) compared the Gulf War situation, where the Allies had almost complete control over the flow of information, with the first Intifada between Israelis and Palestinians that erupted in December 1987. The Israelis had almost no control whatsoever over either the events themselves or the flow of information. Most of the violence was initiated by the Palestinians who were attempting to rise up against the Israeli occupation. The Israelis found themselves trying to constantly take control over the flood of negative stories (some true, others less so) coming out of the territories. It was a logistical nightmare, and although the Palestinians failed in their attempts to end the occupation, they were extremely successful in receiving international recognition and legitimacy for their cause (Lederman, 2019; Wolfsfeld, 1997). The massive amount of international media attention given to the first Intifada was a turning point in the Palestinian struggle against Israel (Daniel, 1995; Wolfsfeld, 1997).

Likewise, Cortell, Eisinger, and Althaus (2009) found that even though the American military could formally control access to the battle areas for Western reporters in the early months of the Afghanistan invasion in 2001, it was unable to restrict access to Arab-language satellite broadcasters who reported regularly on alleged American atrocities. Because they could no longer control access to the battle space for the next major military conflict—the 2003 invasion of Iraq—Cortell, Eisinger, and Althaus found that the American military fell back on the next best thing: manipulating the cultural norms of mainstream journalists by embedding them in military units that were expected to see different types of action.

The Cultural Dimension of Analysis

We will focus our attention here on two variables that have been studied extensively: the level of elite and public consensus in support of leaders' policies in conflict and peace, and the level of overall political discontent among the public. This can be considered yet another measure of the leaders' level of political success, which can then be linked to their level of success in the various forms of media.

Research on the impact of consensus on media coverage has received the most attention with regard to wars. As noted earlier, Hallin's (1989) classic study on the role of the media in the Vietnam war was one of the first to make this connection. Hallin wrote about three spheres of political discourse concerning the war: consensus, legitimate controversy, and deviance. In the early years of the Vietnam War, there was a high level of elite and public consensus in support of the war effort that was reflected and reinforced by the media. The "Cold War" frame dominated political discourse, and the press enthusiastically adopted the frame in all of its coverage. In keeping with the

PMP principle, it took some years before opposition to the war began to spread among the political elite. As the war moved into what Hallin called the sphere of legitimate controversy, more opponents were given voice in the media and reporters began to cover move negative aspects of the conflict. If we want to say something about the "final P," this means that, at the very least, more members of the public were being exposed to a competing frame, and those opposed to the war were in a much stronger strategic position to mobilize others to join the cause.

This general movement from more to less consensus concerning a war effort is fairly common. An interesting exception to this general pattern is again provided by the 1991 Gulf War. Many who lived through that period have probably forgotten that the public and the political elite were deeply divided at first about whether to use military force to drive Saddam Hussein out of Kuwait. After the war began, however, the entire political elite and most of the public became supportive, especially as the war proved to be short and successful (Wolfsfeld, 1997). This was an unusual case in which the amount of consensus surrounding a war effort *rose* and media coverage grew significantly more positive. Thus, although it is the exception rather than the rule, this change in the political environment can either increase or decrease the ability of leaders to have their preferred frames adopted by the various forms of media.

We find the same relationship between political consensus and media coverage with regard to peace processes, and this serves as another reminder of why it is important to consider these two topics together.[5] This brings us back to the comparison between the Oslo, Jordanian, and Northern Ireland peace processes discussed earlier. The data showed that while the level of elite and public consensus in support of the agreements with Jordan and in Northern Ireland were high, the Israeli public and political elite were extremely divided over the Oslo Accords. For this and other reasons, the coverage of the first two agreements was extremely supportive, while coverage of the Oslo Accords was mostly negative (Shaefer & Dvir-Grivsman, 2010).

There are of course other cultural factors in the political ecosystem that could also have an influence on how the media deal with war and peace. Thus, one might want to look at factors such as the degree of hatred for enemies and the extent to which various elites and publics are reluctant to go to war or to carry out violent forms of resistance. Nevertheless, there is good reason why so many previous researchers have focused on elite and public consensus as a critical variable that influences media performance during these historical events.

We want to reiterate that this aspect of the PMP approach can be applied to a wide variety of public policies. It is true that there could be some policies that are less salient and receive less attention in the media. In these cases, questions about political consensus are perhaps less critical. However, when it comes to major policy issues, leaders who are unable to mobilize a wide level of consensus in favor of their positions will find it difficult to take much control over media coverage. The many problems former president Donald Trump had with the American media concerning a multitude of issues perhaps most clearly demonstrate this point (Patterson, 2017). While he and others would claim that the negative coverage can be blamed exclusively on the "leftist media," we would argue that the extremely high level of political polarization in the United States provides a better explanation.

A second important variable that belongs in the cultural dimension of the political ecosystem is the level of overall political discontent among the public. We are referring here to the amount of frustration and anger at authorities that is not necessarily related to any conflict or peace process. An extremely high level of anger will lead some segments of the population to take to the streets. In the digital age, violent protests and rebellions will be organized through the social media. In addition, although the authorities in less democratic regimes will often attempt to block coverage of such collective actions, citizens in most settings will also have some access to media, even if it means relying on foreign news sources.

One of the most extensive tests of the PMP approach was carried out by Wolfsfeld, Segev, and Sheafer (2013) concerning the role of social media in the Arab Spring. The study was designed to counter those commentators who pointed to Facebook and other social media as one of the causes for the violent protests in the Arab world in 2010. Employing the PMP approach, the authors provided strong empirical evidence that the level of political dissatisfaction in the various Arab countries was a far better predictor of the level of political violence than the extent of internet penetration in each country or the extent of Facebook use. The title of the article sums up the major point: "Social Media and the Arab Spring: Politics Comes First."

The study collected a good deal of political, economic, media, and protest data from 20 Arab countries and the Palestinian Authority, and contrary to what many would have assumed, the authors consistently found a strong *negative* correlation between the extent of social media use in each country and the level of political violence. The reason, it was shown, was that those countries with highly developed communications infrastructures were also the wealthiest Arab countries, where the level of political dissatisfaction was the lowest. Also in support of the PMP approach, the researchers provided evidence that any increase in citizens signing up for Facebook was much more likely to come *after* the outbreak of violence, rather than before.

This conclusion was not meant to suggest that the different forms of media were unhelpful in mobilizing people against Arab governments. Those attempting to lead the people to rise up certainly used every form of media at their disposal to organize the various rebellions. In keeping with the PMP approach, the media no doubt served as catalysts for violent protests. The availability of the social media, as well as the extensive exposure to Arab satellite television, certainly facilitated those collective actions. Nevertheless, the data demonstrated that the importance of the various forms of media only came into play in those countries where people were angry enough to risk their lives in order to protest and organize against those regimes.

This study provides an important empirical test of the PMP approach. Not only was it cross-cultural and included a large number of countries, but none of those countries was a Western democracy. In addition, the PMP principle was tested using two different types of tests. The first was a regression approach, which showed that political variables were more important than media factors in explaining the eruption of political violence. The second was a chronological test showing that the eruption of political violence *preceded* changes in usage of digital media. Finally, the study provided a good demonstration of the fact that although politics comes first, the media can still play an important *subsequent* role in what happens on the ground.

Situational Dimension of Analysis

The situational dimension of analysis refers to changes in the political ecosystem that can be related to specific events or circumstances with political ramifications. As noted in earlier chapters, these events can happen quickly. Those that most interest us have a significant influence on media performance and ultimately on political processes.

Such events are fairly easy to discern in the course of violent conflicts and peace processes. One of the things that these events have in common is that they usually happen when those in charge lose control. While the overall lack of control over events was talked about earlier, here we are referring to specific events. In a war, this will often involve an unusually large loss of life among one's own soldiers or among civilians on the other side. In a peace process, it can involve either a major breakdown in the negotiations or acts of violence by one of the participants. The ways in which the various forms of media will react to such events are rooted in other aspects of the political ecosystem.

This all brings us back to the critical importance of elite and public consensus in support of a particular policy. Wolfsfeld (2004) makes this point by comparing the reaction of the local press to the suicide bombing in Beit Lid by Hamas in 1994 and a terrorist attack carried out by the "Real IRA"— a movement that broke off from the main organization by claiming greater ideological consistency than the then-current IRA leadership was providing (Dingley, 2001). The attack was carried out in 1998 in the town of Omagh, Northern Ireland. The goals of each attack were similar: to derail the peace processes. The attacks killed a similar number of people: 19 were killed in Israel and 29 in Omagh.

Wolfsfeld (2004) argued that one can understand how each of these events was covered by examining the extent to which there were competing media frames available for journalists to employ. At the time of the attack at Beit Lid, there were two competing media frames in Israel about the Oslo peace process, which reflected the lack of consensus about Prime Minister Rabin's efforts to come to an agreement with the Palestinians. A "security" frame was promoted by the right-wing opposition to the peace process. Those promoting this frame claimed that the Palestinians couldn't be trusted; they would exploit any accord to launch further attacks on Israel. The competing "peace" frame was promoted by the Rabin government, which argued that the Oslo Accords provided a genuine opportunity for resolving the conflict. In contrast, in Northern Ireland the peace frame dominated media discourse, which reflected the high level of political consensus in support of the process there.

The Israeli press reacted to the Beit Lid attack by fully adopting the security frame and putting a great deal of blame on Palestinian leader Yasser Arafat (Wolfsfeld, 2004). As one would expect in such a situation, the political opposition saw this as a perfect "I told you so" moment. This reminds us that some events have a clear interpretive direction, and this can provide important advantages to one of the competing antagonists (Wolfsfeld, 2011).

The reaction of the leadership and the media to the Omagh bombing in Northern Ireland was exactly the opposite. Given the high level of consensus surrounding the Northern Ireland peace process, the local press enthusiastically adopted the peace frame. Both Catholic and Protestant leaders responded in the media and argued that this attack proved how important it was to *accelerate* the process. Given the extent of elite and public outrage, which was amplified by the press coverage, the Real IRA quickly declared a ceasefire and pledged to refrain from further bombings (Wolfsfeld, 2004).

An even more significant event associated with the Oslo peace process was the assassination of Prime Minister Rabin in November 1995. This was a monumental event, and while there was no guarantee that the Oslo peace process would have succeeded, the death of Rabin made it even less likely. The first reaction of the political and media ecosystems was quite supportive of the process (Wolfsfeld, 2004). It was generally perceived that Rabin sacrificed his life for the process and that the right-wing opposition was at least partially to blame for what happened. There was also a string of events associated with his funeral, where dignitaries from around the world talked about the importance of carrying out Rabin's "legacy." Not surprisingly, although the agreement remained controversial, it reached its height of support immediately following the assassination (Wolfsfeld, 2004).

This event, however, was followed by a series of significant Palestinian terrorist attacks in February and March 1996, and this also had a dramatic and opposite impact on both the political and media ecosystems (Wolfsfeld, 2004). The attacks provided major advantages to those *opposed* to the Oslo peace process, and it was now the government led by Prime Minister Shimon Peres that was put on the defensive. In May 1996, Benyamin Netanyahu defeated Peres in the general elections, and Palestinian terrorism was seen as a major reason for his victory. It is perhaps somewhat unusual for major events that run in opposite directions to take place in such a short period of time. What happened in Israel during these few months demonstrates that there *are* cases in both wars and peace processes in which the political and media ecosystems can change direction very quickly.

There are a large number of cases from violent conflicts for thinking about how a specific event can have a significant effect on political and media ecosystems. Here are just a small number of examples in historical order: the Reichstag fire in Berlin in 1933, the attack on Pearl Harbor in 1941, the dropping of the atomic bombs on Hiroshima and Nagasaki in 1945, the Tet offensive in Vietnam in 1968, the Sabra and Shatila massacre in Lebanon in 1982, and the attack on the Twin Towers and the Pentagon on September 11, 2001. Each of these cases led to significant changes in the political ecosystem, and in each case the role of various types of media was an important element in all that followed.

The Communication Ecosystem

In this section we are interested in identifying some of the most important variations in communication ecosystems that shape the stories elites and publics receive about violent conflicts and peace processes. This is directly linked to the "media selection and transformation" proposition, which claims that the media do not merely reflect what is happening in the political world: they can also have dependent, independent, and conditional effects on political processes by selecting and transforming political events and issues into stories. We are especially interested in those aspects of the media ecosystem that are either partially or completely independent from the surrounding political ecosystem. The reason is that the ability of the various forms of media to achieve a certain degree of independence with regard to war and peace policies can have an especially significant impact on people's lives. Once again it is helpful to make a distinction between the structural, cultural, and situational dimensions of analysis. It will be useful for readers to refer to the overview table we presented at the beginning of this chapter in order to better understand what follows.

The Structural Dimension

There are a number of aspects of the communication ecosystem that would fall under the structure dimension of analysis concerning peace processes and violent conflict. Many of them have to do with the institutional and economic bases that dictate how the various forms of media collect and distribute information, images, and stories. Examples include the extent to which a public broadcasting system is a major player within a given communication ecosystem, the influence that corporate owners and advertisers have over media content, and the audience reach of different forms of media. In this discussion, however, we will limit attention to two factors: variations in communication technology (that is, the communication infrastructure), and the extent to which antagonist publics share a common media. The first factor will be discussed mostly with regard to violent conflicts, and the second in connection to peace processes. Nevertheless, both types of variables could easily be applied to either realm of study.

The advent of what has been called the digital age is an important demonstration of how media variables can have an independent influence on political processes. It is true that political leaders, including nonstate actors, can either impede or enhance the use of new technologies by those directly involved in conflicts as well as those attempting learn about them. Despite this caveat, there is no denying that the very existence of particular forms of technology is an important part of this story.

When it comes to the changing technology and the coverage of wars, perhaps the most important scholarly source available is Knightley's (2004) book entitled *The First Casualty: The War Correspondent as Hero and Myth-Maker from Crimea to Iraq.* Knightley, a historian, provides an extremely rich set of details about the major impact such changes have had on the differing roles of the ever-changing media technologies in wars.

One example will suffice here: the invention of the telegraph before the American Civil War. As Knightley reports, the arrival of the telegraph led to major changes in both the logistics involved in covering battles and the amount of profit that newspaper publishers could achieve. War correspondents covering the Civil War tried to be as close to a telegraph line as possible so they could get the story out before their competitors. Unfortunately, this sometimes meant they couldn't get very close to the actual fighting and their reporting suffered accordingly.[6]

Technology can influence the level of success antagonists have in taking control over the flow of information. In the digital age, the ability of any political or military leader to maintain control over the flow of information is much more limited. The fact that every citizen has the ability to film and upload many real-time events means that scenes which embarrass certain antagonists are much more likely to reach a wide national and international audience. Perhaps the best-known example in the United States is the Black Lives Matter movement that received increased standing and legitimacy when scenes of policemen shooting unarmed African Americans were filmed and uploaded to the internet (Edwards, 2016; Taylor, 2016).

The 2006 Israel-Lebanon War provides another good example of this phenomenon. Many Israeli soldiers carried their cell phones into battle and every problem, setback, or disaster was quickly spread to their families, the media, and to the general public (Rapaport, 2010). This explains why Israeli soldiers were forbidden to take their cell phones into battle during the following violent conflict with the Palestinians: the 2008 Gaza War, which the Israelis called "Operation Cast Lead" (Rapaport, 2010). Israel also attempted, with only partial success, to keep journalists from entering Gaza.

It may seem to some that given the overall benefits of transparency, these leaks are something to be welcomed rather than cursed. In each of the cases mentioned above, there were certainly some types of information that deserved to be made public. Nevertheless, there are some types of information that should be kept secret for the greater good. If too much comes out about ongoing peace talks, for example, they are more likely to fail (Mitchell, 2000; Wolfsfeld, 2004). Indeed, an Israeli leader who was interviewed on this topic claimed that the secret negotiations in Oslo that led to the peace process between the Israelis and Palestinians would not be possible in today's digital environment (Wolfsfeld, 2017). There are also military operations that are morally justified, and leaks about such actions could also lead to failure.

Finally, it is important to remember that the problem of maintaining control over the flow of information in the digital age is also one that also plagues dissident movements and organizations. It is true that the digital age has been a boon for these groups when it comes to mobilization. At the same time, the ability of both democratic and authoritarian governments, as well as other interested parties, to monitor movement activities with digital media is a major problem for them. Evgeny Morozov (2011), one of the most articulate internet skeptics, seems to be only half-joking when he says: "The KGB used to torture in order to get this data. Now it's all available online."[7]

The second structural factor to be discussed has to do with the extent to which antagonistic publics from two sides of a conflict have any shared media.[8] Wolfsfeld (2004) made this point when he again compared the role of the media in the Oslo peace process with what happened in Northern Ireland. The communication ecosystem surrounding the Oslo process was typical: the Israeli public received almost all of its news from their own domestic press in Hebrew, and the Palestinians received theirs from a large number of Arabic sources. Each side was provided with a constant flow of ethnocentric news about the conflict. Among other things, each population was told that deaths on their side were tragedies carried out by a brutal enemy, while civilian casualties on the other side were rationalized away (Frosh & Wolfsfeld, 2007; Wolfsfeld, Frosh, & Awabdi, 2008).

The media ecosystem in Northern Ireland was exceptional because both sides of the conflict were, for the most part, getting their news from the same sources (Wolfsfeld, 2004). The BBC Northern Ireland employed both

Catholics and Protestants throughout their organization. In fact, it is illegal in Northern Ireland for any employer to discriminate on the basis of religion. In addition, while there were Protestant- and Catholic-owned newspapers, each had a commercial interest in attracting readers from the other side of the divide. It was probably one of the only examples in which commercial considerations were *good* for peace. The extent of shared media led quite naturally to all of these news organs covering the conflict in a manner that bridged the gap between the two communities. Wolfsfeld argued this was one of the reasons that, in contrast to most conflicts, the media in Northern Ireland made a *positive* contribution to leaders' attempts to bring peace to that troubled area.

So once again the advantages of using the PMP approach should be clear. The analysis starts with the level of political consensus about a peace process, which has a clear impact on media coverage of the process. Then one moves to the communication ecosystem, which dictates how the events are transformed into stories, which can then either make it easier or more difficult for leaders to promote their policies.

The Cultural Dimension of Analysis

The questions that most interest us here have to do, more than anything else, with the norms and frames that journalists and those who produce user-generated content have developed concerning the government and the military's actions and policies. It is best to think of these positions running along a continuum where one end involves complete support for government policies, while the other end is characterized by fervent opposition, and there are always many points in between.

We once again need to remind the reader of the massive number of problems when we attempt to say something about "the" media in any time or place. This is especially true in the digital age, when citizens have access to a much wider set of options than ever before. While it is certainly worth studying such variations, this shouldn't prevent researchers from attempting to assess the climate of opinion among journalists and other content providers.

The discussion brings us back to Knightley's (2004) book and especially his subtitle: *The War Correspondent as Hero and Myth-Maker*. As Knightley goes through the ways in which the role of war correspondents changed through so many wars, one begins to appreciate how journalists' norms vary over time and circumstance. For those who think sensationalism in news coverage of wars is something relatively new, the historical picture Knightley paints makes it abundantly clear that this is not the case. In fact, what happens now in Western democracies pales when compared to the way journalists covered wars in the nineteenth century. Journalists from that era were especially likely to demonstrate their patriotism by demonizing the enemy. Reporters in the American Civil War, for example, talked about: "Confederate women who had necklaces made from Yankee eyes, while the 'unholy Northerners' used the heads of Confederate dead for footballs" (Knightley, 2004, p. 21).

It is true that, as discussed, the values and norms of journalists covering violent conflicts and peace processes are heavily influenced by the political ecosystems that serve as their cultural base. However, it is also clear that there are independent financial motivations behind the traditional media's clear preference for sensationalist coverage. Indeed, many argue that publisher William Randolf Hearst's success was rooted in his understanding that sensationalist coverage of war provided the essential ingredient for making his fortune (Nasaw, 2001; Whyte, 2009).

This also explains why peace processes are not considered very newsworthy, unless there is either a breakthrough or a breakdown in negotiations. Wolfsfeld (2004) went so far as to claim that there was an inherent contradiction between news values and the needs of a peace process. A peace process is complicated, and journalists demand simplicity. A peace process takes time to unfold, and journalists demand immediate results. Most elements of a peace process are boring, and journalists are looking for drama. Finally, a peace process requires at least a minimum understanding of the other side's viewpoint, and the news media are inherently ethnocentric.

All of these factors become even more problematic in a sensationalist media environment. Here, too, a comparison between the coverage of the Northern Ireland peace process and the coverage of the Oslo peace process in the Israeli press is instructive (Wolfsfeld, 2004). The media ecosystem in Israel places a much greater emphasis on sensationalism, and this made it even more difficult to promote peace with the Palestinians. Among other things, journalistic norms in the Hebrew press led to hysterical coverage of each terrorist attack against the Oslo process, which helped solidify the opposition in Israel. In Northern Ireland the dominant norms of the media ecosystem are much less sensationalistic, and this was another factor that allowed leaders to move the process forward.

In sum, when looking at the cultural dimension of analysis in reference to the communication ecosystem, one has to think about both those norms and values that are rooted in the political ecosystem and those that can be considered independent of those variations. This hopefully will convince readers why a fuller understanding of the role of the media in violent conflicts must consider both the political and communication ecosystems. Almost all who have come before us tend to focus on either how changes in the ways the media function have an impact on conflicts and peace process (M > P), or how changes in the political environment (such as the level of consensus) have an impact on how the media behave. Adopting the PMP approach forces researchers to consider how both ecosystems and the relationship between them have an impact on violent conflicts as well as attempts at peace.

The Situational Dimension

There are a number of specific events that can have a significant influence on the media ecosystem surrounding the coverage of violent conflicts and peace processes. Examples include decisions to restrict or allow access to conflict areas, physical attacks on journalists covering terrorism or war, and misinformation campaigns initiated by either or both sides.

Here, however, we will return to what happens when there are major leaks about a war effort. In some cases, it makes sense to consider these cases as exceptions to the "politics first" proposition because they can entail a substantial amount of investigative journalism. More often than not, however, one finds a political actor leaking sensitive information in order to sway public opinion.

Two examples will suffice. The first took place in 1971 when Daniel Ellsberg (2003) released a top-secret research paper that provided some extremely embarrassing details about the government and military decisions surrounding disasters during the Vietnam War.[9] The second took place in 2010 and became known as the Wikileaks scandal (Leigh & Harding, 2011; Sifry, 2011). Afghan war documents were released by Wikileaks in 2010 and contained a massive number of military secrets. Here, too, it is clear that the goal was to embarrass the American military.

There are a number of analytical points to be made here. First, the fact that the Ellsberg leak took place in 1971 demonstrates that the problem of leaks did not begin after the creation of the internet. Second, the fact that in both cases the political activists who released the material had political goals tells us that they should not be seen as cases of pure investigative reporting. Thus, they are perfectly consistent with the "politics first" proposition. In addition, they represent a failure of the authorities to maintain control over the flow of information that, as discussed, we attribute to the structural dimension of the political ecosystem. The immediate results of that failure, we argue, led to a situational change in the media ecosystem because it provided journalists with an enormous amount of critical information about the two wars.

The Second P

We come to the final part of the PMP cycle: the subsequent influences of the various forms of media on war and peace. Our central argument is that variations in the political ecosystem are a major factor in explaining variations in the communication ecosystem, but that the various forms of media also have independent interests and norms that influence how they behave (or are used). The political influences work through and are transformed by the communication ecosystem, which then influences political processes—in this case in the areas of violent conflict and attempts to achieve peace. The last stage is what we have labeled the "second P." As noted, we do not consider it the *final* P, because the PMP cycle often involves multiple iterations.

We shall conclude this chapter by demonstrating that it makes sense to look at the full cycle in order to understand the role of the media in these processes. As indicated in the overview table, we will consider three major variables: the overall level of public support for conflict and peace policies; the extent of internal violence; and the level of political, military, and diplomatic success. This is in no way considered an exhaustive list, but it does represent some critical areas of study.

We start with considering the impact that media coverage can have on public opinions about peace. Fortunately, we have an excellent study that looks directly at the ways in which the media can have an independent impact on public opinions about peace. The research was carried out by Sheafer and Dvir-Gvirsman (2010) and returns us to the Oslo peace process. The cycle begins with the lack of political consensus about the Oslo process (the political ecosystem) that was discussed earlier. The situation was then exacerbated by journalists' preference for negative news, which is in keeping with our "selection and transformation" proposition. This second finding about negative news was confirmed in both Wolfsfeld (2004) and Sheafer and Dvir-Gvirsman (2010).

The Sheafer and Dvir-Gvirsman study went one step further; therefore it relates well to the "second P." The authors provided strong empirical evidence that the Israeli public was more likely to respond to negative framing than positive framing. Their conclusion is critical for our argument: "Since most of the coverage of the peace process and conflict focused on negative developments while ignoring positive ones, the media effect on public opinion was that of peace spoilers" (Sheafer & Dvir-Gvirsman, 2010, p. 205).

We now turn our attention to the impact of the media on opinions about war. One of the most important "second Ps" in this area of research relates to questions of how much impact news coverage has on domestic support for an ongoing war. The standard assumption is that when popular support for war moves up or down, it changes because people have received new information about the latest developments in the war. If this support-moving new information was independently selected by professional communicators, then the political impact of this "second P" could be profound because declining popular support for a war almost invariably translates into electoral losses for political parties that are seen as responsible for starting the conflict.

While there is quite a bit of research on this topic, a broad picture of the possibilities is collectively represented in three pieces of research: one by Baum and Groeling (2010), one by Althaus, Bramlett, and Gimpel (Althaus et al., 2012), and the third by Althaus and Coe (Althaus & Coe, 2011). Each of these studies provides clear evidence about the ways that media coverage can *independently* influence popular support for war.

Baum and Groeling (2010) drew similar conclusions about coverage of war to those of Sheafer and Dvir-Gvirsman (2010) concerning Israeli coverage of Oslo peace process. Focusing on popular domestic support for war in the United States, Baum and Groeling argue that journalists' ability to interpret the realities of war lend them to be especially attentive to those who are critical of war. Baum and Groeling show that credible and authoritative political leaders who defy expectations on whether they support or oppose the national leader (as when in-partisans to the American president offer criticisms about the war, or out-partisans offer praise for how the president is handling things) will tend to get news coverage regardless of what is going on with the war. More importantly, when these "costly signals" (as opposed to the more conventional "cheap talk" offered by in-partisans supporting their president or out-partisans criticizing the need for fighting) are carried in news coverage, they appear to have an important impact on changing levels of popular support quite apart from other developments that track the ongoing progress of the conflict.

This conclusion is especially interesting because it runs against our normal understanding that journalists are reluctant to criticize the government and the military during wars for fear of being considered unpatriotic (e.g., Carruthers, 2011; Knightley, 2004). Despite temporary seasons when even journalists "rally round the flag," as at the initial onset of wars, all forms of professional communication put a premium on reporting conflict, including internal conflict, even when the topic is an ongoing war involving one's own country (e.g., Althaus, 2003; Entman & Page, 1994; Hayes & Guardino, 2013). Thus, while journalists may be reluctant to criticize those in charge at the beginning stages of a war, they have a clear professional interest to be on the lookout for early signs of dissent that can provide the conflicts they so desperately need to produce copy. Baum and Groeling's (2010) study shows that this tendency among journalists produces a clear "second P" political impact in shifting the American public's levels of support or opposition to an ongoing conflict.

Another study done on this topic was carried out by Althaus, Bramlett, and Gimpel (2012). It explored what effect local news coverage of American military casualties had on popular approval of President George W. Bush during the early stages of the Iraq War. Although they couldn't analyze local news coverage everywhere in the United States over 18 months, they found a workaround by identifying the date of death and hometown of record for more than a thousand American military personnel killed during that period, and then matched tens of thousands of survey respondents for whether they lived within 25 miles of that casualty's hometown.

Using this innovative strategy, the authors examined whether local war deaths caused changes in people's approval for the president's handling of the war. They found clear evidence for this, and in the expected direction: presidential approval went down when local casualty levels went up, presumably reflecting the local news attention that was being given to the hometown casualty. But they found that these negative effects of local casualties on presidential approval faded after a few months. So when large numbers of "hometown heroes" die, there is a large negative effect on war support in that local area, but after the news of these losses fades into memory, this negative effect goes away.

This study's conclusions hold an important implication for the communication ecosystem's "second P" effects: any independent influence of the "media selection and transformation" proposition on war support is likely to be conditional. Any political impact of the communication ecosystem might be bound by space or time, and understanding these boundaries (and the conditions that produce them) is needed before the full impact of journalistic war coverage can be properly understood.

The third piece of research to mention is a study done by Althaus and Coe (2011) which showed that the most important "second P" impact of wartime news coverage might not have to do with the negativity or the topical focus of that coverage, but rather with the mere fact that a war is being covered at all. Their unprecedented analysis of war support dynamics across all major US military conflicts in the post–World War II era showed that even when accounting for the number of casualties, major wartime events, and how much time had passed since the start of the war, the most important driver of changes in levels of popular support for American wars was simply how much front-page newspaper coverage was being given to the war, regardless of whether things were going well or badly in the war. When the intensity of news attention was high, war support went up; and when news of the war dropped off the front pages, war support went down.

This pattern was consistent, the authors argued, with the idea that news attention to war primed supportive social identities (e.g., "When I'm reminded that we're at war, as a loyal American I guess I had better support the president"), but was inconsistent with the idea that Americans were simply updating their sense of the war's merits based on the latest information about the fighting. Once again, the Althaus and Coe study reminds us that the communication ecosystem's political impact can take unusual and unexpected forms, so that the mere fact that news outlets are focusing on an ongoing military conflict (as opposed to the latest celebrity gossip or political intrigue) can have a profound effect on the political constraints that might be imposed on governmental leaders.

The next list of political processes we think is important to briefly discuss has to do with the extent of internal violence. One understandable concern of many commentators, decision-makers, and scholars is the role of the media in inciting large-scale killings of minority groups. Perhaps the most well-documented case has to do with the role that radio played in the massacre of the Tutsi minority in Rwanda in the summer of 1994 (Kellow & Steeves, 1998; Li 2004; Rothbart & Bartlett, 2008). It is estimated that 800,000 people were murdered in about 100 days. One station in particular, RTLM, was both the most popular in the country and constantly called for more killing (Li, 2004). Li (2004, p. 9) begins his exploration of the subject with a blood-chilling quote from one of the broadcasts: "The graves are only half empty; who will help us fill them?"

Nevertheless, this is also a perfect example of why any serious study of this type of violence must *start* by considering the political ecosystem that preceded it. About 85% of Rwanda was Hutu, but the Tutsi minority had long dominated the country (Mamdani, 2020). The hatred between the two ethnic groups went back long before the massacre. Any serious analysis would also include what happened on April 6, 1994, when a plane carrying then-president Juvenal Habyarimana was shot down. This event would clearly fall into what we have labeled the situational dimension of analysis. Hutu extremists blamed the Rwandan Patriotic Front (RPF) for shooting the plane down, and the massacre began (Mamdani, 2020). So talking about the role of the radio without first talking about the historical background in Rwanda makes no sense. Politics must again come first.

The final political process listed in our overview table has been labeled "political, military, and diplomatic success." If positive journalistic coverage has even a small bearing on the chances that a war will be won, then anything that shapes the chances for positive coverage should contribute to the eventual success of the war. The link between battlefield success and news coverage of war was clearly illustrated by Althaus et al. (2011), whose analysis of *New York Times* coverage given to every major conflict from World War I through the first half of the Iraq War showed that news attention to American casualties went down whenever the prospects for eventual military victory went up. The clear implication is that battlefield success can distract news attention from a multitude of potentially negative topics that would ordinarily be covered when a war isn't going so well. This points to the communication ecosystem's potential to serve as an amplifier (rather than merely a conveyor) of battlefield success, which in turn can bolster a public's belief that the war is worth its costs in lives and treasure.

The larger point is not just that political success leads to media success, but that success with shaping media coverage can independently contribute to further political success. While getting legitimating coverage for a war effort is probably less likely to bring victory on the battlefield than the amount of military force one has at one's disposal, it can certainly have an impact on the outcome. This is likely to be especially true in conflicts that receive international news coverage. Every modern political leader and general has little choice but to keep an eye on how their actions are being covered both locally and internationally. It has become almost a cliché to say that even if one wins on the battlefield, one can still lose on the diplomatic front (Carruthers, 2011; Hallin, 1989; Leuprecht, et. al, 2009; Tumber & Palmer, 2004).

Conclusion

The goal of this chapter was to convince readers that the PMP approach provides a better conceptual map than previous models for understanding the varying roles of media in violent conflicts and peace processes. In way of summary, we will return to the four major ways in which this approach improves upon what has come before.

First, the PMP approach forces researchers to examine a "fuller picture" of the roles the various forms of media play in violent conflicts and peace processes. Hopefully, the large amount of research cited here has provided a convincing case that those who only look, for example, at how different forms of media coverage have an influence on the level of public support for war or peace policies are missing a critical part of the picture. It makes absolutely no sense to ignore what is happening on the ground when attempting to assess any independent media effects. Similarly, those who only look at the impact of what is happening on the ground in various forms of media are also putting on conceptual blinders. A wealth of studies demonstrate that the ways in which the various forms of media select and transform conflict and peace events into stories can also have an independent effect. It is critical then, to examine *both* the political and communication ecosystems.

The second contribution has to do with the distinction between structural and cultural variables. This distinction is important for many reasons, but here only two will be mentioned. First, it allows us to focus on those enduring structural changes in the political ecosystem (such as the level of formal control over the various forms of media) as opposed to cultural changes, that are more likely to vary (such as the level of elite and public consensus in support of conflict and peace policies). Second, this allows for a much better understanding of cross-national similarities and differences.

The third way in which the PMP approach provides something new has to do with our goal of pointing the way for our fellow researchers to contribute to cumulative knowledge. For those who are willing to adopt our approach, it provides some very specific "cells" which can be easily added to in order to move our understanding of the roles various forms of media can play in violent conflicts and peace processes. To give just one example, our hope is that those who are experts on social media will look at how structural, cultural, and situational factors help explain how user-generated content has an impact on the level of support for conflict and peace policies and on the level of internal violence in different countries.

The fourth contribution has to do with our stated goal of increasing dialogue among researchers in different fields of political communication. This should be fairly clear for those readers who take in all of the chapters in this book. Many of the points raised in this chapter should prove especially helpful for those who work in comparative political communication and are looking at the role of various forms of media in election campaigns. All of the cells and many of the variables can be easily adapted to studies that examine similar issues in other fields.

This is also true with regard to what we write in the next chapter, which deals with the role of the media in historical change. At first glance, many will find little similarity between the studies we discussed here and those that deal with the role of media in long-term social and political change. But hopefully, after finishing that chapter, the rationale for using the PMP approach to study both topics will become clearer.

4

PMP and Historical Changes

The purpose of this chapter is to demonstrate how the PMP principle can be helpful in understanding the roles media can play in historical changes in the political world. In this case, we feel comfortable talking about a PMP *cycle* in which changes in the political ecosystem lead to changes in the media ecosystem, which can then have a significant impact on political processes. In addition, we intend to show how the three dimensions of analysis—structural, cultural, and situational—are all helpful in understanding changes in political processes over time. Three cases will be analyzed: two from the United States and one from Israel. The American cases are the civil rights movement of the late 1950s and 1960s, and changes in opinion and policies concerning the death penalty, especially during the late 1990s and the decade starting in the year 2000. The Israeli case has to do with a historical change that also has taken place in other countries: the increasing personalization of politics. In this case, we take an even longer historical period. We look at 16 to 19 election campaigns for the Knesset that took place between 1949 and 2009.

There are two theoretical points to be made before beginning these analyses. Although it is conceptually convenient to think of what happened in terms of one very long cycle, the reality of such changes is that they involve a *series* of shorter PMP cycles. When changes take place in a political process, they often constitute a change in the political ecosystem, which then leads to further change in media practices. This is a further reminder that the "second P" is often *not* the "final P." Researchers would do well to think about both long-term changes and short-term cycles when attempting to apply the PMP principle to historical change.

Thus, the previously discussed changes in opinions and policies concerning nuclear energy in the United States (Gamson & Modigliani, 1989) involved a series of reinforcing changes in terms of anti-nuclear movements "persuading" the media to consider alternative frames that then increased

Building Theory in Political Communication. Gadi Wolfsfeld, Tamir Sheafer, and Scott Althaus, Oxford University Press.
© Oxford University Press 2022. DOI: 10.1093/oso/9780197634998.003.0004

the size and significance of these movements. In addition, as various political leaders became convinced about the dangers of nuclear energy, this also had an effect on the changing media frames about the issue. The point is that the most important historical changes in any country take time and involve a series of shorter PMP cycles.

The second point is that, although we emphasize the role of media in such historical changes, other factors can be equally—or even more—important in bringing about such developments. There are social, economic, technological, and (of course) political forces at work in such cases. We believe that media can play a major role in such changes, but it would be foolish for any social scientist to suggest that changes in media values and practices are the only reason for such changes. As argued earlier, some of these factors work *through* the media, but others have independent influences on political processes. It is understandable that our focus on the media might lead some readers to conclude that our analysis of these historical changes is overly simplistic and incomplete. To a certain extent, this criticism is justified. We leave it to historians to write a more comprehensive account and can only hope that they, as some have already done, also include the role that the media has played in such changes.

We again present an overview table in order to help guide the reader through the discussion (Table 4.1). Nevertheless, the discussion is structured differently than in previous chapters. As this analysis is based on three historical case studies, we will, in essence, be telling three "stories." The major sections are divided along the lines of the three cases: the US civil rights movement, the US anti-death penalty movement, and the change to a more personalized political system in Israel. This also explains why the "variables" are formulated in much more case-specific terms, rather than the more generic labels used in previous chapters. In addition, there will be somewhat less of an emphasis on using the seven analytical cells (including the "second P" cell) that were so central in previous discussions. Although the overview table is still meant to be a reminder of our overall conceptual approach, hopefully readers will find the alternative narrative approach appealing.

Table 4.1 PMP and Historical Change: An Overview Table

Dimension	Political Ecosystem	Communication Ecosystem	"Second p"
Structural	Increasing number and strength of civil rights and anti-death penalty organizations/movements (US) More personalized electoral system (Israel)	Introduction of television (US and Israel) Creation of "race beat" in mainstream media (US)	Passing of civil rights legislation (US)
Cultural	Changing cultural frames about civil rights and death penalty (US) Changing perceptions among elites and public about personalization of politics (Israel)	Changing media salience and frames for covering civil rights and death penalty (US) Changing journalistic norms for covering civil rights and the death penalty (US)	Changing opinions and policies concerning civil rights and death penalty (US)
Situational	Major incidents of anti-Black violence (e.g., Selma, US) Advent of DNA to prove innocence, Illinois moratorium on executions (death penalty, US)	Media storms about civil rights and the death penalty (US) Attacks on journalists during civil rights events (US)	Increasing personalized behavior among legislators and voters (Israel)

The PMP Principle and Civil Rights in the United States

If it hadn't been for the media—press and television—the civil rights movement would have been like a bird without wings, a choir without a song.
    —Congressman John Lewis, as quoted in Roberts and Klibanoff
    (2008, p. 407)

The US civil rights movement provides an excellent starting point for demonstrating how the PMP principle can be used to better understand the role of media in political change. Although there are a tremendous number of books and articles on the civil rights movement, the brilliant and Pulitzer Prize–winning book *The Race Beat*, by Gene Roberts and Hank Klibanoff (2008), is especially helpful for tracing media influences that propelled the movement forward. Roberts and Klibanoff carried out an exhaustive and extremely detailed study of the ongoing interactions between Black leaders and journalists during these critical years. A careful reading of this history provides a clear case in which changes in the political ecosystem (including a major rise in Black activism and the violent reactions by some Southern authorities and citizens) led to significant changes in media values and practices (e.g., more journalists being sent to cover the "race beat" and more sympathetic coverage for the civil rights movement), which led to subsequent, significant changes in the political process (e.g., changes in public opinion and major legislation about civil rights). The authors also provide some important insights into the changing communication ecosystem (especially the introduction of television) during the years in question, demonstrating how this contributed to the political change that took place.

In this section we intend to show why the two central propositions underlying PMP are essential for understanding what happened during those fateful years. The "politics first" proposition tells us that the media are, for the most part, unlikely to initiate political change on their own; they react to what takes place in the political arena. The "media selection and transformation" proposition reminds us that one must also look at the communication ecosystem to understand the full picture. The stories that many journalists chose to tell about the movement and the growing power of television news had a significant impact on the political process concerning civil rights in the United States (the "second P" in PMP). There can be little doubt that without these "wings," political change concerning civil rights would have taken much longer to get off the ground.

The Political Ecosystem Surrounding Civil Rights

The Structural Dimension of Analysis

We start the analysis by looking at the *structural* changes in the political environment that took place during the 1950s and 1960s in the United States. Here, we will focus on one particular structural change: the creation, organization, and expansion of the social movements fighting for the civil rights of Black Americans. A more detailed analysis would also include other important structural changes, such as the *Brown v. Board of Education* decision by the Supreme Court in 1954 to end segregation in public schools (Patterson, 2002) and the fact that two relatively liberal presidents (Kennedy and Johnson) took office in the 1960s (Purdum, 2014). These and other structural changes in the political environment also had a significant impact on media values and practices.

It is important to begin this story *before* race was a major public issue in the United States. There were some protest activities going on in the 1940s, but they attracted little media attention apart from what was then called the "Negro press" and a small number of liberal Southern newspapers (Roberts & Klibanoff, 2008). The *New York Times* established its first Southern office in 1947. The issue of race relations was, for the most part, a non-issue. In many ways, this situation was similar to the early days of the women's movement (Ferree & Hess, 2002; Lind & Salo, 2002), the gay rights movement (Aday, 1996; Clendinen & Nagourny, 2001), and the previously discussed antinuclear power movement (Gamson & Modigliani, 1989).

The four most well-known national organizations at that time were the Student Nonviolent Coordinating Committee (SNCC), the Congress of Racial Equality (CORE), the National Association for the Advancement of Colored People (NAACP), and the Southern Christian Leadership Conference (SCLC; Carson, 1995; Fairclough, 2001; Sellers & Terrell, 2018; Sullivan, 2009). It is noteworthy that although the NAACP was founded in 1909, and CORE was founded in 1942, the two other organizations were founded at critical moments in the civil rights struggle. The SNCC was founded in 1960, and the SCLC was founded in 1957. The first president of the SCLC was the Reverend Martin Luther King Jr.

Their increasing institutional strength allowed these movements to organize an increasingly large number of protests (Andrews & Biggs, 2006; Friedman & Richardson, 2008; Roberts & Klibanoff, 2008; Lee, 2002;

McGhee, 2014). The most well-known are the Montgomery bus boycott that started in 1955, the Woolworth cafeteria sit-ins in Greensboro, North Carolina, in 1960, and the marches from Selma to Montgomery in 1965. These acts and others put increasing pressure on the Black, local, and national press to start following the civil rights movement on a regular basis (Roberts & Klibanoff, 2008). The creation of the "race beat" is a wonderful example of how changes in the political ecosystem can lead to structural changes in the communication ecosystem.

In addition, Andrews and Biggs (2006) show that news media were critical in the disbursement of information about the sit-ins to many other communities in the South. This is yet another example of how media can have a subsequent yet significant impact on the political process (the "second P"). In many ways, one could draw useful parallels between the ways in which the traditional news media served as a catalyst for protest in those days to the role that social media play today.

If one thinks about how these organizations were formed and how they grew in size and importance throughout the 1960s, it is difficult not to think again about a series of PMP cycles at work. These political movements were able to generate publicity for their cause, which brought new members and supporters, which then provided them with further resources for political action and for generating even more publicity.

There is nothing inevitable about social movements achieving this type of success. Many social movements, perhaps even most, are unable to generate enough publicity or public support to enlarge their base. Indeed, the fact that the NAACP was founded at the very beginning of the twentieth century reminds us that political and media success depends on the nature of the political environment at a particular time and place. For some movements it takes an extended period of time before they achieve any progress, and others never succeed in doing so. For the civil rights movement, the creation and political success of these movements catalyzed an important structural change in the political environment surrounding this issue.

The Cultural Dimension of Analysis

No army can withstand the strength of an idea whose time has come.
—Senator Everett Dirksen, June 10, 1964[1]

These dramatic words were stated by Dirksen, the Republican minority leader at the time, for explaining why he changed his mind concerning the passage of the Civil Rights Act of 1964.[2] In the same famous speech, Dirksen referred to a number of other historical changes which were initially controversial until their "time had come."

> Dirksen summarized the long history of once controversial reforms that had become an accepted part of American life, from laws mandating pure food and drugs, to those barring child labor and governing wages and hours, to the creation of the civil service system and the advent of women's suffrage. (Purdum, 2014, p. 292)

These are all excellent examples of how historical changes can eventually become part of the political consensus. The argument we are making is that although the media can often play a critical role in accelerating, shaping, and reinforcing such changes, they rarely *initiate* them. In each of these cases, and in many others, political activists were responsible for promoting these changes, and the media were among the more important tools they used to convince both elites and the public that the "time had come."

The cultural dimension of analysis deals with the aggregate of individual and collective values, beliefs, norms, and actions among political actors concerning political matters within a particular time and place. An important goal of the many protests carried out by the civil rights movement was to increase the *salience* of the issue. The activists' assumption, which proved accurate, was that if they could raise the salience of the issue in the media, this would also raise the salience of the issue among the public and elites. In the field of political communication, the first part of this cycle is referred to as agenda *building* and the second as agenda *setting* (McCombs & Shaw, 1972; Sheafer, Shenhav, Takens, & van Atteveldt, 2014; Weaver & Elliot, 1985).

In their analysis of the role of the media in the civil rights movement, Roberts and Klibanoff (2008) devote quite a bit of attention to the well-known work by Swedish Nobel-laureate economist Gunnar Myrdal, *An American Dilemma*. Despite the fact that it was published in 1944, Myrdal was quite optimistic that once Americans became more knowledgeable about what he called the "Negro problem," they would change their views about what needed to be done. The press, argued Myrdal, was an essential tool for ending people's ignorance:

Myrdal reached the conclusion that would prove to be uncannily prescient. Even before he got to the fiftieth page of his tome, he wrote "To get publicity is of the highest strategic importance to the Negro people." (Roberts & Klibanoff, 2008, p. 6)

As reported by Winter and Eyal (1981), civil rights activists were extremely successful in raising the salience of the issue within the media, and this in turn had a dramatic influence on the salience among the public. Indeed, the change in public opinion about the importance of this issue over the 22-year span they studied (1954–1976) rose from 0% to 52% of Americans naming civil rights as the "most important issue facing the American public today." Another relevant study was carried out by Burstein (1979) that demonstrated that only when well over 50% of the American public expressed support for various forms of civil rights were US legislators willing to pass anti-discrimination laws.

Roberts and Klibanoff (2008) provide an excellent summary of how important the media were in these changing attitudes:

> At no other time in U.S. history were the news media . . . more influential than they were in the 1950s and 1960s, sometimes for the better and sometimes for the worse. There is little in American society that was not altered by the civil rights movement. There is little in the civil rights movement that was not changed by the news coverage of it. And there is little in the way the news media operate that was not influenced by their coverage of the movement. (p. 7)

The Situational Dimension of Analysis: Selma

What happened in Selma, Alabama, in March 1965 provides especially good evidence for why it is important to also examine situational changes in the political ecosystem when attempting to apply the PMP principle. The events there, which are now better known due to the 2014 movie *Selma*, demonstrate that the PMP approach can help us understand the role of media not only in long-term political change but also with regard to more short-term cycles.

The Reverend Dr. Martin Luther King Jr., had decided that Selma, Alabama, would be the perfect place to confront forces aligned against the movement.

There were two important elements in his media strategy that proved essential for the movement's success. The first was the insistence of using nonviolent tactics that would work against those attempting to portray them as extremists (Roberts & Klibanoff, 2008; Lee, 2002). The second, somewhat less known, was to find locations where the authorities were more likely to react to their demonstrations with violence (Roberts & Klibanoff, 2008). Selma Sheriff Jim Clark was known to be quick-tempered and violent. This was critical because without a violent reaction to the protests, activists would never make it on the evening news or the front page of the major newspapers. Indeed, an earlier attempt in Albany, Georgia, failed because the police chief there responded with a minimal amount of force (Roberts & Kilbanoff, 2008).

The most famous incident in Selma was what became to be known as "Bloody Sunday," which took place on March 7, 1965.[3] This was the first of three important marches, and as expected, Sheriff Clark responded with tremendous violence. The scenes of men, women, and children being beaten were televised around the world.[4] The picture of an unconscious Amelia Boynton lying on the infamous bridge also appeared on the front page of many newspapers (Roberts & Klibanoff, 2008).

The political response to what happened was both swift and significant. Thousands of people from around the country traveled to attend the second and third marches that took place on March 9 and March 21. Even more importantly, President Johnson gave a special nationally televised speech on the issue to a joint session of Congress, demanding a new voting rights law. The Voting Rights Act was passed on August 6. It would be hard to imagine that all this would have happened so quickly without the tremendous media coverage of the violence. Our argument, then, is that the political events, the resulting coverage, and the political response that characterized the Selma protest can be seen as a microcosm of what happened more generally with regard to the civil rights movement.

It is important to note that the entertainment media also reacted to the increasing interest in racial issues during these years. The willingness of the entertainment industry to reflect changes in the political climate is another important ramification of the PMP principle. Here are just a few of the important films of the 1960s that dealt with the issue of race: *A Raisin in the Sun* (1961), *To Kill a Mockingbird* (1962), *Guess Who's Coming to Dinner* (1967), and *In the Heat of the Night* (1967). Here, too, the fact that Americans and the US news and entertainment media were discussing these issues also tells us how different types of media can serve to reinforce and accelerate political change.

The Media Ecosystem Surrounding the Civil Rights Movement

To understand the contribution of media to the success of the civil rights movement we turn to the "media selection and transformation" proposition, which states that all forms of media do not merely reflect the nature of the political ecosystem; they can also have an independent effect on political processes by selecting and transforming political events and issues into stories.

The news media were not merely giant megaphones for the events surrounding the civil rights movement; they were also storytellers. Editorial decisions about how and how much to report these events were a critical part of this process. Thinking about this aspect of the PMP cycle provides a number of more general insights about how media frames can change over time and how this change can influence the final outcome.

The Structural Dimension of Analysis

Technological changes represent some of the most important structural variations in the communication ecosystem that can affect the way events are transformed into news. Thus, if one thinks about the many technological changes that have taken place in the coverage of elections (see Chapter 2) and wars (Knightley, 2004) one begins to appreciate the importance of such factors. One reason why this is so important in thinking about our second proposition is that these changes can often be considered *independent* developments in that they are always directly linked to changes in the political environment.

The most important technological change during the late 1950s and early 1960s in the United States was the spread of television to homes around the country. Williams and Delli Carpini (2011) write extensively about the "rise and fall of the age of broadcast news" (p. 51) in their book on the topic. For our purposes, the increasing popularity and perceived credibility of the major television networks during the 1960s are critical. As the authors point out, by 1967, television had become the most important avenue for people to get news. Over these years, television also gained in credibility. By 1968, television was twice as likely to be believed as newspapers (Williams & Delli-Carpini, 2011, p. 61). Thus, television grew into a major force for informing

Americans all over the country of what was happening with regard to a long list of public issues, including civil rights.

While the horrifying still pictures on the front pages of newspapers were also important, there can be no denying that having events such as the Selma marches broadcast into the living rooms of so many Americans had a major influence on the political process. It is not surprising that one of the most racist sheriffs complained about things getting "much worse since television" (Roberts & Klibanoff, 2008, p. 198). Here is the way *New York Times* television critic Jack Gould described the impact of television (as cited in Roberts & Klibanoff, 2008):

> The medium of television is proving an indispensable force in the Negro's pursuit of human rights. Through the home screen, the Washington drama of mass protest was brought to life in virtually every household in the nation, a social phenomenon inconceivable before the age of electronics. . . . The gentle entrance and exit of so much petitioning humanity was an editorial in movement. Its eloquence could not be the same in only frozen word or stilled picture. (p. 348)

In addition, given the fact that television was relatively new in the 1960s, one can assume that the experience of seeing such images must have been very different than it would be today. One also has to wonder whether Sheriff Clark and other segregationist law officials had any understanding of what would happen when their actions were being broadcast around the world. In contrast, the police and military of today are all very aware of the impact such images can have, especially in the age of cell phone cameras and YouTube (Wolfsfeld, 2017; Wolfsfeld & Tsifroni, 2018).

There was another relevant structural change in the mainstream news media, but in contrast to the spread of television, this one was directly related to the ongoing changes in the political ecosystem. We are referring to the increasing use of African Americans as legitimate news sources.[5] This is a critical element in changing media coverage because it gives minorities and other challengers a voice in public discourse. There can be little doubt that the creation of a "race beat" contributed to this change (Roberts & Klibanoff, 2008). The fact that Martin Luther King became a nationally recognized figure was also an important part of this changing landscape.

An important turning point with regard to Black sources was a documentary about the Freedom Riders produced in 1961 by Harry Smith of CBS. As reported by Roberts and Klibanoff (2008):

What made the program remarkable was that for the first time in a major national forum, black citizens in the South were given equal time with whites in discussing a city's racial problems. They didn't hold back. . . . Whites, at best, came across as defensive. (p. 251)

In thinking about news frames, it is interesting that many critics of Smith's broadcast complained that he wasn't being "objective." His response was instructive; he claimed that demands for objectivity on this issue are the "equivalent of saying that truth is to be found somewhere between right and wrong, equidistant between good and evil" (Roberts & Klibanoff, 2008, p. 252). In the end, however, it would seem that in 1961 the American audience was not yet ready for such a change. Smith was forced to resign from a CBS position he had held for over two decades.

The Cultural Dimension of Analysis

When discussing the cultural dimension of analysis with regard to the communication ecosystem, we are referring to the changing norms and values of content producers covering a certain issue. The very fact that, as discussed, the mainstream media were giving increasing attention to civil rights during the 1960s is ample proof that professional norms were changing. In addition, as is made abundantly clear by Roberts and Klibanoff (2008), many journalists were also becoming convinced that "the time had come" for equal rights for Blacks. It is worth repeating here the final part of a quote cited above: "And there is little in the way the news media operate that was not influenced by their coverage of the movement" (Roberts & Klibanoff, 2008, p. 7).

It is interesting, however, to remember that not all journalists were changing their views on this issue. When comparing major events coverage of the Northern, Southern, and Black press, one finds that each of these audiences was exposed to very different interpretations of what was happening (Lee, 2002; Roberts & Klibanoff, 2008). Thus, while major civil rights protests were reported in the Southern news media, they were rarely placed on the front page, and the frame would more likely be questions of "law and order" rather than "injustice" (Wolfsfeld, 2022). This is not to suggest that there was no change taking place among some Southern journalists about this issue, or that there were not important variations with that part of the media. However, as Roberts and Klibanoff (2008) pointed out, even Southern journalists who were more conflicted about what was happening on the ground had to moderate their writing, so as not to anger their audiences.

Two points are worth mentioning here. First, it is always a problem when we refer to "*the* media." This is especially true in recent years because many news organs have become more partisan, in addition to the spread of social media. When journalistic norms about covering an issue or leader change over time, the degree and speed of change will vary among different news outlets. Second, when talking about "cross-cultural" variations, we need to think not only about differences among countries (which will be discussed in Chapter 5), but also about cultural differences *within* countries. Thus, as one applies the PMP principle, it is important to think about such differences when attempting to assess both the political and communication ecosystems.

The Situational Dimension of Analysis

The situational dimension of analysis refers to changes in the communication environment stemming from major events or circumstances that can influence how content producers collect, construct, transmit, and validate political information. The history of ongoing interactions between journalists, activists, and opponents over civil rights provides a wealth of incidents that could be used to demonstrate the utility of this dimension. As in the earlier discussion about the political ecosystem, we are interested in *short-term* changes in the communication ecosystem that have an impact on how journalists operate. Here we will provide just one example as an illustration.

What happened in Little Rock, Arkansas, in 1957 (Anderson, 2010) is well-known to most Americans who lived through that period or studied it in school. The Supreme Court had issued a decision to force the nation's schools to desegregate. By 1957, the NAACP had registered nine Black students to attend Little Rock Central High School. On the day the children were supposed to start studying, an angry crowd of segregationists gathered, and the scenes of their racist shouts and spitting proved to be an iconic moment in news coverage of the civil rights movement. One photograph in particular came to symbolize the good-versus-evil theme that would come to dominate a good deal of the subsequent news coverage during the 1960s: the scene of 15-year-old Elizabeth Eckford walking alone through the angry crowd as she attempted to enter the school (Margolick, 2011).[6] Eventually,

President Eisenhower was compelled to send federal troops to ensure that Black students could enter the school safely.

Here we want to focus on two situational components that are relevant to the present analysis. The first has to do with the fact that during these events many journalists were severely beaten by the angry crowd (Roberts & Klibanoff, 2008). This would not be the first or last time such violence took place, but these attacks made it perfectly clear that the reporters were considered by many local whites to be the enemy. While the sympathies of most Northern reporters were formed before Little Rock, it would be difficult to argue that this had no impact on their ongoing coverage of future events. The argument is that there are certain specific events, often associated with some form of violence, that reporters find impossible to forget, and the impact can sometimes be long lasting. This is why we see such events as best categorized within the situational dimension of analysis.

The second component is that the scenes at Little Rock were so shocking that they even had an effect on the normally pro-segregationist Southern press. As reported by Roberts and Klibanoff (2008), the events at Little Rock led 67% of the newspapers in the North and 68% in the South. Attacking children was simply too ugly to be dismissed. For the first time, a significant number of the Southern newspapers expressed a certain amount of sympathy for the Black children. The *Arkansas Gazette* lost a good deal of advertising and subscription money because of this coverage and eventually had to issue a pro-segregationist editorial in order to prevent further damage (Roberts & Klibanoff, 2008, p. 174).

The point of this example is to show that researchers need to understand how situational variables can also influence journalists' norms and values. We also discussed this issue in Chapter 3, which dealt with the role of media in conflict and peace processes. This resulting coverage can then have a significant influence on the political process that is consistent with the media selection and transformation proposition. Whether the effects are short- or long-term in nature will vary over time and circumstance.

In Sum

In sum, the story of the civil rights movement provides strong evidence of the how the PMP approach helps explain the role of media in political change. As with many other successful movements, it begins with activists struggling to gain public attention and sympathy for their cause. If they succeed in carrying out newsworthy events and mobilizing a sufficient amount of political support for their cause, content producers start taking notice, and news frames begin to change. In addition, different media have their own norms, routines, and interests, and it is critical to think about how journalists transform issues and events into news stories. There is also significant variance in how different journalists and different types of media cover an issue. In the next, but certainly not the last, part of this cycle, the news stories themselves have an impact on elites and on the public and, in some cases, the new interpretive frames are adopted by an increasing number of people. In the most successful cases, such as the struggle for civil rights, this can lead to significant changes in policies and laws.

It is intriguing to think about how the role of media in the civil rights movement would have been different if the movement was active in the digital age. In fact, given what happened in the United States and other countries in 2020, researchers will be given a multitude of opportunities to study just this question. There are commentators who believe that the video of George Floyd being killed by police in May of that year and the massive number of demonstrations related to that event could represent a tipping point in terms of how the United States deals with racism. There can be little doubt that political communication researchers will be attempting to assess the role of various forms of media in what has taken place and what will transpire in the future. Hopefully, this chapter can convince some that the PMP approach could offer a useful analytical tool for examining this and similar issues.

PMP and the Death Penalty in the United States

The second example of how PMP can be helpful in explaining the role of the media in political change comes from the debate over the death penalty in the United States. The fact that we are no longer talking about changes concerning minority rights is important, for it demonstrates that the PMP cycle can be applied to different types of political change.

Here we will rely extensively on one important piece of empirical research: Baumgartner, De Boef, and Boydstun's (2008) *The Decline of the Death Penalty and the Discovery of Innocence.*[7] The authors employed a different theoretical approach to the issue, and the PMP principle is not mentioned in the study.[8] Nevertheless, the massive amount of evidence they have collected on the topic provides strong support for the PMP approach. Equally important, while the case being made for applying PMP to the civil rights movement was based on a historical analysis, here the evidence is also quantitative. This should help persuade some social scientists who prefer this type of data.

As before, we start by talking about changes in the political ecosystem, especially changes in the cultural and situational dimensions. We then talk about ways in which the American communication ecosystem changed concerning the death penalty and how this served to accelerate changes in both public opinion and public policies addressing the death penalty. In the interest of brevity, we shall not employ all six dimensions of analysis as we did in previous discussions. Nevertheless, we did suggest in our overview of Table 4.1 how some of the variables would easily fit into the various cells.

Changes in the American Political Ecosystem Concerning the Death Penalty

While political change concerning the death penalty is in some ways very different from what happened with regard to civil rights, there are also critical similarities. The story again begins with a group of activists (mostly law students this time) working hard to fight against the death penalty in the United States. The media were again a major tool for bringing about a change in public opinion and policies. As Baumgartner et al. (2008) convincingly demonstrate, a good deal of these groups' success can be attributed to their successful promoting of a new frame—the "innocence frame"—to the American news media and to a growing number of political elites. As a result, news media practices for covering death penalty cases changed significantly. Journalists gave much more attention to the issue, and the innocence frame gradually came to dominate media discourse. This in turn was one of the factors that led to a change in both public opinions and policies, including many states placing a moratorium on executions (the "second P").

It is helpful to again begin by talking about the "pre-change" period. There was extremely strong support for the death penalty among Americans. For many years, about 80% were in favor of executions (Baumgartner et al., 2008). The debate over the issue often focused on questions of deterrence, morality, and constitutionality (i.e., cruel and unusual punishment). Given the continually strong support for the death penalty, it is clear that few of these anti-death-penalty arguments resonated with most of the American people in those years.

Baumgartner et al. (2008) provide a very careful chronology of the founding and growth of the innocence movement. In the 1980s, a number of research and legal aid organizations were founded with the goal of "providing research and legal assistance to wrongfully convicted defendants serving long sentences or waiting on death row" (p. 63). As the authors point out, the fact that these "innocence projects" were mostly located within major universities was important, not only because it provided a good supply of bright, young, motivated individuals, but also because it made the organizations more newsworthy and legitimate. It could be argued that this was a *structural change* in the political ecosystem in that new institutions were being created that facilitated the promotion of the innocence frame. Here is what the authors said about this change:

> News that college students have helped to free an innocent man from prison tells a fundamentally different story than news that high-powered attorneys have accomplished the same feat. When lawyers win their clients' release, the public may assume that some ploy was involved; people may assume the defendant was guilty, even if the charges were dropped. . . . This is not typically the reaction when an underfunded, overworked, inexperienced, and unpaid group of students unearths clear evidence that an obscure inmate sitting for years in a state penitentiary was convicted erroneously or, even better, identifies the guilty party and brings a real criminal to justice. (p. 63)

The major point for demonstrating the utility of the PMP principle has to do with the major *cultural change* in the political environment that took place in the late 1990s and the decade starting in the year 2000. As discussed in earlier chapters, the cultural dimension of analysis includes changes in beliefs and values about major social issues as well as levels of political consensus among elites. Only a few years earlier, the legal and political momentum was moving in the opposite direction. In 1994, President Clinton passed the Violent Crime and Law Enforcement Act that expanded the federal death penalty to 60 additional crimes.[9]

The promotion of the innocence frame by anti-death-penalty groups was a major change in their approach, and this resonated with a large number of journalists, elites, and publics. Thus, a structural and cultural change in the political ecosystem led to a more general cultural change within a number of important actors (the "second P"). The authors emphasize that although anti-death-penalty groups were critical, they were not the only important changes that took place during these years. This was *not* simply a case of successful public relations, but rather a series of reinforcing events, all of which contributed to a significant change in media coverage, public sentiment, and public policy.

The year 2000 was a critical turning point in this dramatic change in the political ecosystem. The following words come from an article (Lutton, 2000) published in that year in the progressive magazine *In These Times*. The piece is entitled, "The End of Executions?" and the author quotes both Mike Farrell, who was president of an anti-death-penalty group based in California, and JoAnn Patterson, whose son was on death row.

"A confluence of events came to a head," Farrell says. "There was the conference on the wrongly convicted at Northwestern University in Chicago, the whole explosion of the issue of innocents on Death Row, Governor Ryan's [from Illinois] decision to declare a moratorium, the *Chicago Tribune*'s articles, the movie of Sister Helen Prejean's book *Dead Man Walking*—there were so many things that were happening. All of these things kind of collided at a time and . . . people suddenly began to wake up. And I think it has established a momentum that in my view is irreversible. . . . This has left activists somewhere between dumbstruck and giddy. "It was like they finally heard us," says JoAnn Patterson, mother of Illinois Death Row prisoner Aaron Patterson, who has worked with the Illinois Death Penalty Moratorium Project.[10]

In some ways, this statement reminds one of the quote by Senator Dirksen about the civil rights movement and an idea "whose time has come." Cultural assumptions about the death penalty had changed, and these changes were reflected and reinforced in the communication ecosystem.

The Situational Dimension of Analysis

As alluded to earlier, there were a number of events that helped advocates promote the innocence frame to both the media, political leaders, and the general public. In Table 4.1 we point to two such events that are especially notable: the advent of DNA analysis and the Illinois moratorium on executions (Baumgartner et al., 2008).

It is clear that as DNA analysis became more acceptable as a solid piece of evidence in criminal trials, this had a critical impact on the ability of those promoting the innocence frame to make a more convincing argument. Here was supposedly uncontroversial, scientific "proof" that innocent people were being sentenced to death. The reason we put the world "proof" in quotation marks is that some scholars claim that DNA results are not as conclusive as most believe (Aronson & Cole, 2009). Some readers might find it problematic that we place this event within the political ecosystem. It can be argued that these types of *real-world* events provide important ammunition for political activists and thus can be considered political events.

The second event that is listed in Table 4.1 is the Illinois moratorium on executions. In January 2003, Republican Governor George Ryan blanket-commuted the sentences of 167 inmates condemned to death. But the official moratorium was declared in 2011 by Democratic Governor Pat Quinn, who declared that he was abolishing the death penalty because he had become convinced that it was impossible to create a system that could completely prevent innocent people from being put to death (Warden, 2012). This was a precedent that clearly had an effect on other states around the country. Not all would follow the Illinois example, but it was clear that it provided important ammunition for those trying to achieve similar goals.

The fact that Illinois and other states made this decision could also be considered a "second P," a subsequent effect of what had happened in previous years in both the political and economic ecosystems. The point to bear in mind is that, as stated earlier, there is no reason to think about the "second P" as the "final P." There is often a feedback cycle where changes in the political process lead to *further* changes in the communication ecosystem that lead to further changes in political processes.

Changes in the Media Ecosystem Surrounding the Death Penalty

The key decade for change in media practices concerning the death penalty was the 1990s. There were two major changes, both of which were a godsend for all of those working to end capital punishment. The first was a dramatic rise in the *amount* of media attention given to those sentenced to death. Part of the reason had to do with the increasing success that activists and lawyers were having in getting their clients exonerated. As Baumgartner et al. (2008) point out, however, this was only part of the story. They compared two time periods: 1992–1998 and 1999–2005.

> The number of exonerations increased over this time from an average of three per year in the early years to seven per year in the more recent period. This is an important increase, to be sure. But, because each individual exoneree has become more newsworthy, the yearly average of stories has multiplied almost twenty-four times. The average number of stories that an individual exonerated from death row today is likely to get is more than thirteen times the number that someone exonerated in the pre-innocence frame could expect. Something changed, and it was not the facts. Exonerees are simply more newsworthy today than before the innocence movement began. (p. 97)

This analysis is a perfect example of those instances in which the changes in media values and practices create an added impetus to political change. These editorial decisions can probably be attributed to both the changing political ecosystem surrounding the death penalty (a dependent effect) and commercial considerations about the drama associated with exonerees (an independent effect).

The second major change in media practices noted by Baumgartner et al. (2008) was that journalists increasingly adopted the innocence frame to cover the issue. The authors were able to track eight major frames that were used in media discourse to cover the death penalty from 1964 to 2005. A good deal of early news stories used an "eye for an eye" frame or a "constitutional" frame. The innocence frame gradually became the most salient frame employed by the American news media. During the 1990s, the innocence frame "completely dominated media discussion, with no alternative frame existing" (Baumgartner et al., 2008, p. 148).

The empirical evidence provided by Baumgartner et al. offers strong support for the PMP approach. The changes concerning the death penalty in the United States began in the political ecosystem in large part because activists were enjoying an unprecedented amount of success in convincing journalists, legal experts, and political leaders that innocent people were being executed. This led to a dramatic change in media practices, which included far more attention to exonerees and adoption of the innocence frame in a good deal of the coverage. As with the case of the civil rights movement, this change in coverage served as a powerful catalyst for accelerating the rate of political change. Fortunately, as discussed below, the authors were able to empirically isolate the net influence of media coverage on the political process.

It is also worth noting another change in the communication ecosystem during this time period. The entertainment media began putting a major emphasis on DNA testing as one of the primary ways of proving either the innocence of guilt of suspects. Television shows such as CSI, as well as many movies, helped reinforce the idea that the advent of DNA was a definitive change in the criminal justice system (Ley, Jankowski, & Brewer, 2012).

The Subsequent Influence on the Political Environment Concerning the Death Penalty

This brings us to the "second P": the evidence telling us that the changes in media practices concerning the death penalty led to subsequent changes in the political process. This is always the trickiest part of the equation because attempting to isolate media effects from all other factors that can have an effect on the political world is never easy. Fortunately, Baumgartner et al. (2008) carried out an extremely careful analysis of this relationship and found strong support that the "net tone" of media coverage did indeed have an independent effect on both public opinion and public policy concerning the death penalty.

We start with the issue of public opinion. As the authors point out, American opinions about the death penalty were extremely stable for many years. One of the reasons is that these opinions are closely tied to people's religious and ethical beliefs, and such attitudes are especially resistant to change. In their analysis, Baumgartner et al. (2008) were able to employ hundreds of surveys conducted on the issue between 1976 and 2006. In the end, they found two major factors that had statistically significant effects on changes in public opinion: the number of homicides and the "net tone" of media coverage. As homicide rates go down and the net tone of media content is more oriented toward the innocence frame, public support for the death penalty goes down. As the authors point out, one can only understand these changes by charting the variables over an extended period.

What all this means in plain English is that public opinion does indeed respond to homicide levels and to the net tone of media coverage about the death penalty. But the change is sluggish and not immediate. Opinion slowly drifts in response to important changes to the tenor of the debate as expressed in the media and to the violent crime rate. This opinion shift is sensible and important, but it is not immediate. (Baumgartner et al., 2008, p. 192)

It is also important to note that the authors found that the overall impact of the net tone of media coverage was equal to the influence of homicide levels during the 40 years they studied. This finding again tells us that the editorial decisions made by journalists can indeed have a subsequent and significant impact on a political process.

An even more important influence of the news media on the political process surrounding the death penalty concerns the number of death sentences issued. This is a critical test for the PMP approach because it has to do with changes in public policy. Public policy about the death penalty is reflected in decisions by governors to declare a moratorium on executions, prosecutors deciding whether to push for the death penalty, and decisions by juries about whether to impose the death penalty on defendants. The most objective measure of these policy shifts is the number of death sentences issued. As pointed out by Baumgartner et al. (2008), between the years 1961 and 2005, the yearly number varied greatly, from a low of 50 to a high of 357. Especially relevant to the present discussion, between the years of 1997 and 2005 there was a 60% drop in the number of death sentences.

Here, too, the researchers' main goal was to determine the major factors that best explained the rise and fall of death penalty sentences over that long period of time. There were three factors that were important: the number of homicides, changes in public opinion concerning the death penalty, and media framing (net tone). The most important conclusion in support of the PMP principle was the extremely significant impact of the net tone of media coverage on death sentences. In fact, net tone was *four times* more important in explaining the number of death sentences than the number of homicides during a particular year.

These findings demonstrate the "media selection and transformation" proposition: content producers can also have a subsequent and independent impact on political processes due to the ways in which they select and transform political events into stories. While the number of homicides can have an effect on policies concerning the death penalty, the way that media told these stories had the most important impact.

To summarize, the massive and painstaking research carried out by Baumgartner et al. (2008) provides an extremely rich illustration of how the PMP principle helps explain the role of media in political change. Changes in public opinion and policies concerning the death penalty in the United States begin with significant changes in the political ecosystem (activists promoting the innocence frame) that led to a measurable change in the way American media covered the issue, which in turn led to dramatic changes in both public opinion and a significant drop in executions.

We are not arguing here that this all took place in one linear path. There can be little doubt that all of these processes, as well as many other events, reinforced one another. As the authors of *The Decline of the Death Penalty* point out, it is best to see the relationship between politics and media on this issue as not only intertwined but *iteratively* intertwined. There were at least three other mechanisms fueled by the shift in media coverage: an increasing wariness on the part of juries to select a death sentence, an increasing tendency of defense attorneys to bring up the innocence claim, and a growing reluctance of prosecuting attorneys to seek the death penalty (perhaps so as not to risk a poor performance record).[11]

Here again, there is often a "feedback" loop in any PMP cycle where the changes in the political environment brought about by changing media coverage lead to further changes in the political (and legal) process. Nevertheless, researchers need to also think about the long-term cycle that led (and perhaps continues to lead) to a more just society in the United States.

PMP and the Growing Personalization in Israeli Politics

The third case study looks at a very different type of political change in a completely different cultural setting. We will be using the PMP principle to explain the growing personalization of politics in Israel. While the previous two cases dealt with opinions and policies, here we focus on political behavior, and we will move our analysis to a different country.

We will primarily focus on two empirical studies. The first was entitled, "The Personalization(s) of Politics: Israel, 1949–2003," by Gideon Rahat and Tamir Sheafer (2007). It is worth noting that, in contrast to the studies mentioned until now, testing the PMP principles was one of the specified goals of the research. The second study was carried out by Meital Balmas and Tamir Sheafer (2013) and is entitled, "Leaders First, Countries After: Mediated Political Personalization in the International Arena." Although the PMP principle was not mentioned in the article, the historical perspective adopted in the study provides powerful evidence in support of our approach.

In order to understand what happened in Israel, it is important to first define what is meant by the term *personalization*. Personalization is seen as a process in which the political weight of the individual actor in the political process increases over time, while the centrality of the political group (i.e., the political party) declines (Brettschneider & Gabriel, 2002; Kaase, 1994; Rahat & Sheafer, 2007). Rahat and Sheafer (2007) suggest a typology of three types of personalization. *Institutional personalization* refers to "the adoption of rules, mechanisms and institutions that put more emphasis on the individual politician and less on political groups and parties" (p. 66). A good example would be a move from a party vote (as is the case in many parliamentary democracies) to a direct vote for the prime minister or the president (as is the case in the United States). This type of change clearly falls under the *structural dimension* of the political ecosystem. When a country or a political party changes the way they choose their candidates for office, it is an *institutional* change.

Rahat and Sheafer's (2007) second category is *media personalization*, which refers to "a change in the presentation of politics in the media, as expressed in a heightened focus on individual politicians and a diminished focus on parties, organizations and institutions" (p. 67). When journalists change their norms and routines about covering the political world, we consider this as falling under the cultural dimension of analysis. When journalistic norms, values, and routines change, either because of previous changes in the political ecosystem or due to more independent forces, this is considered a cultural change in the communication ecosystem.

The final type of personalization is *behavioral personalization*. Here it is helpful to provide a subdivision between the behavior of politicians and the behavior of the public. The process of personalization in the behavior of politicians is expressed in an increase in individual political behavior and a decline in party activity. Thus, an increase in the submission and adoption of private member bills in a Parliament would be considered a good indicator of personalization in the behavior of politicians. Personalization in the behavior of the public is best thought of in terms of electoral behavior. When citizens increasingly relate to candidates rather than parties in making their voting decisions, this is a clear indicator that personalization has influenced their behavior.

Based on the premise of the PMP principle, Rahat and Sheafer (2007), and later, Balmas, Rahat, Sheafer, and Shenhav (2014), hypothesized that institutional personalization leads to more personalization in the media, which then leads to more personalization in the behavior of politicians and the public. Israel provides an excellent test case to study this question. Political parties in Israel were the dominant actors in politics for many years (Galnoor, 1982; Lissak & Horowitz, 1989). Israel has a parliamentary system, and in the general elections, citizens cast votes for parties, not candidates (except for a short period in the 1990s, where direct vote for the prime minister was introduced and then was later canceled).

Rahat and Sheafer's study also allows for testing a second hypothesis that has to do with a structural change in the communication ecosystem: the introduction of television to Israel. Television only came to Israel in 1969. Because of its visual nature, television tends to focus on personalities rather than on abstract entities such as parties and groups. The introduction of television was also raised in discussing the boost given to the American civil rights movement in the 1960s. In accordance with our previous discussion, we see this development as an excellent example of an independent change in the communication ecosystem in Israel.

In order to put the PMP principle to a statistical test, the researchers needed empirical measurements of the four types of personalization. We will briefly present these here; for more details, please refer to Rahat and Sheafer (2007) and to Balmas et al. (2014).

Except for the short-lived adoption of direct elections for the prime minister in Israel (1996–2001), the relevant changes for institutional personalization at the national level occurred within the intra-party arena. These were changes in the nature of candidate selection methods, in particular at the level of inclusiveness of the selecting body of party members (Rahat & Hazan, 2001). The inclusiveness of each selecting body was estimated, from the most exclusive nominating committee, which was completely autonomous in determining the composition and ranking of the candidate list, through a larger selected party agency and to all party members, who were completely free to determine the composition and ranking of the candidate list.

Personalization in the news was measured through a content analysis of the news coverage of all 16 election campaigns for the Knesset (the Israeli parliament) that took place in Israel between 1949 (the first elections) and 2003. Each election-related news item was coded based on whether its main focus is mainly the parties, the candidates, or equally both.

The measurement used for identifying personalization in the behavior of politicians was the percentage of the laws that were passed in each Knesset that originated in private member bills out of the total number of bills passed in a specific term. To those who are not familiar with parliamentary systems, it helps to point out that the initiation and adoption of private member bills are the exception rather than the rule in this kind of government system. This is summarized in the "90% rule" that holds that in parliamentary systems "... about 90 percent of bills come from the executive, and that around 90 percent of its bills become law" (Hague, Harrop, & Breslin, 2001).

Finally, the measurement used for identifying personalization in the behavior of voters was the percentage of respondents in election surveys who mention the party leader as their determining factor in voting for a party, vis-à-vis the percentage of respondents who claim that they make their electoral decision based on identification with a particular party (Balmas et al., 2014).

Figure 4.1, which presents the first three types of personalization, provides strong support for the PMP hypothesis, according to which changes within the political ecosystem initiate the process (P), the

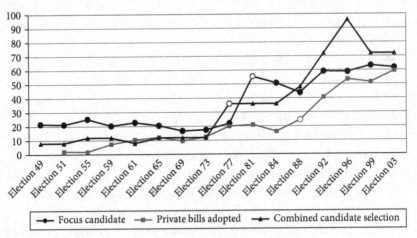

Figure 4.1. Personalization of politics: A combined look.

Note: Entries represent the sum of the inclusiveness measure of the selectorates that selected the candidates; percentage of legislation in each Knesset term that originated in private member bills; and percentages of personalization news items that focused mainly on candidates. The empty dot on each of the personalization lines indicates the time in which personalization has started to take off. Taken from Rahat and Sheafer (2007, p. 75).

communication ecosystem responds (M), and this then influences the conduct of politics (P). As can be seen, institutional personalization (combined candidate selection) is the first indicator to take off, in the 1977 elections. These elections were the first time in Israel that a party (Likud) delegated to its central body of party members the right to select the list of candidates for the Knesset. Small incremental media and behavioral personalization(s) occurred since the 1950s; but only later, after the personalization of candidate selection methods started to peak, did the trends accelerate. Second, in the subsequent election campaign (1981), journalists apparently recognized this change and reacted to it with an upsurge in personalized news coverage (a focus on candidates). Third, after the media changed their pattern of coverage, politicians made a significant effort to demonstrate personal activism, in order to make themselves more visible to the media and to their voters in the party elections. The overall incremental increase in the percentages of legislation that originated in private member bills started to peak in the 11th Knesset (1984–1988).

Balmas, Rahat, Sheafer, and Shenhav (2014) added an analysis of the fourth type of personalization—the behavior of voters. This analysis is based on respondents' answers to direct questions regarding their voting preferences: Do they vote based on identification with a party, or with the party's leader? As can be seen in Figure 4.2, there has been in general an increase over time in the percentage of survey respondents who mention the party leader as their determining factor in voting for a party, with a simultaneous decline in the percentage of respondents who claim that they make their electoral decision based on identification with a particular party. Over a period of six elections, Israeli voters generally voted more on the basis of their leader preferences and less on the basis of their party identification. This shift becomes more visible when comparing the ratio between the two preferences (the thick gray line in Figure 4.2).

As discussed, we see the introduction of television in Israel as an excellent example of how nonpolitical variables can also influence the media ecosystem. While some technological innovations, such as the extent to which citizens have relatively easy access to the internet, can be more easily linked to the political ecosystem, the introduction of television in Israel is better seen as an independent change. Based on the second PMP claim, we would expect this change to have an independent influence on the process of personalization.

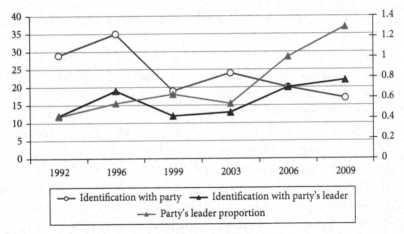

Figure 4.2. Behavioral personalization of voters.

Note: The Y-axis represents the percentages of respondents in national surveys who mentioned identification with the party leader or identification with the party when asked about their determining factor for voting. The right Y-axis represents the proportion of the voters deciding to vote on the basis of their identification with the party leader out of the decision to vote on the basis of the voters' identification with a party. Taken from Balmas et al. (2012, p. 16).

In the statistical analysis they conducted, Rahat and Sheafer (2007) assigned to the television variable a value of 0 until 1973 and a value of 1 from that year (in 1969, the year television was introduced in Israel, there were too few homes with televisions to allow for any impact). Their analysis shows that the introduction of television has a positive, strong, and significant independent effect on media personalization (please refer to table 1, p. 76 in their article). In other words, the introduction and penetration of television to Israel clearly brought an upsurge in media personalization, in addition to the effect of institutional personalization on media personalization. These findings demonstrate how *both* political and nonpolitical factors can lead to changes in the political ecosystem.

In sum, we find that once again the PMP principle helps us understand the roles of the political ecosystem and the communication ecosystem in political change. The processes of personalization in Israel began with institutional changes in the way party leaders were chosen, which led to more emphasis on individual candidates in the press. These changes in media coverage then led, in turn, to politicians being increasingly eager to initiate private member bills in the Knesset, and to voters being increasingly focused on party leaders when making electoral decisions.

Conclusion

The goal of this chapter was to demonstrate that the PMP principle can be a powerful analytical tool for better understanding the role of media in historical changes. In the first two cases, the civil rights movement in the United States and the debate in that country over the death penalty, the PMP cycle began with activists attempting to change opinions and policies. In both cases media were seen as important, but not exclusive, tools for accomplishing those goals. In both cases there is also considerable evidence that media coverage changed significantly and that this change was an important factor in the subsequent political changes that took place. The third case analyzed was different in that it dealt began with structural change in the political ecosystem, and it took place in a different country. Nevertheless, the PMP principle was given additional empirical support by analyzing the increasing personalization of Israeli politics over a long historical period.

Two additional points are worth reiterating here. First, in thinking about the PMP principle, it is critical not to forget what we have referred to as the "media selection and transformation" proposition. Despite our argument that politics comes first, the media are not merely passive transmitters for what takes place in the political realm. In each of these cases, it has been demonstrated that the media can serve as major catalysts for promoting change when making critical editorial decisions about what to cover and how to cover it. Equally important, there are some changes in media norms, values, and routines that can be seen as independent of what is going on in the political world. The advent of television was a critical factor in what happened in the US civil rights movement and in increasing the personalization of politics in Israel. Other technological and economic factors are also important factors to be considered when thinking about political change.

The second point is that all three cases came from Western, democratic countries. It would be interesting to study the role of media in similar types of historical change within partial democracies and authoritarian regimes. The ability of social movements to bring about policy changes and the extent to which a controlled media can play an active role in these processes are just two examples of the types of issues that are likely to arise. Nevertheless, it is clear that different forms of media do play a role when major political changes occur in non-WEIRD countries, and that the PMP approach can be a helpful conceptual addition for those who think about this issue.

5

PMP and Comparative Political Communication

The field of comparative political communication has gained a great deal of attention in recent years (de Vreese 2017). This is a welcome addition to political communication research, because only by taking on a comparative perspective can one begin to understand the wide range of variations when it comes to issues such as communication effects and the interdependence between the political and communication ecosystems (Blumler, McLeod, & Roengren, 1992; Mancini & Hallin 2012; Pfetch & Esser 2012). Looking at what happens in one particular country at a particular time provides a very limited perspective on the major research questions that concern us.

To preview the chapter, we start by presenting what we see as the most important "PMP question" at the macro level, and an answer to that question, as provided by the most influential comparative study in the field of political communication. The question is whether and to what extent political systems and institutions affect communication systems and institutions. The most influential answer to date is provided by Daniel Hallin and Paulo Mancini, in their book *Comparing Media Systems* (2004). They argue that the structure of the political system plays a significant role in shaping the media system, so differences in political systems produce differences in media systems. And although political and media systems evolve together, it is a country's political system that matters most. We will get back to that question later in the chapter.

Our goal in this chapter is to demonstrate that using the PMP approach as a conceptual map for understanding and improving comparative political communication research is advantageous for at least five reasons.

First, the PMP approach makes a clear distinction between the role of structural and cultural variables in comparative political communication research. This allows researchers to better consider two implications. One is what types of structural and cultural variations in either the political or communication ecosystems create similarities and differences in the roles played

Building Theory in Political Communication. Gadi Wolfsfeld, Tamir Sheafer, and Scott Althaus, Oxford University Press.
© Oxford University Press 2022. DOI: 10.1093/oso/9780197634998.003.0005

by various media in different countries and political processes. Also, and highly related, the PMP approach directs the attention of scholars to possible sources of change in political communication performance and in the role of political communication in the democratic process. As such, this approach also tells us where to expect changes over different periods of time.

Second, the PMP approach provides an excellent set of analytical "cells" for researchers to make definitive statements about how their work contributes to cumulative knowledge in the field of comparative communication. These cells can be seen in Table 5.1. For example, while one study can look comparatively at a certain cell (such as comparing the structural dimension of the communication ecosystem in various countries), another can look comparatively at relations between cells (such as comparing how the structural dimension of the political ecosystem relates to the structural dimension of the communication ecosystem in various countries).

Third, the PMP conceptual map provides a good platform for dialogue with other fields within political communication. A good example would be scholars who study the role of media in election campaigns, as discussed in Chapter 2. Scholars addressing a single country would be in a much better position to cite findings from similar studies carried out in comparative political communication. Also, those working in the comparative field would be better placed to relate to single-country studies. If both groups of scholars are using similar conceptual categories when designing their studies, their ability to learn from each other grows considerably.

Fourth, the PMP conceptual map helps researchers to "see the full picture." One of the major limitations of individual comparative political communication studies is that the vast majority of them cover only a small part of the overall map. A useful way to demonstrate this problem is to look at a summary article by de Vreese (2017), in which he divided the research in this area into four categories: (1) media and political systems; (2) political and election news; (3) political communication in the European Union; and (4) political journalists. What the field is still lacking, however, is a broader theoretical perspective that links these various topic areas and provides a conceptual map for moving toward a more comprehensive understanding. We believe that the PMP approach represents such a conceptual map.

Fifth, by using the PMP approach and its conceptual map—two ecosystems, each with three dimensions—and by "seeing the full picture," one can better identify theoretical arguments that have strong empirical support,

Table 5.1 PMP and Comparative Communication: An Overview Table

Dimension	Political Ecosystem	Communication Ecosystem	"Second P"
Structural	Type of political system	Level of commercialization of media system	Level of political elites' responsiveness to communication media
	Level of political power concentration	Level of media-party parallelism	
	Electoral system		
Cultural	Politicians' representational conceptions: delegates vs. trustees	Levels and types of media logic in the news	
		Level of political power concentration in the news	

and others in which further comparative empirical analysis is needed. We present examples of this issue throughout the chapter.

Comparative political communication scholars are likely to find at least some of these five contributions familiar, as they occasionally appear in various forms in their own studies, some of which are mentioned in this chapter. These scholars have done an excellent job of pushing comparative political communication research forward in a rather short period. We believe that the PMP conceptual map can help them to continue this important trend.

We start with an example of the utility of this conceptual map in comparative political communication research, summarized in Table 5.1. This table is slightly different from the tables in previous chapters. It still represents the same conceptual map: two columns of ecosystems (political and communication) plus a third "second P" column, and rows for the structural and cultural dimensions (we do not present the situational dimension in this chapter, for reasons explained below). The difference is that here we use Table 5.1 to explore possible connections between the ecosystems and dimensions regarding one theoretical issue: *the extent to which political elites are responsive to various forms of media*. This issue focuses on the circumstances in which political elites use "media logic" to mold their behavior to fit the needs and values of various forms of media, and the extent to which they do so. "Media logic" refers to the "production of media culture in general and of the news in particular" (Mazzoleni, 2008). It is the set of unwritten rules journalists follow in producing the news. News production has changed over the years from emphasizing a political logic directed at the public's good to a media logic directed at what the public is interested in. What is important to emphasize, from our perspective, is that media logic varies over time and space. First, it (mostly) increases over time (Altheide, 2004). Second, it might vary between political cultures (e.g., stronger in one country compared with another country, see Altheid, 2004; de Vreese, Esser, & Hopmann, 2017b). Third, it might vary in content and strength between media, and particularly between mass media and social media (de Vreese et al., 2017a; Klinger and Svensson, 2015).

The variables in the table are not exhaustive by any means, but merely illustrative of the types of factors found to be relevant in previous studies. As noted above, presenting various theoretical questions in such a table can enrich our understanding regarding the relations between variables and can identify areas (represented by cells in the table) in which more comparative research is needed.

Therefore, the following discussion focuses only on several examples that are related to how the PMP approach is constructive for understanding political elites' responsiveness to communication media from a comparative point of view.

The Utility of the PMP Conceptual Map for Understanding Political Elites' Responsiveness to Communication Media

Political leaders depend on communication media as an information resource about public opinion and current affairs, for communicating their messages to the public, for re-election, and more. While their level of dependency on the media is much lower than that of citizens because they have access to other sources of information, this dependency is nevertheless quite extensive (Van Aelst & Walgrave, 2017; Walgrave, Sevenans, Zoizner, & Ayling, 2017). Much of what they do is driven by their belief in the power of media (Cohen, Tsfati, & Sheafer, 2008), so they anticipate the needs of the communication media and behave accordingly (Cook, 2006; Sheafer, Shenhav, & Balmas, 2015; Strömbäck & Esser, 2014). However, the extent to which political elites are dependent on communication media varies considerably across the political and communication contexts in which they are operating, partly as a function of the structural and cultural factors that are dominant in both ecosystems.

We deliberately chose to start with this example because it is one of the most researched questions in political communication. In addition, it is designed to serve as a link to Chapter 6, where we talk extensively about how important the notion of responsiveness is to questions about the optimal role of the communication ecosystem in supporting political performance. So while you read the examples presented in the next few pages, it will be helpful to refer to Table 5.1.

Consider the impact of the electoral system—a structural variable in the political ecosystem (the top left cell in Table 5.1)—on the extent to which political elites are responsive to the communication media (the "second P" column). At the political party level, candidates required to compete in primaries are expected to be more dependent on gaining favorable media coverage in order to be elected, compared with instances where party lists are decided by party leaders or by small selectorates (Rahat & Kenig, 2018). Also, the responsiveness of political elites to the various forms of media is greater in electoral systems with large multi-member districts than in small, single-member districts (Amsalem et al., 2017). The reason is that, in small single-member districts candidates have more direct access to their voters, while the nature of political representation differs sharply in districts of greater magnitude, in which direct constituency efforts are generally ineffective. So, in large districts politicians are more dependent on media for re-election. And the more they depend on media for re-election, the more they simplify their rhetoric to fit various media considerations of newsworthiness (Amsalem et al., 2017).

Moving one cell down in the table, an example of the association between the cultural dimension of the political ecosystem (the bottom left cell in Table 5.1) and the extent to which political elites are responsive to communication media can be presented as follows: politicians' political representation conceptions affect the level of their responsiveness to the communication media. Specifically, politicians who view themselves as conduits of the public (that is, as delegates) may be more responsive to communication media (which convey signals about public opinion) than those who act on their own judgment (that is, as trustees) (Zoizner, Sheafer, & Walgrave, 2017).

One example in Table 5.1 regarding the association between the political ecosystem and the communication ecosystem is provided by Vos and Van Aelst's (2017) study about variation in media visibility of politicians across 16 Western democracies. They found that in countries where political power is more equally distributed across politicians (see "type of political system" and "level of political power concentration" in the upper left cell), a broader range of politicians with different institutional functions makes it into the news ("level of political power concertation in the news"; see the cultural dimension in the communication ecosystem cell).

Finally, there seems to be somewhat less research that directly connects the structural dimension of the communication ecosystem with political elites' responsiveness to the communication media. Assuming this observation is correct (we may have missed some studies), it demonstrates the usefulness of the conceptual table, which can direct researchers to important "missing links" in research. For example, it is logical to think that political elites living in countries with higher levels of media commercialism will be more responsive to communication media than political elites in countries with lower levels of commercialization. Why? Because the more commercialized the communication ecosystem, the more we'll find media logic shaping interactions between politicians and the communication media.

Below we expand the scope of evidence for the utility of the PMP approach to comparative political communication research. The examples below are not necessarily mentioned in Table 5.1, but in the discussions we clearly state the cell to which they belong.

As noted, this chapter does not deal with the situational dimension of analysis, which focuses on the ways in which significant events in the political ecosystem can have an impact on the various forms of mediated communication. We chose to leave this out of the current discussion mostly because our overall approach in this chapter deals with multiple countries, and at the time of this writing there was simply not enough empirical work to say anything definitive about particular situational factors as a larger theoretical matter. This, in itself, demonstrates the need for something like our conceptual table to begin identifying and organizing related work.

The Political Ecosystem

The Structural Dimension

The most basic "PMP question" at the macro level is the degree to which the political system and political institutions tend to shape communication systems, values, practices, or the other way around. A good deal of the comparative research in this area relates to the role of the structural dimension of the political ecosystem.

As noted at the beginning of the chapter, in talking about the type of political system, we rely heavily on Hallin and Mancini's (2004) seminal work, *Comparing Media Systems*, which is often considered the most influential comparative study to date in political communication. The authors' major argument is that "[t]he state plays a significant role in shaping the media system in any society" (p. 41). All of their main research hypotheses deal with the impact of political system characteristics on the characteristics of media systems (their language predates the widespread advent of social media, so today it might be more appropriate to use the term "communication system" to be more inclusive of newer media types, although both terms ultimately point to the same thing). The political system variables "are more general and deeply rooted aspects of social structure and culture than are the media-system characteristics" (Hallin & Mancini, 2004, p. 47).

Hallin and Mancini present major political system variables, such as political history (early vs. late democratization) and the type of government (consensus vs. majoritarian), which are independent variables in the hypotheses the authors generate concerning the association between a political system and a media system. Media systems have several characteristics relevant to their argument, such as the extent to which media outlets in a given country possess political affiliations with political parties; the level of journalists' professionalization, which refers to the development of journalism as an autonomous profession with distinct norms and ethics; and the level of state intervention in the communication media industry. Overall, Hallin and Mancini demonstrated how the political system affects the extent to which the government and political parties have control over communication media.

In their concluding chapter, Hallin and Mancini (2004) asked whether changes in media systems are caused by or have an effect on the political system:

> To a large extent, media system change is certainly a result of the deeply rooted [political] processes summarized previously, which have undercut the social basis of mass parties and of group solidarity and of a media system connected with them. It is clearly also true, however, that processes of change internal to the media system have been at work and it is quite plausible that changes in European media systems have contributed to the process of secularization. (p. 268)

Hallin and Mancini preferred to present this process as a "coevolution of media and political institutions within particular historical contexts" (2004, p. 297). Our reading is somewhat different, in accordance with the PMP principle. Consider, for example, the process of secularization mentioned by the authors. Most evidence points to a unidirectional process that is driven by politics at large. For example, Inglehart and Welzel's (2005, p. 75) empirical analysis of 64 countries suggests that the process of secularization is identified with change over time in a country's political values. Our claim can also be observed from a "negative" example. Aalberg, van Aelst, and Curran (2010) analyzed general trends of media commercialization, looking to determine whether a worldwide convergence toward a commercial market model has been developed that overrides important political differences across countries. They found that this did not happen: political system differences still matter and they continue to shape media markets.

The communication media are almost always best seen as *catalysts* for change, rather than first causes of change, in keeping with the PMP approach. The relationship between a country's regime type and the relative freedom of the media could easily be considered the most obvious manifestation of the "politics first" principle in the realm of comparative politics. Although this issue is more complex than some might assume, it is important to begin with the most basic understanding that a free press is one of the cornerstones of any true democracy. In authoritarian regimes, by contrast, opposition forces find it difficult to gain access to the media, and this severely limits their ability to mobilize against governments. Thus, from a comparative perspective, people living within these societies are also less likely to be exposed to dissident views, both in the communication media (the cultural dimension of the communication ecosystem) and in the speeches and behavior of political elites (the "second P"). This is, of course, precisely why such regimes often make such an effort to take control of all forms of media.

Variations in political ecosystems lead to variations in media practices, even when one compares among two or more non-democratic states. There are significant differences among both non-democratic and democratic states in terms of how much control they attempt to exercise over all parts of the communication ecosystem and how they attempt to exercise that control. Starting with two well-known examples of authoritarian regimes, we can consider the differences between the level of media control in North Korea and China.

North Korea is a state where the government has almost complete control over the entire communication ecosystem (Byman & Lind, 2010; Dukalskis, 2017; Lankov, 2014). The government's willingness and ability to take this level of control over all forms of communication serves as an important example that even in the digital age, some authoritarian leaders are still in a position to make it extremely difficult for citizens to gain access to unofficial sources of information. This is not to suggest that the country can be hermetically sealed, but the level of control over the flow of information is far greater in North Korea than in probably any other country in the world.

China takes a very different approach to controlling the communication media. Dukalskis (2017) compared the attempts by three authoritarian regimes (North Korea, Burma [Myanmar], and China) to take control over the public sphere. Although Chinese media are far from free, the government has allowed the internet to grow enormously. Thus, Dukalskis reported, internet usage rose from 2% in 2000 to over 45% by 2013, a growth of over

500 million users in the course of only 13 years (Dukalskis, 2017, p. 174). This has led to what Lei (2017) has called a "contentious public sphere." Compared to many other authoritarian regimes, the authorities in China find themselves fighting for control over this sphere. But unlike the North Korean regime, which blocked any expression of opposition, the Chinese chose a different strategy. A large-scale analysis of censorship in Chinese social media networks showed that while government criticism was allowed (somewhat surprisingly), calls for collective action were censored (King, Pan, & Roberts, 2013). So it is acceptable for Chinese citizens to vent their political disappointments through social media, as long as they do not mobilize for political action (for another such analysis, see Repnikova, 2017).

Comparative use of the PMP approach also helps explain how differences between multiparty parliamentary systems and two-party presidential systems, as well as between proportional and non-proportional systems, are connected with differences in the communication ecosystems in those countries. For example, consider the extent to which the various forms of media provide sufficient time and space for diverse voices to be heard. As can be seen in Table 5.1, we are placing this latter variable (represented as "level of political power concentration in the news") in the cultural dimension of the communication ecosystem. Given that news media serve as a major venue for public discourse, the amount and range of access given to varied political actors, ideologies, and voices can be considered a critical component in assessing the health of the democratic process.

Several studies have indicated that the level of idea diversity in the news varies across countries and that the type of political system is a critical determinant of these differences. Sheafer and Wolfsfeld (2009) compared the visibility of oppositional actors in Israel and the United States and expected to find a significant difference in the amount of attention given to dissident voices between higher-consensus, two-party democracies (such as the United States) and lower-consensus, polarized, multiparty democracies (such as Israel). More pluralistic news media were expected to both reflect and reinforce this difference between the two types of political systems. The empirical findings provided strong support for this argument. Thus, structural differences in the political ecosystem (type of electoral system) led to cultural differences in the communication ecosystem (the range of sources used, see also Baum, 2013) and, at the very least, exposed the average Israeli to a more diverse set of viewpoints relative to the average American (a clear "second P").

Diversity and competition in the political and communication ecosystems are expected to have political consequences. For example, Nir (2012) developed and tested the notion that political-institutional contexts (the structural level of the political ecosystem) provide incentives that facilitate or inhibit discussion, expression, and political information acquisition among citizens (the "second P" variable). Based on survey data from 12 European countries, Nir showed that individuals' frequency of discussing politics is determined not only by individual differences (such as level of political interest), but, more importantly, by the competitiveness of the political system of the country in which a person lives. So, higher levels of political discussion among citizens were found in countries with more competitive political systems. The conceptual map in Table 5.1 shows that this analysis goes directly from the "first P" (the left column) to the "second P" (the right column). Table 5.1 helps reveal that intervening elements within the communication ecosystem are missing from this analysis. Indeed, Nir pointed to the need to add media systems and other communication-related variables to future comparative analyses of political discussion (2012, p. 565).

An example of a comparative analysis that focuses on the communication ecosystem is the relationship between the type of electoral system (the structural dimension of the political ecosystem) and the extent to which media coverage of political elites is personalized (the cultural dimension of the communication ecosystem). There was a discussion of changes in the degree of personalization in Israel over time in Chapter 4. Now we look at the same issue cross-nationally. The question that researchers studying this phenomenon usually ask concerns the extent to which professionally produced news coverage focuses on political institutions versus individual politicians.

In his study of six European democracies, Kriesi (2012) found that the level of personalized coverage does vary across political systems. The most significant difference in personalized media coverage was between France, which had higher rates, and five other countries (the United Kingdom, the Netherlands, Germany, Austria, and Switzerland), which had lower levels of personalized coverage. Kriesi attributed this difference to the institutional arrangements in those countries: France is characterized by its semi-presidential system, whereas the five other countries are parliamentary states. Here, too, a personalized electoral system naturally leads to more personalized media coverage (for additional related studies, see Balmas & Sheafer, 2013; Van Aelst et al., 2017).

The Cultural Dimension

Here we provide several examples regarding the role of political culture variables in the PMP sequence, from a comparative viewpoint. One might be described as the culture of governance. There are many dimensions of governance culture, including respect for institutional authority, quality of regulatory controls, adherence to the rule of law, and control of corruption.[1] This political culture variable is highly related to a country's political structure, such as the level of democracy. So, in many new and establishing democracies, aspects of governance culture may be less internalized and therefore more unevenly implemented compared with more established democracies.

Governance culture might play an important part in understanding the role of strategic media framing (a variable that belongs to the cultural dimension of the communication ecosystem) in shaping levels of political cynicism among citizens (a "second P"). This provides an effective demonstration of the whole PMP sequence from the political ecosystem (i.e., type of political system at the structural dimension and governance culture at the cultural dimension—the upper and lower cells on the left column in Table 5.1), through the communication ecosystem (i.e., strategic media framing at the cultural dimension of the communication ecosystem, which would be in the bottom cell of the middle column in Table 5.1), to political behavior (various levels of cynicism toward politics—a "second P" variable—which would be in the right column in Table 5.1).

Schuck, Boomgaarden, and de Vreese (2013) studied the impact of strategic media framing on political cynicism in 21 countries during the European elections and found significant variations among countries. Specifically, in countries with high levels of democratization, exposure to strategy frames increased cynicism toward the European parliament, while no such impact was detected in low-democratization countries. The authors suggest:

> In contexts in which the quality of governance and democracy is lower to begin with such news will hardly contribute to changes in levels of cynicism. This is in line with previous research stressing that in a news environment in which negative news is the norm, positive news has the potential to stick out more and be more effective. (p. 34)

Cultural variables are, naturally, more elusive and harder to measure than structural variables. For example, consider the general tendency of politicians to rely on media logic (the core values that drive decisions in the communication ecosystem) to achieve political goals. This is similar to what mediatization scholars (e.g., Esser and Strömbäck, 2014) refer to as the extent to which the political system has internalized media logic (instead of political logic) into its conduct. Although this variable is hard to measure, a comparative design often helps to identify it. Let us return to the example we presented at the beginning of the chapter, of the study by Amsalem et al. (2017) about the differences in the extent to which politicians in Canada, Belgium, and Israel are responsive to communication media.

As noted, the responsiveness of politicians to the communication media is greater in electoral systems with large multi-member districts (such as Belgium and Israel) than in small single-member districts (such as Canada). The reason is that candidates in small single-member districts have more direct access to their voters, while the nature of political representation differs sharply in districts of greater magnitude. The greater the extent to which politicians are dependent on the communication media for re-election, the more they simplify their rhetoric to fit the media's newsworthiness considerations.

The elusive and somewhat confusing—but interesting—thing is this: in Amsalem et al.'s (2017) research, the independent variable is the electoral system (a structural variable at the political ecosystem), while the dependent variable (the "second P' variable) is the level of politicians' simplicity/complexity of rhetoric. Going a step forward, it is reasonable to argue that a Belgian politician does not measure the size of her district in order to simplify her rhetoric accordingly. Rather, the political structure has probably created a political culture in which communication-related values have been strongly internalized (and hence this is a variable that we place in the cultural dimension of the political ecosystem).

What makes this argument especially interesting and relevant is that it points to the cyclical nature of politics and media, which the PMP approach depicts so nicely. That is, the level of internalized communication values in the political culture (which varies between countries) drives politicians to be responsive (more or less) to these values and to mold their rhetoric accordingly (to be more simplified or complex), which further molds the political culture, again and again. Such a resonance of the "second P" with the "first P" does not change the political culture quickly, but may act over time to slowly erode or enliven aspects of political culture through longer-term forms of cumulative influence.

Another example of the general tendency to use the communication media for achieving strategic goals can be seen in the study of political agenda setting.

The research field of political agenda setting is engaged with the question of who sets the agenda, and thus who has the upper hand politically. Do communication media follow politics, in the sense that they cover issues raised by legislators and the executive? Or do politicians respond to media attention and handle issues highlighted by communication media? Although scholars find reciprocal effects, many studies have found that politicians follow the news more often than the other way around (e.g., Bonafont & Baumgartner, 2013; Edwards & Wood, 1999; Walgrave, Soroka, & Nuytemans, 2008; Zoizner, Sheafer, & Walgrave, 2017). Social media appear to have a similar impact. Barbera et al. (2019) found that the political agenda of US legislators is influenced by issue priorities conveyed in Twitter messages.

Yet, looking at political agenda setting from a comparative perspective provides a more complex picture. For instance, Vliegenthart et al. (2016) compared political agenda setting in seven European countries. They found that in countries with a single-party government, legislators from the opposition followed communication media in their political activity to a greater extent than those from the opposition in political systems with multiparty government. At the same time, legislators from the governing coalition in countries with multiparty governments relied more on communication media than legislators from the governing coalition in countries with a single-party government.

Fitting this example into the conceptual map presented by the PMP approach points at the following net of connections: the form of government (single party vs. coalition—a political-structural variable) influences the extent to which politicians are dependent on communication media for achieving political goals. The dependence of politicians on communication media for achieving political goals is itself a political-cultural variable. The greater the extent to which political elites need communication media, the more they are likely to respond to the topical agenda of communication media (a communication-cultural variable) in their own political agenda (a "second P" variable). Using the conceptual map also helps to focus interested researchers on the areas that most need further research. In this case, politicians' relative need to use communication media for achieving political goals is the weak link that demands more direct empirical evidence.

One final example of a political-cultural variable is the extent to which a populist political climate exists in a particular time and place. Mudde (2004) referred to this as the "populist zeitgeist." There has been a great deal of interest in how populist leaders around the world have exploited all forms of media in recent years in order to promote themselves and their political parties. Here, too, we find significant cross-national differences in the impact these leaders have had on communication media, and subsequently on their ultimate electoral success.

Unsurprisingly, there are many definitions of populism (Abromeit et al., 2015; Arditi et al., 2005; Müller, 2017). We will use Mudde and Kaltwasser's (2017, p. 6) definition: "a thin-centered ideology that considers society to be ultimately separated into two homogeneous and antagonistic camps, 'the pure people' versus 'the corrupt elite', and which argues that politics should be an expression of the volonté générale (general will) of the people."

In terms of PMP, we start by considering the prominence of these views among elites and the general public in different countries. Unsurprisingly, the level of prominence has a significant impact on the degree to which populist leaders obtain publicity and are in a position to use communication media to recruit citizens to their cause (Aalberg et al., 2017; Engesser, Ernst, Esser, & Büchel, 2017). What is especially important from a PMP perspective is that the "populist zeitgeist" in different countries is an important starting point to examine. In Germany, for example, the political establishment has an inherently strong cultural antagonism toward populist parties, which also has an impact on both the ability of such views to be spread and the amount of hostility those views generate in communication media (Aalberg, de Vreese, & Strömbäck, 2016). In other countries, leaders and citizens are more willing to accommodate these parties; they have a less antagonistic "populist zeitgeist." In countries where populist views become less controversial, the traditional and digital media become less hostile toward populist voices. However, the study of populism still requires a better comparative perspective that would go beyond insights based on specific cases (de Vreese et al. 2018; Reinemann, Matthes, & Sheafer 2017).

The Communication Ecosystem

At the core of the PMP approach are the connections between the political and communication ecosystems and their linkages back to the political world, as represented by the "second P" variable. Here we further elaborate on the role of the communication ecosystem from a comparative point of view.

The Structural Dimension

The structural dimension in the communication ecosystem refers mainly to institutional arrangements, such as the strength of public vs. commercial media organizations, the proliferation of digital infrastructure, and the level of independence between communication organizations and political organizations (or, in Hallin and Mancini's term, the level of media-party parallelism).

Hallin and Mancini (2004) made a distinction between three types of media systems: the Mediterranean or Polarized Pluralist Model (France, Greece, Italy, Portugal, and Spain), the North/Central Europe or Democratic Corporatist Model (Austria, Belgium, Denmark, Finland, Germany, Netherlands, Norway, Sweden, and Switzerland), and the North Atlantic or Liberal Model (Britain, United States, Canada, Ireland). These models differ on various dimensions, such as political parallelism (the extent to which communication media have a clear political orientation, which is highest in the Mediterranean model; see "media-party parallelism" in Table 5.1), professionalism of journalists (lowest in the Mediterranean model), and market commercialization (highest in the North Atlantic model). These structural variables result in different levels of media freedom (cultural dimension of the communication ecosystem), which, according to Hallin and Mancini (2004), is higher in the North Atlantic and the North European models than in the Mediterranean model.

As discussed above, one of Hallin and Mancini's (2004) central arguments is that a country's political system directly determines its media system. Therefore, if a certain country belongs to the North European model in its political system, it will belong to this model in its media system as well. Those authors found further confirmation for this argument in their second edited book (2011), which moved beyond Western Europe and the United States to include countries such as Poland, South Africa, Russia, the Baltic countries, Brazil, and China. Based on this argument and using our PMP conceptual map (as in Table 5.1), one should expect to find strong connections between the top left and top center cells. The simplest example of that, which has been already mentioned, is the high similarity between the levels of political freedom and the level of press freedom in a country.

Another example of strong connections between the top left and top center cells in our conceptual table is the development of digital communication infrastructure. Comparative political communication research on the "digital divide" explores why wealthier countries are much more likely to have a more developed internet infrastructure and a higher proportion of citizens with access to the various digital channels than poorer countries (Guillén & Suárez, 2005; James, 2011; Vaccari, 2013; Van Dijk, 2017, 2020). Elaborating on this causal connection between the structural dimensions of the two ecosystems, Van Dijk (2017, p. 3) presented a "resources and appropriation theory" which argues, among other things, that (1) categorical inequalities in society produce an unequal distribution of resources (top left cell in Table 5.1), and (2) an unequal distribution of resources causes unequal access to digital technologies (top center cell in Table 5.1). Once again, organizing conceptual elements in a common framework helps direct the attention of other scholars to gaps in existing research and importantopportunities for developing new theoretical insightsor empirical tests.

The Cultural Dimension

Comparative political communication studies envision the cultural dimension of the communication ecosystem as comprising the values that direct the actions of the various actors in this diverse ecosystem, and the actual nature of the communication output, whether it is news in offline and online outlets or exchanges in social media networks. Here, we show how the PMP approach can be helpful for understanding the various forces that play a role in molding the cultural dimension of the communication ecosystem. We attempt to show that communication output is molded by political forces (both structural and cultural), as well as by the structural dimension of the communication ecosystem.

Pfetsch and Esser defined political communication culture as the orientations, attitudes, values, and norms that govern the relationship between political actors and media actors (Pfetsch 2004; Pfetsch & Esser 2012). At the center of this definition is the relationship between the political and communication ecosystems. Pfetsch and Esser attempted to identify the roles that various forces play in molding political communication cultures. They focus on variations in political and media systems as well as the impact these systems have on how journalists view their relationship with politicians and how "close" they feel to them (Esser & Pfetsch, 2004).

For example, Pfetsch, Mayerhöffer, and Moring (2014) examined journalists' perceptions about the political pressure they face. The authors found that different political cultures have developed in Southern and Northern European countries, where journalists in Southern cultures experience high levels of political pressure, while those in Northern cultures report low political pressure. Pfetch and Voltmer (2012) found that the political communication cultures in Poland and Bulgaria—two Eastern European emerging democracies—differ from those of Western Europe due to political-structural variables such as their relatively short periods of democratic practice. Nevertheless, journalists in these countries are also quite different from each other, due to the very different transformational paths to democratization. Generally, the bottom-up transformation to democratization in Poland has led to the development of a rather professional and independent political communication culture. Bulgaria's top-down transformation to democratization resulted in a closer network of relationships between journalists and politicians that sometimes threatens the integrity of journalistic independence. The effect of the political ecosystem on the communication ecosystem is quite clear.

One of the main pillars of the cultural dimension of the communication ecosystem is journalistic culture. This concept was studied intensively in a large comparative project led by Thomas Hanitzsch (Hanitzch, 2007; Hanitzsch et al., 2011). Journalistic culture is defined in that project as "a particular set of ideas and practices by which journalists legitimate their role in society and render their work meaningful" (2007, p. 369). Hanitzsch and his colleagues explained that "the concept captures the field of journalism as being constituted and reaffirmed by a set of culturally negotiated professional values and conventions that operate mostly behind the backs of individual journalists" (Hanitzsch et al., 2011, p. 273).

Hanitzsch, Hanusch, and Lauerer (2016) looked at the determinants of "interventionism" in 21 countries. Interventionism is conceived as the willingness of journalists to set the political agenda, to influence public opinion, and to advocate for social change. The authors examined various sets of variables that are hypothesized to have an effect on journalists' interventionism. Overall, they found that journalists' interventionism was contingent on the level of freedom in their country; their willingness to take an active role was higher in less politically free countries.

Journalists' culture may often clash with communication forces as well. Mellado et al. (2020) looked at the gaps between journalistic role conceptions and the performance of media organizations in nine countries from Latin America, Western Europe, and Asia. Generally, they looked at the differences between what journalists deem important from a normative point of view (such as having a watchdog role), and what they published in their newspapers. The authors found that structural communication variables played the greatest role in explaining these gaps. In particular, journalists working in state-owned newspapers (a structural variable in the communication ecosystem) demonstrated the greatest gap between the importance they attributed to the interventionist role and the way this role has been reflected in the news items they have written.

These analyses of journalistic culture are of great value. However, looking at our conceptual map (Table 5.1), one area that might deserve more comparative research is the connection between a country's journalistic culture (the cultural dimension on the communication ecosystem) and various "second P" political consequences. As argued above, stating exactly where more research is needed can be seen as an important contribution of the PMP approach to building cumulative knowledge in the field.

Another set of comparative studies focus on news performance (de Vreese, Esser, & Hopmann, 2017). Some of these studies were conducted as part of a large-scale project by NEPOCS (Network of European Comparative Political Communication Scholars). This is a network of scholars from more than 15 countries (de Vreese, Esser, & Hopmann, 2017; Esser, 2012). This project looked at the representation of six main concepts in the news of 16 Western democracies: strategy and game framing, interpretive journalism, negativity, political balance, personalization, and hard and soft news. The study found that variations in the presence of these concepts in the news of different countries can be explained by political-structural variables, such as the level of federalism in a country's political system, and by communication-structural variables, such as the level of competition in the communication market (see, in particular, de Vreese et al., 2017, and Reinemann et al., 2017). For example, Aalberg, de Vreese, and Strömbäck (2017) found variations in the extent to which the news in these countries is dominated by strategic and game frames. Consistent with the PMP principle, their analysis attributed these variations to both political and communication ecosystem variations. They found that the role of public service broadcasting (structural dimension of the communication ecosystem) appeared to matter most, but that the number of parties in parliament (structural dimension of the political ecosystem) also had an effect: "the fewer political parties, the greater the use of strategic game frames, suggesting that more clear-cut competition might lead to a stronger focus on the game" (Aalberg, de Vreese, & Strömbäck, 2017, p. 48).

The prevalence of online disinformation (also known as "fake news") is a good example of a media content variable that is part of the cultural dimension. Humprecht, Esser, and Van Aelst (2020) published a cross-national study that summarizes a great deal of research in this field. Their analysis returned to the 18 countries depicted in Hallin and Mancini's (2004) study and referred to three clusters of countries, based on the amount of disinformation that online news users have reported being exposed to (we consider this to be a cultural variable in the communication ecosystem). The cluster with the least amount of online disinformation includes most Western European countries and Canada. These are countries with mostly consensus-based political systems and a strong welfare state (two structural variables in the political ecosystem), as well as low levels of polarization (a cultural variable in the political ecosystem), and a strong public broadcasting system (a structural variable in the communication ecosystem).

The second group of countries, which has higher levels of reported exposure to online disinformation, is termed the "polarized cluster," which has substantial partisan and ideological divisions (two cultural variables in the political ecosystem). These are mostly Southern European countries. The only country in the third cluster is the United States, which is characterized by a polarized environment with low levels of trust in the government. The United States also has a highly competitive and commercial media market (two structural variables in the communication ecosystem) and is the country where disinformation is most likely to take root, according to the authors.

The examples provided here (and there are numerous other studies not presented) show that communication output (the cultural dimension at the communication ecosystem) is molded by political forces (both structural and cultural), as well as by the structural dimension of the communication ecosystem. Looking again at the conceptual map presented in Table 5.1, these are horizontal forces (from the political ecosystem to the communication ecosystem), and vertical forces (from the structural dimension of the communication ecosystem to the cultural dimension of the communication ecosystem). However, our understanding of the forces that mold communication output—be it news or social media exchanges—remains far from complete, since high levels of variation between countries are still unexplained (e.g., Esser et al., 2012; Reinemann et al., 2017).

From Politics to Communication and Back: The Second P

The conceptual map presented in this chapter (Table 5.1) improves our understanding regarding the network of connections from the political ecosystem, through the communication ecosystem, and back to the political world—the "second P." There are many ways in which the various features of political and communication ecosystems can affect political elites, the public, political events, and political processes. Recently, there has also been considerable comparative research on this topic, some of which has already been mentioned in this chapter. The studies mentioned above looked at "second P" outcomes such as the political agenda of politicians, the level of politicians' responsiveness to the communication media, the level of political discussion among citizens, and the level of political cynicism among citizens. Scholars have looked, and should look, at many more outcomes, such as voting turnout, public policy, electoral results, collective action, political trust, and violent conflicts and wars, all by employing various comparative research designs.

Because most of the studies mentioned above look at political outcomes within the political ecosystem, we focus here on the less obvious relations between the communication ecosystem and the "second P." One example of the association between the structural dimension of the communication ecosystem and individual political behavior is provided in a comparative analysis of 74 countries (Baek, 2009). That study explored how political communication institutions affect cross-national differences in voter turnout in democratic elections. Baek argued that institutional settings that reduce information costs for voters will increase turnout. The empirical analysis showed a positive correlation between the amount of money allowed for running advertisement campaigns (the structural dimension of the communication ecosystem) and the levels of voter turnout. The size of public broadcasting system in a country (another structural variable in the communication ecosystem) was also found to have a positive association with voter turnout.

A related variable that belongs to the structural dimension of the communication ecosystem is media commercialization. Ariely (2015) analyzed the association between the level of commercialization in a country and the level of political trust (a "second P" variable) in 33 European countries. Higher levels of commercialization in a country's communication ecosystem were found to be related to lower levels of political trust. The overall rationale is that an emphasis on conflict and sensationalism (which is expected to be higher in more commercialized media) is more likely to increase public cynicism toward politics (see also Aarts, Fladmoe, & Strömbäck, 2012). Note, however, that while the argument is that what drives cynicism is news focusing on conflict and sensationalism (which belongs to the cultural dimension of the communication ecosystem), the empirical analysis looked only at the structural level of the communication ecosystem (i.e., the extent of commercialized media). This is not to say that the argument is invalid. Rather, as discussed in other instances above, the PMP conceptual map presented in this book helps readers to more easily identify areas in which further comparative empirical analysis is needed.

Conclusion

The central premise of the comparative approach to the study of political communication is that connections between ecosystems, as well as within each ecosystem, are *conditioned* by specific political and communication-related variables that are responsible for differences between various actors, such as countries, political parties, individual politicians, and media organizations. When we say that such connections are conditioned, we mean that the connections between politics, communication, and politics are not universal, but vary according to the specific political and communication contexts that govern the ecosystems of each actor or each case study. Schematically, the nature of the connection between politics, communication media, and politics (PMP), is likely to differ if it occurs in environment A or environment B, when A and B have different characteristics.

We believe that this chapter provides a powerful demonstration of the usefulness of the PMP approach for understanding the relationship between politics and communication from a comparative perspective and to direct future research into promising but understudied elements of complex dynamic processes. We want to reiterate five of the main contributions of the PMP approach to comparative political communication.

First, the approach makes a clear distinction between the role of structural and cultural variables in comparative political communication research. Second, it provides an excellent tool for researchers to improve their knowledge about processes in political communication, and about the relations between various dimensions in the political and communication ecosystems, as well as between these ecosystems and the "second P." Third, using the PMP conceptual map provides a good platform for dialogue with other fields in political communication, as scholars can fit non-comparative case studies in relevant comparative "cells," revealing interesting differences and similarities. As noted, this might be helpful for integrating larger numbers of country-level case studies as pilot studies for future comparative analyses. Fourth, the PMP conceptual map helps researchers to "see the full picture." The result of seeing the full picture is our fifth contribution: it helps to identify gaps in theory and focus the attention of comparative scholars on those gaps—that is, on arguments that are currently underdeveloped in comparative empirical evidence and that require further research. We believe that political communication is all about the relations among politics and communication—or, as the central premise of this book puts it, from the political ecosystem, through the communication ecosystem, and back to politics.

Throughout this chapter we have consciously used terms such as "connection" and "correlation" instead of "influence" or "effect" to describe the nature of the findings presented in the comparative analyses. We did this because the methodological designs of many comparative analyses usually show connection/relationship/correlation, while "influence" and "effect" often require different designs and further empirical support. Nevertheless, while urging caution regarding these terms, the empirical evidence firmly supports the argument that the most common direction is from the political ecosystem, through the communication ecosystem, and back to the political world.

Finally, we have seen that PMP is a cyclical process, in which the political ecosystem molds the communication ecosystem, which feeds back to various political behaviors and phenomena, which in turn slowly shapes the political ecosystem.

6

Using the PMP Approach to Assess Media Performance in Both Democratic and Autocratic Regimes

Political communication research usually assumes that communication ecosystems should be independent from political ecosystems, and that this independence should be encouraged and protected. However, we rarely consider why the political autonomy of communication ecosystems should be important from a normative perspective, or what aspects of political performance are expected to suffer when media independence is diminished. Normative theories of democracy offer little assistance in this regard, as the philosophers developing these theories rarely seem to consider media performance as being interesting or worthy of comment. Although media performance should matter for political performance even in autocratic regimes where communication systems are tightly controlled, conventional approaches to theorizing media independence in the political communication literature have little to say about non-democratic countries. This is a problem for cross-national comparative research, where it has been difficult to develop or apply a single normative framework that is suitable for comparing media performance across regime types.

This chapter uses the conceptual leverage provided by the "politics first" proposition and the "media selection and transformation" proposition to address these challenges. Along the way, we will apply the PMP approach developed in previous chapters to demonstrate its usefulness for answering one of the more vexing and awkward bigger-picture questions that political communication researchers regularly have to face: What is communication supposed to do for politics? This question is vexing because no simple answers have yet emerged from the past few thousand years of philosophical reflection on the nature and purpose of politics. It is awkward because few political communication researchers possess the philosophical skills necessary to

Building Theory in Political Communication. Gadi Wolfsfeld, Tamir Sheafer, and Scott Althaus, Oxford University Press.
© Oxford University Press 2022. DOI: 10.1093/oso/9780197634998.003.0006

weave a compelling answer together from obscure strands of normative political theory that were never part of their graduate school training.

This chapter applies the PMP approach to develop a normative framework
for clarifying why media independence is an important concept for political communication. We specify some core representational activities that
can be used as central criteria for evaluating media performance, and explore sources of tension in the representational dynamics between communication ecosystems and political ecosystems that create friction for political
performance. These representational dynamics are rooted in the conceptual
leverage provided by our Politics-Media-Politics (PMP) approach, and the
framework we develop in this chapter can be applied to autocratic regimes as
easily as democratic ones, so that media performance can be assessed from
multiple normative perspectives across the full spectrum of regime types.

This chapter introduces readers to a basic conceptual framework that can
be used to clarify whether a communication ecosystem is enhancing or degrading political performance in any place, at any time in history, and for any
type of political regime. The framework is able to accomplish this because it
is set at a high level of abstraction. It is so high and so abstract that it can be
used to quickly address the "so what?" questions that underlie a wide range
of political communication research covering structural, cultural, or situational dimensions of either political or communication ecosystems (or both)
in nearly any kind of political system, from feudal monarchies to modern
democracies. We also hope to show how useful an abstract concept map can
be for sharpening research questions and motivating falsifiable hypotheses.

In this chapter we develop a compelling way to succinctly answer the question of "What is communication supposed to do?" The short answer that we
will eventually come to is this: *the communication ecosystem enhances political
performance when it promotes responsiveness and accountability.* However,
we will require the whole chapter, and the conceptual leverage provided by
the PMP approach, to unpack some of the most thorny issues: responsiveness to what, accountability to whom, and the reasons why communication
ecosystems struggle to supply both. When this PMP-derived framework is
properly laid out, it will become clear that a better way to ask the big question
would go something like this:

How is political performance enhanced or diminished by communication
performance in a dynamic interplay of mutually dependent ecosystems
structured by different representational logics?

We would not be able to readily pose the question this way without starting from basic insights derived from the PMP approach. Our ability to whittle things down to a sharp answer illustrates what other researchers might be able to do with a good conceptual map. If we succeed in making our case, we may have moved a small distance toward our ambitious dream of revolutionizing the "throwaway normative paragraph" into something that might actually be useful.

What Is Communication Supposed to Do?

It is difficult for political communication researchers to say with certainty what communication is supposed to do for governance. Disseminate politically relevant information? Definitely. Raise levels of popular knowledge about politics? Sure. But beyond that, it is unusual to meet a political communication researcher who can easily articulate how this information and this knowledge are supposed to serve the larger purposes of democratic politics. This difficulty partly reflects a lack of clear guidance from theorists of democracy: political philosophers have said surprisingly little on the subject. Hobbes, Locke, Rousseau, Montesquieu, Bentham, and the like must have had more important things to worry about, because the communication systems required for effective governance are hardly mentioned at all in canonical works of democratic theory. John Stuart Mill's *On Liberty* urges that even bad opinions should be allowed to spread freely in a democracy, without ever detailing the necessary systems or information channels required to serve this purpose. Thomas Jefferson offered a few pithy quotes and Tocqueville's two-volume *Democracy in America* devotes a few laudatory pages to the value of newspapers (in Chapter 6 of Part II). However, by and large, the eighteenth- and nineteenth-century designers of democratic institutions had surprisingly little to say about what exactly communication ecosystems were supposed to do for politics.

The question is also difficult to answer because the most compelling and thoughtful responses depend on underlying (and usually unstated) assumptions about what proper governance is supposed to look like— assumptions that are themselves debatable and highly contested. Republican theorists of democracy insist that good politics must be broadly participatory and deliberative because the common good only emerges when different opinions clash against one another. Liberal pluralists criticize the republican theorists as expecting too much of ordinary citizens (who among us is really that interested in politics anyway?). Instead, they view good governance as the end product of a process that channels healthy competition among rival groups operating under fair rules into collective bargains that are binding on the whole. In this view, good governance means that the strongest pressure group wins, as long as it follows the rules. Competitive elitists scoff at the liberal pluralists for assuming that groups can effectively defend—let alone articulate—even their own narrow interests when the world is so complicated that not even university professors can agree on causes and solutions to pressing problems of the day. Good governance, from the perspective of elite theorists, means rule by teams of experts who have the best chances of really understanding what is going on and solving political problems. As long as citizens have the opportunity to freely choose among rival groups of experts, theorists favoring competitive elite models would say that the best governance requires getting ordinary citizens out of the way: let them vote every once and a while, but mostly just leave politics to the specialists. However, the competitive elitists are then criticized by the republican theorists for holding a view of politics that is hardly democratic at all, and the cycle goes round and round without any clear winner. Assumptions are contested all the way down.[1]

As if those two strikes were not enough, the question of what communication is supposed to do for politics is also hard to answer because social scientists are trained to avoid drawing normative judgments of any sort. In this view, "good" political communication research should not really care what the news ought to do, because answers to such questions cannot be derived from careful observation alone: they are not very "science-y." But qualitative researchers know better; they know that normative assumptions are always lurking behind empirical observations. Like describing the meaning of cross-sectional covariance without using any causal assumptions at all (try it sometime), it is harder than we think because we easily fall into well-worn ways of reducing complexity with intuitive hunches. Empirical observation is usually guided by normative intuitions, which is not a problem. The problem is when empirical observers are unaware of these hidden simplifiers. Qualitative researchers know that empirical analysis is always motivated by normative expectations of one sort or another, regardless of whether the analyst is aware of them: simply claiming that a finding is important assumes some ability to answer the "Important for what?" question, and any compelling answer will rest on value assumptions that are loaded with normative freight.

Our approach to assessing how the communication ecosystem helps or hinders the performance of the political ecosystem addresses all three of these problems. Because it is organized around two essential activities that are common to all models of representative governance—responsiveness and accountability—this framework can be used with a wide range of normative assumptions and institutional structures, regardless of which particular theory of governance one might prefer (or assume). Because it is set at a level of abstraction that does not require researchers to make any particular normative assumptions, it can be used in purely descriptive research projects as readily as for philosophical theorizing.

This chapter aims to equip researchers with a conceptual road map to quickly and easily address one of the central but most difficult questions in political communication scholarship: How does the communication ecosystem help or hinder the performance of the political ecosystem? We begin by elaborating the separate systems of representation that are implicit in each of the PMP's two ecosystems.

Separate Systems of Representation

We can think of the political ecosystem and the communication ecosystem as following separate systems of representational logic. To keep things simple for the moment, we focus on exploring these representational systems within the familiar context of democratic politics illustrated in Figure 6.1. Starting with the political ecosystem, political actors learn what the citizens want and either ignore that information or do something about it. The degree of responsiveness to citizen preferences is a key measure of how well the political ecosystem is delivering on what the people want. In turn, the citizens learn what political actors have done (or left undone), and they either reward or punish the political actors in some way. This accountability mechanism ensures that political actors are ultimately answerable to the citizens, who can, for instance, vote political leaders out of office at the next election if they wanted to. In short, the political ecosystem is where political representation happens.

Political representation doesn't happen in an informational vacuum. To work well, political actors need to learn what citizens want, and citizens need to learn what political actors have done. The information circulating between citizens and political actors is supplied by the communication ecosystem

Political Ecosystem

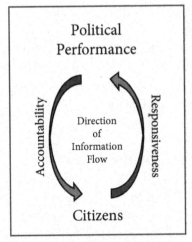

Communication Ecosystem

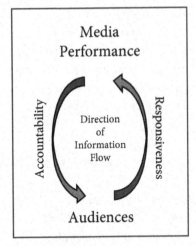

The political ecosystem is where political representation happens

The communication ecosystem can enhance or inhibit effective governance

Figure 6.1. Parallel representational systems in democratic regimes.

and, as stated in the "politics first" proposition, the communication ecosystem will usually reflect, amplify, or emphasize things that originate in the political ecosystem. Likewise, the "media selection and transformation" proposition reminds us that the information circulated by the communication ecosystem can produce dependent, independent, or conditional effects on the representational logic of the political ecosystem.

The communication ecosystem is not answerable to all citizens in the same way as the political ecosystem. Different parts of the communication ecosystem are answerable to different groups of citizens, and ultimately the audiences for various media institutions end up driving a large amount of informational circulation within that ecosystem. Figure 6.1 reminds us that successful media institutions tend to give audiences the informational content that they want because it is often difficult to sustain media operations without demonstrating a proven capacity to keep and hold audience attention. This creates a separate cycle of representation within the communication ecosystem, where audiences hold content producers accountable for how well they have supplied the information that the audiences demand.

Depending on how well aligned the demands of audiences are with the needs of citizens, the communication ecosystem can enhance or inhibit effective governance by influencing the flows of information that circulate between citizens and political actors in the political ecosystem. Before we can develop the implications of this core insight from the PMP approach, however, we must first properly define some key terms and clarify what we mean (and do not mean) by effective governance. To do that, we must step away from the PMP approach to develop a new concept map that captures the core elements and essential activities of political representation.

Three Elements of Political Representation Everywhere

Political philosophers can disagree on the details of just about anything, but most would admit that feasible systems of governance for groups much larger than very small villages require some form of political representation, and all systems that require political representation share a small number of conceptual elements. These elements form the foundation of our theoretical framework for defining effective governance. Disagreements among the various normative models and theories of institutional design tend to focus on the particular ways of defining and implementing these conceptual elements within a particular institutional setting. These disagreements tend to center on the kinds and qualities of political representation that various types of institutional arrangements might provide. At the heart of these disagreements are differences over first principles and starting assumptions, but rising above them is a common set of basic structural elements—building blocks useful for any theory of political representation—that shape what effective governance looks like. These basic structural elements include an individual or group holding sovereign political power, a set of governing institutions, and some means of impersonal communication that allow the government to learn what the sovereign political power wants. These means of impersonal communication must also allow the individual or group holding sovereign political power to assess whether governing institutions are doing what is wanted.

For any system that requires political representation, we can say that *effective governance occurs when the will of the sovereign political power is carried out by the governing institutions (we call this activity "responsiveness") and when the sovereign political power can effectively reward or punish the governing institutions for how well or poorly they have carried out the sovereign's will (we label this activity "accountability").* Before moving on to explore how the PMP approach can use this formulation to give researchers analytical leverage on a wide range of political communication topics, it is important to pin down what we mean (and do not mean) by formulating things in this simplistic but analytically powerful way.

Governing Institutions

Some polities are so small that all the work of governance can be carried out by the entire group of individuals who are governed. In such extreme cases, governance is direct rather than representative. Once a polity gets much larger than a small village, the challenges of scale will tend to require the citizens to hand over day-to-day control of their institutions of governance to a chosen set of political actors. Larger polities require more elaborate divisions of labor between the citizens and the governing institutions, so that the governing institutions operate, to some degree, independently of the citizens, while still being guided in some way by the citizens. Within the language of the PMP approach, we might say that *governing institutions are enduring systems of structural and cultural elements within the political ecosystem.* In the special case of democratic regimes, governing institutions are independent from the citizens, but are charged with carrying out the will of the citizens.[2]

Governing institutions are important in authoritarian regimes as well. Any tin-pot dictator can overthrow a government and assert sovereign power by force of arms, but holding onto that power and consolidating it for effective rule requires something more. This is why the most long-lived and politically effective authoritarians rely on what Jennifer Gandhi and Adam Przeworski call "nominally democratic institutions" for having their will put into action (Gandhi and Przeworski, 2007). Institutions like legislatures and ruling parties provide tangible benefits for authoritarian rulers to dole out to supporters, while simultaneously addressing the usual problems of governing at scale. The upshot is that effective autocratic regimes often end up adopting governing institutions styled after those in democratic regimes.

Means of Impersonal Communication

When governance is carried out directly by the citizens, as in very small villages, everyone can have basic knowledge about which problems are most pressing and who has done what to address them. However, when governance is carried out by political representatives, the citizens must somehow let their representatives know what they want, while also monitoring the actions of those representatives to ensure that governing institutions are doing what they asked for. As the size of a polity grows, effective governance will increasingly depend on means of impersonal communication that do a few things for the polity, as James Carey described in a famous essay.[3]

First, means of impersonal communication (as opposed to purely one-to-one communication, such as a telephone conversation) are needed to convey information back and forth between the citizens and the governing institutions. Carey (1988) called this the "transmission view" of communication, and it aims to overcome the challenge of social and physical distances that separate the citizens from the places where governing actually happens. When the legislature passes a bill in a distant capital, the people back home want to know.

Transmission of politically relevant information is an essential part of effective governance, but Carey reminds us that there is also a second type of politically important communication. Because societies are continually changing, they risk forgetting parts of their past in ways that unmoor them from the boundaries of their better desires. Therefore, impersonal means of communication not only transmit useful information, but also help a polity maintain its first principles, core beliefs, and enduring value commitments by serving up regular reminders that these things are important to the polity. Carey called this second function the "ritual view" of communication because this sort of impersonal communication raises societal eyes to higher principles and guiding beliefs that a society deems to be collectively important. This second type of communication can take many forms, and among the important ones is reminding the citizens what they valued in the past as a way to guide their desires for the future. This ritual view of communication is especially important for large polities in which many millions of individuals, distributed across large spaces, may have little in common, apart from whatever happens to be carried to them through common channels of societal communication. Impersonal means of ritual communication help remind citizens to want the right things from governing institutions and to hold those institutions accountable in the right ways.

We can sum this concept up as follows. Representative governance in democratic regimes needs *impersonal means of communication* that allow the citizens to do three things: tell governing institutions what to do, find out what those institutions have actually done, and help them project their own will into the future by maintaining fidelity with their desires from the past.

The Sovereign Political Power

The opening chapter in this book pointed out that an important limitation of much political communication theory is its narrow roots in and application to countries that are WEIRD: Western, educated, industrialized, rich, and democratic (Henrich, Heine, & Norenzayan, 2010). As a result, most theoretical perspectives in the field with expectations for media performance do not seem to travel well to the non-WEIRD world. For this conceptual framework to be broadly useful for cross-national comparison, it must deal explicitly with the wide variation in regime types and institutional arrangements that are found outside the WEIRD zone. The linchpin in this framework that does the hard work of transitioning between WEIRD and non-WEIRD polities is the concept of political sovereignty.

Thus far we have talked about "the citizens" because we have been keeping the conversation focused on the special case of democratic regimes. However, to broaden the application of this conceptual framework to include non-WEIRD countries, we must shift away from "the citizens" to focus on the role that citizens play in democratic political systems. At this more abstract level, the role played by citizens in democracies is quite similar to the role played by kings and queens in hereditary monarchies or by dictators in authoritarian regimes. Although their various systems of governance take quite different forms, the role of citizens, queens, and dictators within their respective political systems is basically the same: they are the sovereign political power.

Sovereign political power can take many forms, but behind those forms is a common set of attributes that emphasize the role played by the sovereign power within a system of representative governance. Two definitions provide good starting points for describing these critical attributes. The *Blackwell Encyclopedia of Political Thought* defines sovereignty as "the power or authority which comprises the attributes of an ultimate arbitral agent—whether a person or a body of persons—entitled to make decisions and settle disputes within a political hierarchy with some degree of finality" (King, 1991, p. 492). The *Encyclopedia of Modern Political Thought* puts it slightly differently:

> *Sovereignty* is the authority vested in the highest offices and institutions of states: their supremacy over all other authorities in a country as defined by constitutional law, and their political and legal independence from each other, as recognized by international law. *Supremacy* means the highest and final authority from which no further appeal is available. A sovereign is not subordinate to anybody. *Independence* means constitutionally separate and self-governing. A sovereign is not somebody else's dependency. Exercising sovereignty is having the final word. (Jackson, 2013, p. 761)

Some finer points could be brought in here. For example, even though power and authority are two attributes that all political sovereigns possess, these might be held in different ways or to different degrees. We will pass over such nuances for now to keep an eye on the main ideas. The *sovereign political power* is the individual or group that is empowered or authorized to serve as the final word and ultimate decider of disputes regarding the political performance of governing institutions within a polity.

Sovereignty is sovereignty regardless of its institutional framework, but it tends to take different forms in authoritarian regimes than in democratic ones. As a shorthand for the sort of sovereign political power that democracies are designed to respect, we use the term *popular sovereignty* to refer to a particular type of sovereign political power consisting of all responsible adult citizens in a polity. Something like popular sovereignty is the rule for all modern democracies, where the power of governing institutions is formally checked by regular elections in which nearly all adult citizens are eligible to take part.

Identifying the sovereign political power in autocratic regimes is more challenging, because, as Mary Gallagher and Jonathan Hanson note, "lack of clarity about the locus of power is a distinguishing feature of authoritarian systems" (Gallagher & Hanson, 2015, p. 368). Sovereign political power in autocratic polities can be exercised by a vast collective or concentrated in a small group. At the extreme end of this spectrum, an absolute monarch like King Louis XIV of France can correctly declare, "I am the state," because as the sole sovereign power in a clearly structured regime, he certainly was the state's ultimate and final authority, independent of any other power and answerable to none other but perhaps God alone.

While modern democratic countries tend to vest formal power to choose leaders in electorates that are fairly universal in scope, modern autocratic regimes face a more complicated terrain for thinking about sovereign power. At least two forms of sovereign power enter the calculations of autocratic leaders. In recent authoritarian regimes, leaders typically secure their hold on governing institutions by co-opting or securing assent from a group of powerbrokers. Following Bruce Bueno de Mesquita and coauthors (Bueno de Mesquita, Smith, Siverson, & Morrow, 2003), we can call this group that embodies manifest forms of sovereign political power the *selectorate*. Although selectorates are often groups of insiders forming a ruling elite who directly benefit from supporting the status quo, selectorates in competitive autocracies can take more complex forms. For example, Melanie Manion (2014) observes that China's selectorate consists both of elite insiders (in the case of China, leaders within the Chinese Communist Party) and of voters in local congresses who play a limited role in nominating party leaders within controlled elections. In either form, the selectorate is the first and most concrete locus of sovereign political power that shapes the representational contours of authoritarian rule.

Even autocratic leaders must also attend to popular opinion, because their control of governing institutions risks coming to an abrupt and decisive end through coups, assassinations, and popular uprisings. The possibility of rebellion by groups excluded from the selectorate represents a latent form of sovereign political power that no dictator can safely ignore. Following the memorable phrasing of William Zimmerman (2014, p. 3), we can call the set of groups that make up this latent kind of sovereign power the *ejectorate*. These outsiders represent a simmering potential threat that authoritarian leaders need to defuse, avoid, co-opt, or crush. For example, Chinese leaders have developed an extensive censorship system designed to reduce the possibility that citizen frustrations could ever be mobilized into collective action like mass protests that might threaten the state's rule (King, Pan, & Roberts, 2013, 2014; Roberts, 2018). The ejectorate is the second and more abstract form of sovereign political power that marks the outer bounds of authoritarian rule.

Summarizing the dual face of sovereign power in authoritarian regimes into selectorates and ejectorates has limitations when applied to the diverse range of institutional arrangements and power structures found in these systems (Gallagher & Hanson, 2015). For example, some despotic systems are basically ruled by a single person or extremely small coterie (think of the Kim regime in North Korea or Putin's Russia). In such cases, the notion of a selectorate exercising authority over such a dictator is something of a stretch. In practice, selectorates can be large or small, with powers that vary in scope and kind from system to system. Their composition can be difficult to pin down with confidence, but something like a selectorate seems to serve as a sort of final authority in controlling the formal institutions of autocratic government. For the uncommon exceptions to this rule, such as the so-called Color Revolutions that swept through the countries of Georgia, Ukraine, and Kyrgyzstan in the early 2000s, it is the will of the ejectorate that carries the day. The ejectorate's potential for mobilization in authoritarian regimes reflects the inherent instability of any political system that remains misaligned with the needs, wants, and values of the governed. Empowering the few at the expense of the many always creates structural uncertainty about the durability of politics as usual.

Even with these conceptual limitations, a simple distinction between selectorates and ejectorates as dual sources of sovereign political power in authoritarian regimes offers a useful heuristic that serves several important purposes for this framework. First, it not only encompasses a broad spectrum of contemporary autocracies, but can also fit Aristotle's four basic types of non-popular rule in the ancient world (monarchy, tyranny, aristocracy, and oligarchy). This allows the same conceptual framework for understanding how communication performance affects political performance to be used across both ancient forms of governance and current varieties of authoritarian rule. Second, because this way of thinking about sovereign power in authoritarian regimes offers a direct corollary to popular sovereignty in democratic regimes, the same conceptual framework can be used across both regime types. With this approach, even though authoritarian regimes differ in many ways from democratic regimes, both kinds of systems can be usefully compared within the same conceptual framework despite differences in the composition of their respective sovereign political powers. Third, and most important, distinguishing between selectorates and ejectorates as alternative sources of political sovereignty allows an analysis of media performance in autocratic regimes that evaluates not only how a communication ecosystem enhances or diminishes the performance of autocratic rule, but also the degree to which popular interests are underrepresented within that system. This provides conceptual leverage to understand whether the communication ecosystem in any particular autocratic regime might be increasing or relieving representational tensions between those who hold power and those who are excluded.

The Two Essential Activities of Effective
Governance Everywhere

Thus far we have posited that political regimes in both WEIRD and non-WEIRD countries share three common elements that shape how things get done politically: governing institutions, impersonal means of communication, and some type of sovereign political power at the bottom of it all. The key implication is that because even autocrats must rely on impersonalized institutions to put their wills into action, authoritarian regimes depend on political representation to get things done just as much as democratic regimes do.[4] This means that even autocrats have to be concerned about the degree of responsiveness and accountability that their governing institutions provide. However, responsiveness and accountability look very different in democratic and autocratic regimes, so before defining what exactly these terms mean and explaining how they are important to effective governance even in authoritarian systems, it is important to first lay out what the essential activities of responsiveness and accountability look like in these two different political contexts.

The three elements and two essential activities of political representation are summarized graphically in Figure 6.2 for the familiar case of democratic regimes. The representational process starts in the lower right of the figure, where the sovereign political power (which we label "the citizens," even though it would be unusual for *all* of the citizens to make demands on government) tells the governing institutions to do something. The citizens have a voice, but no direct power to make the governing institutions do what they want in any particular way, and their voice must be carried to the governing institutions through impersonal means of communication. We can think of these impersonal means of communication as serving to elevate the governing institutions so they can hear what the citizens want and so the citizens can see what governing institutions are doing. When the governing institutions receive information about what the citizens want, they ignore the information or they do something about it. What they do (or leave undone) is then made visible to the citizens by the impersonal means of communication, and in the lower left of Figure 6.2 the citizens judge whether governing institutions should be rewarded or punished in some way as a result. The dotted line moving back to the right reminds us that, depending on whether they rewarded or punished the governing institutions, the citizens might demand the same thing as before or something different. And the representational cycle continues.

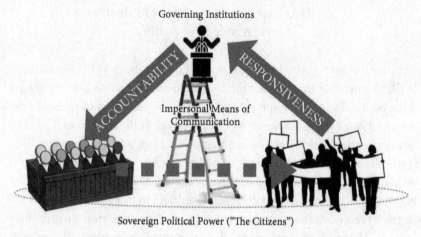

Figure 6.2. Elements of political representation in democratic regimes.

An illustration of this cycle is provided in the sequence of events that led up to the United Kingdom withdrawing from membership in the European Union. British prime minister David Cameron fulfilled a campaign promise in 2016 by holding a referendum on continued membership in the European Union, which he expected would produce a clear "remain" vote. When 52% of voters in the non-binding referendum voted instead for Brexit ("Brexit" is short for "British Exit"), an embarrassed Cameron was forced to resign. His replacement, Theresa May, attempted to move the Brexit process forward in Parliament, but her failure to implement a deal created popular backlash against her government that eventually forced her resignation as well. Boris Johnson took over as prime minister and finally completed the process of leaving the European Union on January 31, 2020, after two general elections and several harrowing passes through the representational cycle in Figure 6.2.

The representational cycle in autocratic regimes looks somewhat different, even though the component elements and essential activities are the same. Figure 6.3 shows that instead of "the citizens," sovereign political power is exercised primarily by a selectorate that supports the authoritarian leadership. It is the selectorate (or the leadership supported by the selectorate) that demands things of governing institutions and rewards or punishes those institutions for how they respond. This process still requires impersonal means of communication, but there is a kind of repressive lid imposed

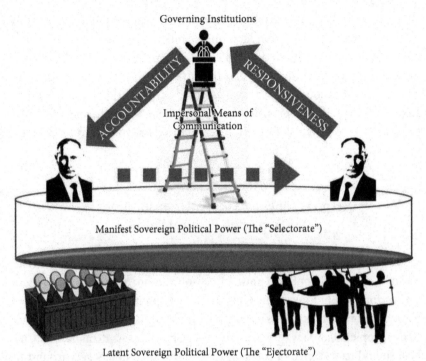

Figure 6.3. Elements of political representation in autocratic regimes.

from above on the citizens who are excluded from the selectorate. Although these citizens can still observe (to some extent) what governing institutions are doing, their demands are unlikely to be taken seriously unless the pressure from below becomes so great that it threatens to blow the lid off. When tainted infant formula in China killed six babies and left as many as 300,000 others hospitalized, the resulting popular outrage forced the Chinese government to pursue criminal convictions of the perpetrators and visibly demonstrate an increased commitment to safeguarding the food supply (Yang, 2013). Only under threat of bringing the whole system crashing down will the representational cycle take some part of the ejectorate's will seriously, and even then, governing institutions will do only what is required to reduce the pressure from below to sustainable levels while still respecting the sovereign power of the selectorate. But public opinion has to be taken into account, even by authoritarian leaders.

Within our highly abstracted conceptual map, representational dynamics within the political ecosystem look quite similar, regardless of whether the regime is democratic or not. In both cases, a continual process of back-and-forth information transfer between the sovereign political power and the governing institutions supports two essential activities that are common to all theories of political representation: responsiveness and accountability. We are now in a position to define what each of these essential activities actually involves.

Responsiveness of Governing Institutions to the Sovereign Political Power

Responsiveness addresses the ability of governing institutions to carry out the will of the sovereign political power. In absolute monarchies, responsiveness means doing the bidding of the king or queen. In polities with popular sovereignty, responsiveness entails hearing and acting in accordance with the voice of the people in some way. For example, when protestors demand that City Hall should fix a stretch of road, and the mayor then finally gets around to sending a repair crew, we can call this an instance of responsiveness. But theories of representation differ on whether this might be an appropriate kind of responsiveness. Who is authorized to speak for the sovereign, what parts of the sovereign's voice should be listened to, and what should follow after that voice is heard are important questions that do not have easy answers. This is the level at which real differences among various theories of representation start to emerge, because the activity of responsiveness to the sovereign power can take quite different forms under different models of representation and there is no agreement on which forms are most important. The conceptual framework developed here is, for better or worse, wholly indifferent to them all; its purpose is merely to provide a common set of reference points broad enough to bracket important differences among theories of representation, while still being useful for assessing the performance of the communication ecosystem.

Nonetheless, two kinds of responsiveness are so basic and so potentially important to political communication research that they should be distinguished briefly. They go by different names in different theories, but we can label them agenda responsiveness and preference responsiveness. *Agenda responsiveness* occurs when the agenda of government action is shaped to reflect the topical concerns of the sovereign power. The Chinese government's rapid responses to citizen concerns about food safety following the 2008 baby formula scandal is an example of agenda responsiveness. This type of responsiveness features prominently in the most recent work of Jürgen Habermas and the classic writings of Edmund Burke. The familiar trustee model of representation can be construed as having a special concern with agenda representation, where trustees respond to (and anticipate) the underlying interests of their sovereign while potentially ignoring the sovereign's preferred course of action. *Preference responsiveness* occurs when the policies advanced by government action are shaped to reflect the preferences of the sovereign power. The United Kingdom's eventual exit from the European Union following a clear signal from voters in 2016 is an example of preference responsiveness. This type of responsiveness corresponds to the delegate model of representation and was important for early pollsters like George Gallup and institutional designers like James Madison, among others. Delegates respond to (and anticipate) the stated needs and desires of their sovereign, while potentially ignoring any interests of the sovereign that they have not been instructed to address. This distinction is potentially fruitful for political communication research, because only certain kinds of information conveyed through the communication ecosystem might be relevant for preference representation (for example, petitions, opinion poll results, or individual expressions of policy preference), but nearly all kinds of information carried through impersonal means of communication could potentially be relevant for agenda representation.

We are deliberately skirting around important questions about what it means to represent and how the sovereign is supposed to be represented in governing institutions. We are ignoring distinctions among types of responsiveness and also blurring distinctions among such phrases as "will of the sovereign," "interests of the sovereign," or any combination of "what the sovereign wants/needs/values." Doctoral degrees are conferred for novel ways of dividing and refining such terms, so we should note that our casual mixing of these concepts is an academic slash-and-burn over artfully arranged landscapes of philosophical rapture. However, since our inconsiderate sweeping across one of political philosophy's most meticulously crafted mandalas leaves a brown sandy pile that serves our purposes perfectly, we can just write "Philistine" on our name tags and get on with the argument.

Accountability of Governing Institutions to the Sovereign Political Power

Accountability addresses the ability of the sovereign political power to exercise ultimate control over governing institutions. Think of a jury hearing a case in court. The court is a set of governing institutions that defines a process and a set of possible outcomes for the trial, but it is the jury that makes the final decision on whether the defendant is guilty. In this kind of trial, while the jury is sovereign, it has only a single and very limited task: to pass judgment on whether the governing institutions have presented a strong case. Accountability looks like juries and courtrooms. Systems of political representation require accountability mechanisms to ensure that governing institutions remain subservient to the will of the sovereign, and there are many mechanisms to choose from. The more familiar ones are *formal mechanisms* for checking government power, such as elections, impeachment proceedings, and requirements for holding political office. Such formal mechanisms are set up to define boundaries of permissible action or to create decisive points of intervention for the sovereign to reward or punish governing institutions for what they have done (or have left undone). There is also a diverse array of *informal mechanisms* for checking government power that bring pressure to bear on governing institutions through rewards and punishments that take less than decisive forms. Petitions, protests, opinion polls, and publicity (adverse or otherwise) are among the informal mechanisms of accountability that could potentially motivate a sovereign to intervene at some future point through formal accountability mechanisms. Such informal mechanisms of accountability are less decisive than formal ones, but they are no less important for checking the exercise of government power. The court of public opinion often has far more power to hold governing institutions to account than any election: just ask any number of once-powerful officials who no longer enjoy the perquisites of office due to scandal or publicized incompetence.[5]

Although the framework developed here tries to draw a clear distinction between responsiveness and accountability, in practice the line between them can be blurry. If we think about these activities as a paired sequence (responsiveness followed by accountability), it becomes clear that whether governing institutions are rewarded or punished for how they responded to the will of the sovereign could shape the sovereign's next demands. If rewarded, the sovereign might ask for even more of the same or for something entirely different. If punished, the sovereign might insist that governing institutions try again, but get it right this time. In non-democracies, this insisting is not done nicely. North Korean dictator Kim Jong Un has reportedly executed senior leaders with anti-aircraft guns and flamethrowers, among other extreme methods, presumably to send strong signals to other leaders that they had better not let the Supreme Leader down.[6] Because what happens in the accountability stage has an impact on what the sovereign will want government to do in the future, at some level accountability feeds back into responsiveness. They are not completely independent from one another, but they can be distinguished conceptually.

Effective Governance

Political representation entails both responsiveness and accountability, and the communication ecosystem contributes fundamentally to effective governance when supporting these essential activities. In all but the most unusual instances of direct governance and a few other odd cases, the term "effective representation" is more or less synonymous with "effective governance," but "effective governance"—as we use the term—is different from "good governance," so before moving on it is important to briefly distinguish the two.

By *effective governance* we mean that the system of representation allows the sovereign political power to direct and control the governing institutions in some appropriate way. This is a very narrow concept. Effective governance occurs when the necessary conditions are in place for the sovereign to exert power over governing institutions, but this does not mean that the representation is done well. For example, the 2016 election of Donald Trump to the presidency of the United States followed precisely the institutional rules for American national elections, but also contributed to increasing levels of political polarization (Finkel et al., 2020), greater propensity to believe in conspiracy theories (Golec de Zavala & Federico, 2018), and decreased trust in government (Citrin & Stoker, 2018). Despite these negative outcomes, Americans in 2016 got the candidate they wanted (at least according to the arcane rules of the US Electoral College system). We can therefore say that the US governance system was effective from a representational standpoint in allowing the sovereign power to exercise control over governing institutions, both by bringing Trump to the presidency and then showing him the door four years later, even if voters didn't end up getting what they hoped for when Trump was first elected. As we use the term, *effective governance* is therefore more closely related to accountability than to responsiveness.

Good governmental performance is different and is probably closer to what most people have in mind when they imagine how government is supposed to work. For our purposes, we can say that *good governance* occurs when the governing institutions actually deliver what the sovereign political power wants. The Brexit case is an example of good governance, even if it produces buyer's remorse after its effects are fully known: UK voters sent a clear signal in 2016 that they wanted to withdraw from the European Union, and governing institutions eventually delivered that outcome four years later. But even here, "good governance" has nothing to do with "the correct (or best possible) outcome" but merely that the representational system does what the sovereign power demands. There can be no consensus on what good governance would even look like, so we have not attempted to define any such characteristics for the purposes of this conceptual framework. Our narrow point is merely that good governance—understood here in its most general sense as somehow delivering on what the sovereign power wants—is more closely related to responsiveness than to accountability.

In summary, good governance emphasizes the performance of governing institutions in delivering certain outcomes, while effective governance focuses narrowly on the structural connections that allow the sovereign power to hold governing institutions accountable in the first place. In the way we separate these terms, you can have effective governance without good governance (as when the sovereign's will is clearly conveyed, but political leaders fail to act and are therefore thrown out of office in the next election) and also good governance without effective governance (as when the sovereign's will is carried out by accident). Our conceptual framework is only concerned with effective governance, and even here we offer no specific vision of what effective governance looks like. Therefore, we have nothing at all to say about "good governance," even though delivering on what the sovereign wants (or ought to want) is, of course, the ideal result of effective governance.

This distinction is crucial for maintaining the normative agnosticism of our conceptual framework. Normative theories quickly part ways on the quality, quantity, and type of representation that political systems should produce. These are the key ingredients for defining "good governance" from different vantage points and also fighting words for political philosophers, but our approach ignores the conflict altogether. What makes our framework potentially powerful is that almost any definition of good governance—as well as specific types, qualities, and quantities of representation—can be imported into it from nearly any theory of politics because the framework's simple features do not imply any particular definition. Instead of emphasizing good governance, this narrow emphasis on effective governance is concerned only with increasing the chances that the will of the sovereign political power is somehow represented in the activity of governing institutions, without actually specifying a particular type, quality, or minimal threshold of representation. More responsiveness and accountability should generally lead to more effective representation of the political sovereign's will, so "more is generally better" within this framework, but only up to a point. It is possible to have too much responsiveness and excessive accountability, but since ideal amounts of both will vary by model of governance and so many other starting principles, it is difficult to specify boundary conditions in a way that might generalize across a broad swath of theoretical starting points. So while we omit those details from our conceptual framework, it should be compatible with nearly any amount or variety of these key representational activities.

We made earlier reference to "effective governance *everywhere*." Before exploring how the communication ecosystem might help or hinder political representation, it is first important to take a closer look at how political representation works in non-democratic regimes and why the framework's equivalence across regime types actually makes good sense.

Political Representation and the Communication Ecosystem in Authoritarian Regimes

If effective political representation entails responsiveness and accountability to a sovereign political power, even in authoritarian regimes, the communication ecosystem should be nearly as important for political performance in autocratic states as in democratic ones. Of course, we recognize that the ultimate source of power in a police state comes from having a governmental monopoly on the use of force: daily pronouncements from the *Pravda* newspaper were probably helpful to the Soviet Union, but the threat of tanks, troops, and gulags were quite enough on their own to keep the masses in line. However, a large gap remains between "keeping the masses in line" and "effective governance," and even police states benefit from communication ecosystems that facilitate effective political representation (of the autocrat's will, of course, rather than the ejectorate's). This insight helps explain why hybrid "competitive authoritarian" regimes often allow independent media outlets to flourish despite the obvious political risks of doing so (Kiriya & Degtereva, 2010; Levitsky & Way, 2002, 2010): autocrats depend on impersonal communication for getting things done in much the same ways as democrats do. More generally for dictators, ballots are a more legitimate and cost-effective means of securing power than bullets (Levitsky & Way, 2020). And to be seen as legitimate, elections usually require at least the appearance of give-and-take, even in the communication ecosystems supporting authoritarian regimes.

The value of this insight for the research community may not be obvious, as no self-respecting political communication scholar daydreams of helping autocrats gain a tighter grip on their citizens. When viewed from within the PMP approach, however, it becomes clear that the very process of relying on impersonal means of communication for getting things done creates perverse incentives for autocrats to relax their grip on citizens, at least in the communication domain. Politics comes first, especially for autocrats, but even autocrats have strong incentives to let the communication ecosystem have its turn as well. This is because the informational transmissions required for effective accountability and responsiveness to what the autocrat wants should become easier to sustain when the communication ecosystem is at least somewhat independent from government control. To see why, let us take a separate look at what effective accountability and effective responsiveness look like from the standpoint of the autocrat in charge.

Effective accountability is enhanced when the sovereign political power receives accurate information about what officials are doing within all levels of the governing institutions. Autocrats want to minimize their own accountability to any other source of sovereign power, while also maximizing their chances of holding lesser officials to account for what they do (or leave undone). We can refer to this desire of autocrats to maximize accountability for officials at lower levels of the governing apparatus, while minimizing their own accountability at the top of the organizational chart, as *insulated accountability*. Insulated accountability is a difficult balance to achieve within complex governing institutions when the communication ecosystem is rigidly controlled by the state, because such strict control over information flows tends to dampen accountability at all levels of the governance structure simultaneously. However, as illustrated by the pathbreaking analysis of

Chinese censorship practices by political scientists Gary King, Jennifer Pan, and Margaret Roberts (King et al., 2013, 2014), social media censorship in contemporary China is designed to provide precisely this insulated type of accountability: citizens are provided ample opportunities to criticize both local and national political leaders, but little chance of publishing messages that might stimulate collective political action with potential for bringing about leadership change. In this system, if accountability happens, it is because existing leaders want it to, and since leaders at the top have more power than those at the bottom, this system effectively supports a kind of insulated accountability that helps more powerful leaders hold their less-powerful colleagues accountable for acts of corruption and incompetence brought to light by citizen communicators.

Effective responsiveness is enhanced when the will of the sovereign political power is accurately conveyed to governing officials. Regimes of any size need impersonal means of communication to do this, so even autocrats are affected by the "M" of PMP because the structural, cultural, and situational factors that influence media selection and transformation of activity emerging from the political ecosystem tend to shape what kind of responsiveness is privileged within the communication ecosystem. Autocrats want to ensure not only that governing institutions respond to their own desires, but also that the political ecosystem as a whole should effectively relieve certain types of destabilizing pressure that might build up to dangerous levels within the ejectorate. Zheng Su and Tianguang Meng (2016) used the term *selective responsiveness* to describe the Chinese government's tendency to be more responsive to citizen requests for improving economic performance than to other types of policy demands. We have borrowed that term to capture more generally the desire of autocrats to favor a type of responsiveness that promotes the will of the selectorate while finding politically safe ways to relieve only the most dangerous forms of destabilizing pressure that might be building up in the ejectorate. Selective responsiveness aims to sustain a political ecosystem that addresses the will of the selectorate without having to satisfy all (or even most) of the ejectorate's demands.

The key point is that even in dictatorial systems where sovereign power is vested in an individual or small group of leaders, some degree of responsiveness to popular opinion is still required for maintaining the autocrat's continued hold on power, and the communication ecosystem has an important role to play in conveying the demands of ordinary citizens to authoritarian leaders so they can reach for the right pressure-release valve. Even Adolf Hitler required a communication ecosystem that allowed his regime to respond to citizen concerns as the Second World War progressed, although, as detailed by Aryeh Unger (1965), this means of communication was intended for "leader's eyes" only, not popular access. The Nazis set up a private network of communication that passed ground-level Gestapo reports and other surreptitious observations of citizen behavior through successive layers of governmental bureaucracy. The problem for Hitler, as for other authoritarian rulers, is that a communication system that filters information through self-interested governmental bureaucrats is no honest broker; leaders at every level of the Nazi regime had strong incentives to report that all was well in their part of the Reich, regardless of how restive the local populace actually was. When compounded upward across multiple layers of governmental bureaucracy, Unger's analysis shows that the view of the Reich's internal status reaching Hitler's inner circle from this "leader-only" communication channel bore little resemblance to reality and proved useless for monitoring the ejectorate's degree or type of restiveness.

What was true of the Third Reich holds true in contemporary autocracies as well. Political scientist Daniela Stockmann (2013) coined the term "responsive authoritarianism" to describe an important and intentional byproduct of China's tightly regulated, but market-driven communication ecosystem. Stockmann pointed out that when citizens can openly voice their frustrations without fear of government reprisal, and when journalists are relatively free to publish news reports that reflect those frustrations, authoritarian rulers gain a double benefit. First, leaders gain accurate information about the actual levels of restiveness in their citizenry, which allows them to monitor the ejectorate's threat potential without having to bear the costs of actually repressing anyone. Second, because news attention is itself a symbolic form of responsiveness, leaders benefit from the appearance that something is being done about citizens' frustrations without ever having to bring about real change. Stockmann noted that China, like many authoritarian regimes, also has a private communication system that journalists use to convey information to leaders about topics that are too sensitive to publish. But it is the market-driven media system that produces these important benefits for Chinese leaders by permitting symbolic responsiveness to act as a pressure-release valve that simultaneously defangs the ejectorate and informs the sovereign power about where they really stand in the eyes of their citizens.

A related conclusion about the purpose of authoritarian censorship strategies was proposed by Margaret Roberts (2018), who pointed out that fear-based censorship strategies premised on credible threats of reprisal against individual citizens are both expensive and ineffective. Instead, she demonstrated how more porous censorship strategies that only make it slightly difficult to access uncensored information produce most of the benefits of a more rigid censorship system at a fraction of the cost. According to Roberts, allowing citizens to expose minor flaws in the political ecosystem also benefits authoritarian rulers by increasing the system's efficiency while giving the appearance of responsiveness when incompetent or corrupt officials are punished following exposure by an outraged public. In addition, this porous censorship, combined with permissiveness toward airing limited critiques of lower-level government performance, is usually sufficient to protect more powerful authoritarian rulers from being held accountable for their political performance.

To be clear, autocrats often and perhaps usually "respond to citizen concerns" in order to defang or manipulate popular opinion, rather than to champion the needs, wants, or values of their citizens. However, even maleficence can produce a form of unintended responsiveness that arises simply from becoming aware of what restive citizens want. Political scientist Larry Jacobs called this inadvertent responsiveness to citizen demands the "recoil effect" (Jacobs, 1992). The recoil effect is a natural consequence of any governmental monitoring of popular opinion, even when the goal is to sidestep or manipulate citizen demands. As Jacobs put it, manipulation leads naturally to responsiveness. As he showed in the case of American and British efforts to reform their respective healthcare systems, this is because governments naturally begin taking public opinion into account—even if only to better manipulate their citizens—as an unintended byproduct of developing good systems for monitoring what that citizen opinion actually is. The sort of responsiveness produced by the recoil effect may be only partial or limited in scope, but it is responsiveness nonetheless—and it is a clear example of the "media selection and transformation" proposition at work.

Summing Up and Getting Back to PMP

The preceding section introduced a generic and highly abstracted conceptual scaffolding made up of not-very-controversial elements that can fit a wide range of regime types and normative assumptions about how political representation ought to work. We have shown that even autocrats need to be concerned about how communication affects the political ecosystem. Democrats and dictators both benefit from means of impersonal communication that promote responsiveness and accountability to their respective sovereign political powers. Dictators who want to stay in power have additional incentives to foster communication systems that help detect and relieve political pressures within the ejectorate; pressures that, if left untended, could spill over into coups d'état, insurrections, or other forms of destabilizing resistance. In short, because the same sort of informational problems common to democratic regimes make it difficult for dictators to control their institutions of government, both need to be concerned about the vital role that political communication plays in governance. Now that this basic groundwork has been laid, we can leverage the PMP approach to clarify why communication ecosystems so often struggle to support effective governance in WEIRD countries, and why they have such potential to undermine autocratic control in the rest of the world.

Two Ecosystems, Two Sovereign Powers

Effective representation within anything other the tiniest political ecosystem requires some means of impersonal communication. We can say that *effective political communication occurs when the means of impersonal communication increase the responsiveness and accountability of governing institutions to the will of the sovereign political power.* However, few elements of typical communication ecosystems should naturally be responsive and accountable only to the will of the sovereign political power and nothing else. One reason for this is that all but the tiniest communication ecosystems are at least partly designed to represent the will of a different sovereign power than the one holding sway in politics.

When we use the PMP approach to conceptually separate the political ecosystem from the communication ecosystem, we can more easily observe that, in most polities, these two entities will be governed to some degree by different sovereign powers. While the performance of the political ecosystem hinges on the degree to which governing institutions are responsive to the sovereign political power and held accountable by that sovereign power for what the institutions have done (or have left undone), the performance of the communication ecosystem responds in varying degrees to the sovereignty of audiences providing the critical resources of attention and engagement that serve as coin of the realm for communication power. Social media systems are an extreme case in point: even in authoritarian regimes, the individual preferences of ordinary people influence (to at least some degree) which messages get broadly disseminated on social media and which do not. An autocrat might be able to prevent certain messages from being shared, and can even hire large numbers of people to flood social media with positive messages, as China does with its "50 cent army" (Roberts, 2018), but there is little that an authoritarian regime can do to force individuals to disseminate its propaganda if the messages are not interesting or amusing enough to pass along.

Therefore, just as the sovereign political power holds the theoretical reins in the political ecosystem, we can say that there is something like a sovereign audience power holding ultimate authority in a communication ecosystem. However, unlike in the political realm, where the sovereign might be defined by statute or fiat that provides a fairly distinct and enduring identity to the theoretical holder of ultimate power, sovereign power in the communication ecosystem is fluid and fleeting. Evolving opportunities afforded by particular combinations of structural and cultural factors within the communication ecosystem motivate communicators to temporarily assemble particular kinds of audiences that provide resources for sustaining the communicator's continued existence, as well as for accomplishing particular kinds of goals (Hamilton, 2004, 2007; Stroud, 2017). These resources might be supplied by subscriptions or page views or ratings points or numbers of followers; whatever form they take, the attention economy of communication ecosystems prizes enumerated metrics of audience engagement as coin of the realm (see esp. Hindman, 2018). Communication actors compete with one another across complex multidimensional markets to assemble diverse and lucrative audience segments that can be monetized, used to signal reputational status, or converted into other forms of communicative power. This competition inclines self-interested communicative actors to be responsive and accountable (in varying degrees) to desirable audience segments. Nor are state-owned or state-controlled media completely immune to the pressures of audience attention: stiff competition from the commercial sector increasingly forces state broadcasters to justify their continued (expensive) existence by demonstrating how they serve unique audience segments,[7] while Russia's Channel 1 and China's CCTV can only fulfill their domestic propaganda potential if they attract and retain the attention of significant audience shares (e.g., Esarey, 2005; A. Esarey, 2006; A. W. Esarey, 2006; Kiriya & Degtereva, 2010; Stockmann & Gallagher, 2011; Tang & Iyengar, 2011).

For the sake of convenience, we can call this complex and ever-shifting foundation of communication power *sovereign audience power* to distinguish it from sovereign political power, as long as we keep in mind that the communication ecosystem is responsive and accountable to both producers and consumers of information, as well as other third-party stakeholders. For example, audience demand for political information is at least partly structured by the available supply of informational options (e.g., Althaus, Cizmar, & Gimpel, 2009; Baker, 2002; Prior, 2007; Van Aelst et al., 2017). Likewise, the economic incentives that drive available advertising revenue encompass a dual market consisting of advertisers and audiences (e.g., Hamilton, 2004; Napoli, 2003; Picard, 1989). In such systems, advertisers pay content providers for the privilege of messaging desired audience segments, which motivates content providers to supply informational options that are attractive to those segments. Success in attracting audiences (of a certain type) becomes a valuable type of sovereign power that, when amassed in particular ways, allows advertisers and content providers to achieve their respective goals while simultaneously satisfying the preferences of their audiences. Audiences are the ultimate target of attention, but the sovereign power that they exercise within this distributed power system is shared with the firms trying to reach them: if the firms were not trying to get their attention in the first place, cumulative audience numbers would hold less value as a resource to be pursued. To the extent that strategic behavior in pursuit of diverse revenue streams can create and distribute important types of power within a communication ecosystem, sovereign audience power gets divided in complex ways among firms and the demographic segments they are trying to reach. When highly segmented communication markets privilege increasingly complex types of sovereign audience power, the potential for strong alignment of sovereign powers across the communication and political ecosystems quickly grows dim.

Sovereign audience power as a seat of ultimate communicative authority takes different forms across communication modalities, as well as between WEIRD and non-WEIRD countries. Even in authoritarian contexts, where media systems may be entirely controlled by governing institutions, some degree of sovereign audience power always remains in two foundational choices: whether to pay attention or not, and whether to trust transmitted information or not. In the end, no amount of political control over information flows will have much political impact if the intended audience discounts or ignores that information. As there is always the choice to tune out, so there exists, even in authoritarian regimes, a communicative version of Jacob's "recoil effect" that requires governing institutions to first satisfy audience preferences for content provision before any intended political messaging can be effectively placed before them.

Sovereign audience power in authoritarian regimes is also enhanced by the technological difficulty that governing institutions increasingly face in controlling rapidly developing digital media networks (e.g., Reuter & Szakonyi, 2015; Roberts, 2018). Even in China, the rapid spread of high-profile social media posts can easily outpace the ability of censors to quickly pull them down, citizens can break through the government's "Great Firewall" system without much effort to access banned information sources, and widespread use of encoded language designed to avoid censorship detection allows Chinese citizens to maintain vibrant forums for critical dialogue despite the efforts of the state to silence them (Rauchfleisch & Schäfer, 2015; Roberts, 2018). So, while audiences may not rule the communication roost in autocratic regimes, they still hold considerable power for shaping the information flows that have the potential to enhance effective governance.

How this potential translates into real communicative power is difficult to predict or even describe outside of particular communication markets, but it will register through the "media selection and transformation" proposition in the MP part of the PMP cycle. Whereas sovereign political power at least appears simple enough in the abstract, the fluid and fleeting nature of sovereign audience power makes it complicated to pin down right from the start. While sovereign political power often relies on formal accountability mechanisms like elections and laws to exercise control over governing institutions, sovereign audience power is more apt to rest on informal accountability mechanisms, not only because the resource opportunities that combine to form incentives for acquiring and stewarding communicative power are often already shaped by formal regulatory systems (such as laws that disallow certain types of advertising or restrict particular kinds of ownership patterns), but also because these incentives are dynamically structured by strategic decisions about opportunity costs and returns on investment that are difficult to regulate, routinized, or even anticipate. Regulatory systems and other structural elements imposed by the political ecosystem are certainly important factors that shape the forms and nature of sovereign audience power, and the "politics first" proposition should hold even more strongly in authoritarian regimes than in democratic ones. However, because audience dynamics ultimately structure economic resourcing opportunities within the communication ecosystem, sovereign audience power remains an important shaper of information flows within the communication eco-system, even in autocratic regimes. As mentioned in the previous chapter, the way in which this audience sovereignty influences political performance in the "second P" of the PMP cycle will depend on characteristics of the re-gime type, as well as of the particular forms of sovereign power that carry weight in a given regime's political and communication ecosystems.

These differences in the nature and forms of sovereign power have pro-found implications for the ability of communication media to support effec-tive governance, because neither ecosystem stands alone. Both depend on the other for proper functioning, and both influence the other as a byproduct of responding to the wills of their respective sovereigns. The PMP approach not only provides a conceptual map for orienting researchers within this complex theoretical space, but also can be used to generate predictions about how political performance across regime types is likely to be affected by the inherent tensions produced by misalignments between the sovereign powers underlying the political and communication ecosystems.

How Mutually Dependent Ecosystems Affect Political Performance

Effective representation of the sovereign's will in the political ecosystem is enhanced or diminished by the type, amount, and quality of information that flows between the sovereign and governing institutions. However, the con-tent of these informational flows is shaped to varying degrees by the ways that political developments are picked up and transmitted through the com-munication ecosystem. This is invariably a selective process that not only has the potential to filter politically relevant information for consumption by the sovereign audience power, but also to emphasize those activities or messages emanating from the political ecosystem that are particularly interesting or important for certain audience segments.

The PMP approach does far more than merely postulate the mutual de-pendence of these two ecosystems. As illustrated in Figure 6.4, when we join the conceptual framework for political representation developed in the present chapter to the basic PMP model, we can see more precisely how and why this mutual dependence should influence political performance. More importantly, this PMP-derived approach to understanding how the communication ecosystem might improve political performance can be fruitfully applied to develop and test hypotheses that cumulate knowledge for the political communication research community, while simultaneously moving its attention beyond the familiar WEIRD cases to encompass the full range of polities for which political communication should matter for effective governance.

This enhanced PMP approach is illustrated in Figure 6.4. The PMP cycle starts with events or developments that affect the political ecosystem, and the political ecosystem follows its internal representational logic in producing visible responses to these stimuli (for example, bills passed, hearings held, statements made). These visible indicators of political performance are then picked up or ignored by the communication ecosystem, which follows its own representational logic in selectively amplifying and distributing politically relevant information according to the opportunities afforded by its sovereign audience power. The communication ecosystem's visible responses to the initial set of political stimuli then feed back in turn to the political ecosystem, to be picked up or ignored by political actors who selectively amplify and respond to the politically relevant information being conveyed through the communication ecosystem. And again the cycle continues.

At every turn in the cycling process, the full range of structural, cultural, and situational factors germane to each ecosystem will potentially

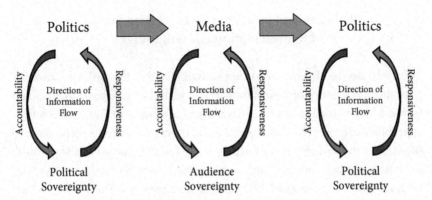

Figure 6.4. A PMP framework for understanding how the communication ecosystem enhances or diminishes political performance.

be in play to shape the responses of institutions, groups, and individuals operating within each ecosystem, but those responses will ultimately be influenced to some degree by the will of each ecosystem's particular sovereign. This is why better alignment between the sovereign powers underlying both ecosystems should tend to increase the likelihood that media performance will support effective governance: different factors will affect each ecosystem at each stage in the PMP cycle, but both ecosystems will ultimately be serving the same sovereign power. It comes as no surprise that countries with vibrant public broadcasting systems dedicated to serving the informational needs of all citizens tend to enjoy higher average levels of political knowledge (e.g., Soroka et al., 2013). But when the two ecosystems generally respond to different sovereign powers, increasing degrees of misalignment between sovereign powers will tend to create friction between the political and communication ecosystems that affects the ability of media performance to support effective governance. When an advertising-driven communication ecosystem makes it easier to encounter videos of squirrels on waterskis than news of the latest parliamentary debate, the differential opportunity costs required for finding politically relevant information should tend to diminish citizen awareness of (and concern for) what government is doing (e.g., Iyengar et al., 2010). As the next section will demonstrate, the novel implications of this enhanced PMP approach follow from the different forms of misalignment across sovereign powers governing the two ecosystems, and from the starkly different outcomes that such misalignment has for democratic and authoritarian regimes.

Dilution and Distortion as Important Forms of Representational Misalignment

This PMP-derived framework is not so much concerned with the amount, type, or sufficiency of representation as it is with the more basic question of whose will is being represented in a particular ecosystem. When the sovereign audience power that has the final say in the communication ecosystem is the same as the sovereign political power that has the final say in the political ecosystem, the communication ecosystem has strong potential for enhancing responsiveness and accountability to the sovereign political power. When both ecosystems serve the same sovereign power, political communication might naturally tend to support effective governance. This is one reason why public service broadcasting tends to produce political news coverage that supports effective governance in democratic polities: public service models of inclusive and reasoned news coverage are explicitly designed, regulated, and resourced to supply the basic informational needs of all citizens, regardless of ideological leaning or relative interest in politics.

However, when these sovereigns are not identical—that is, when each ecosystem represents a different will, to varying degrees—the representational dynamics of the two ecosystems create friction that can work against effective representation of the sovereign political power's will. In the case of democratic polities, if the voice of some people but not all is somehow privileged by the representational dynamics of the communication ecosystem, then the rest of the people risk having a diminished voice in the governance process. This can happen when the communication ecosystem becomes increasingly commercialized, so that information flows come to be shaped more by audience segments that are particularly desirable to advertisers than to all citizens equally (Hamilton, 2004; Hindman, 2008, 2018; Katz, 1996). However, this enhanced PMP approach shows that a similar misalignment of sovereign powers can also happen in autocracies, where a tight grip on power in the political ecosystem is matched by the somewhat more open hand in the communication ecosystem required for producing insulated accountability and selective responsiveness. To the degree that a communication ecosystem in an authoritarian regime grows responsive and accountable to the preferences of audiences who are excluded from political power, as with China's heavily advertising-driven media ecosystem (Stockmann, 2013), that ecosystem becomes less likely to consistently produce information flows aligned with what an autocrat might want.

The key question in either case is whether the representational dynamic within the political ecosystem is focused on the whole sovereign and nothing but the sovereign. Our PMP-inspired approach clarifies why a separate representational dynamic occurring within the communication ecosystem can shift this ideal focus in profound ways. There are a few odd cases (like North Korea) where formal communication institutions may be so tightly controlled by governing institutions that the sovereign powers underlying both ecosystems are difficult to distinguish. However, it follows from the model developed here that, as a general rule, *communication ecosystems that develop with some degree of independence from political control should tend to be at least partly misaligned to the needs of political representation.*[8] Such misalignment should tend to prioritize (or de-prioritize) the informational preferences of some groups more than others in ways that undermine the ability of the sovereign political power to generate effective forms of responsiveness and accountability through the communication ecosystem.

In keeping with the framework's emphasis on basic elements that are as agnostic as possible to contested governance models and normative assumptions, our PMP-derived approach emphasizes a particular kind of alignment problem: misalignment stemming from differences in the composition of each ecosystem's respective sovereign. By composition, we mean simply the number, identity, and variety of included voices that constitute a sovereign. *Compositional misalignment* can take one of two forms: when one of the sovereigns includes groups or individuals that are not part of the other; and when one of the sovereigns provides more weight, power, or voice to some groups or individuals than they have in the other. An example of the first form is when transnational media originating from outside a polity play important roles in its communication ecosystem even though the polity's sovereign political power consists only of domestic citizens. An example of the second form is the United Kingdom's unelected House of Lords, which exercises political checking power over the elected House of Commons, but has no parallel representation in the audience structure for the British television market.

Such compositional misalignments between the sovereign powers of the communication and political ecosystems should be fairly common. Many of these misalignments should have little practical bearing on effective governance, but some will. Two types of communicative influence on effective governance stemming from compositional misalignment between the sovereigns of each ecosystem are particularly important: dilution and distortion of representational power. *Dilution* of the sovereign political power can occur when the communication ecosystem is responsive or accountable to a larger, more inclusive, or more diverse set of voices than holds sovereignty in the political ecosystem. This is China's problem with its vibrant social media system. *Distortion* of the sovereign political power can occur when the communication ecosystem is more responsive or more accountable to some subgroups than others holding sovereign political power. This is the United States' problem, with its highly commercialized media system. Here is another way to think about these two forms of misalignment: they both undermine equal political representation of all dimensions or parts of the political sovereign's will, but dilution empowers voices that are excluded from sovereign political power, while distortion empowers some aspects of the sovereign political power's voice more than others.

This is where it gets interesting. To the extent that representational questions are addressed at all in the political communication literature, research conducted within and about WEIRD countries can be understood as being concerned mainly with distortion. For example, research documenting the unfortunate influence of commercial incentives on the production of quality political journalism is sometimes concerned with whether profit motives in general or the consumer interests of audience segments desirable to advertisers are becoming so central to the calculus of news producers that journalistic organizations are producing too much political-process news and too little basic reporting on political issues (e.g., Dunaway, 2008). This is a concern about distortion of the sovereign political power's will, brought about by misalignment between the two ecosystems. Likewise, research into ways in which "horse-race journalism" squeezes out substantive coverage of policy issues (e.g., Banducci & Hanretty, 2014; Dunaway & Lawrence, 2015) or on the potential for social media to amplify false information over true (e.g., Allcott & Gentzkow, 2017; Bennett & Pfetsch, 2018) can be understood as expressing concern over the distortion of sovereign political power that might result from the internal logic of the communication ecosystem.

Concerns about dilution are less common in the research literature, but they matter more for non-WEIRD polities where political power is less widely shared, consolidated, or stable. Autocrats want to share power as little as possible, but the representational dynamics of communication ecosystems should tend to consider a broader range of preferences than just those of the sovereign political power, if only to develop appealing content to attract audience attention in pursuit of political control. The more open and independent the communication ecosystem, the greater the risk that voices excluded from sovereign power will be represented in the information flows that feed back to the political ecosystem. Likewise, the growing domestic popularity of transnational media like Al Jazeera and BBC World in the Arab world creates a number of representational problems for authoritarian regimes, which all serve to dilute or at least challenge the powers that hold sway over disenfranchised citizens (e.g., Nisbet & Myers, 2010; Nisbet & Stoycheff, 2013). In both cases, dilution of the sovereign political power's will by the communication ecosystem is a threat to authoritarian rule and a potential boon to reformers who would prefer to organize regime politics around a broader and more inclusive sovereign power. We can understand this within the PMP approach as a special problem for autocrats involving the MP stage of the cycle.

Our desire to more fully integrate non-WEIRD regimes into a unified conceptual framework is an important reason why this chapter's PMP-derived concept map focuses on effective political performance rather than "good governance." Compositional misalignments between sovereign powers can degrade political performance in democratic regimes, generally in ways that diminish representation of the popular will. Those of us in WEIRD countries are accustomed to thinking of this as a bad outcome for regimes governed by rule of the people. However, in authoritarian regimes, where sovereign political power is vested mainly in a selectorate, the same kinds of misalignment between sovereign powers can inadvertently work to enhance political representation of the ejectorate's preferences. Within this alternative scenario, which has received little attention within political communication research, any resulting decrease in effective governance is a good outcome for champions of more inclusive rule, because it represents a loss of despotic control over governing institutions.

In summary, distortion and dilution are two forms of representational misalignment that can be brought about by compositional differences in the sovereign powers that underlie political and communication ecosystems serving any given polity. Dilution of sovereign power is the more likely risk for autocracies, but even democracies are increasingly concerned about foreign sovereigns affecting domestic instances of political representation (e.g., the 2016 presidential election in the United States and the 2016 Brexit referendum in the United Kingdom were both affected by Russian interference in their respective communication ecosystems). The more obvious risk for democracies is the distortion of sovereign power, but even autocracies are apt to be affected by power imbalances and shifting alliances within different parts of their selectorates. In whatever form, clarifying the types of compositional misalignment between sovereigns will help identify the groups or individuals that gain disproportionately more or less representational influence in the communication ecosystem relative to that in the political ecosystem.

Applying the Framework in Political Communication Research

At the beginning of this chapter we promised to develop a compelling way to reframe the standard question of "What is communication supposed to do?"

We are now in a position to more fully expand the reframed question that we opened the chapter with:

> How is political performance (encompassing political responsiveness and political accountability to the sovereign political power) enhanced or diminished by communication performance (encompassing media responsiveness and media accountability to the sovereign audience power) in a dynamic interplay of mutually dependent ecosystems structured by different representational logics?

This more appropriately reframed question leverages the conceptual road map developed in the PMP approach to open up clearer and more broadly relevant theoretical vistas for future research to tackle. In demonstrating the value of the conceptual brush-clearing that the PMP approach affords, this chapter paves the way for future researchers to ask (and to be well positioned to answer) novel research questions that would not have been so easy to pose without the PMP-derived framework introduced here. Although they do not exhaust the possibilities by any means, these starting questions not only suggest new opportunities for cumulating knowledge across subfield literatures, but also hold potential for eventually generating a broad range of testable hypotheses that can further contribute to building out our understanding of a much broader range of political communication phenomena than currently seems the case:

- How do different cultural and structural factors that affect the work of professional journalists enhance or diminish the potential for effective governance?
- How do different economic models for funding professional journalism enhance or diminish the potential for improving responsiveness and accountability?
- Which factors in the communication ecosystem are most likely to enhance particular forms of political responsiveness and accountability?
- Which factors in the communication ecosystem are most likely to influence the distortion and dilution of sovereign political power?
- What are the most common patterns and consequences of compositional misalignment across the different sovereign powers that underlie political and communication ecosystems?

- What are the most common kinds of representational gaps introduced by misalignments of sovereign audience power and sovereign political power?
- Can alignment between sovereign powers most effectively be increased by tightening or loosening regulatory control over the communication ecosystem?
- Are the representational dynamics across authoritarian and democratic regimes affected in similar ways by the communication ecosystem?
- Do the factors that produce insulated accountability and selective responsiveness operate differently in democratic regimes than in authoritarian regimes?
- How and to what degree do communication ecosystems in authoritarian regimes represent the will of groups that are excluded from sovereign political power?
- Which factors in the structural, cultural, and situational dimensions incline communication ecosystems in authoritarian regimes to represent the will of groups excluded from sovereign political power?

When we are positioned as a discipline to ask the most fruitful questions, we will be oriented to pursue the most fruitful answers. Furthermore, if two scholars share a common conceptual map for clarifying how one's question is related to the other's, it will be possible to position one's contribution in ways that have clear relevance for the other. The PMP approach is just a start, and a fairly simplistic one at that, but we hope that this chapter has demonstrated the power of even a fairly simplistic conceptual commons for motivating a wide range of scholarship with strong potential for innovation and connective utility across diverse strands of scholarly interest.

Conclusion

When talking to graduate students in our field, we often offer the following advice. Think about the big questions in the field. You won't be completely accurate in your conclusions; when you go big, you make mistakes. But being totally accurate when asking small questions is not the best way to spend your professional career. We hope that most readers will come to the conclusion that this what we were trying to do in this book.

Our overall goal was to present a conceptual map that could be used to contribute to the joint effort of building cumulative knowledge in the field of political communication. It was argued in Chapter 1 that what was needed was an approach that could allow us to better integrate and synthesize research findings from across fields, that could be applied cross-nationally and over time, that could assess how media performance might usefully contribute to successful political performance, that would be applicable to a wide range of regime types and information systems, that would create a basis for dialogue across diverse and specialized research communities, and finally that could increase the efficiency, relevance, and practical importance of research on political communication practices. While there is still a great deal of work to do to achieve these goals, it is hoped that this book does provide an initial map for getting there.

The basic structure of our conceptual map has two central claims, and three dimensions of analysis. We apologize for repeating them once again, but it is important to do so.

The first claim was the "politics first" proposition: *The role of all forms of media in politics can best be understood as one in which variations in political ecosystems are the most important factors leading to variations in communication systems, values, practices, and resources.* If there is one thing that we hope readers will take away from this book, it is that it makes no sense to ignore political context when attempting to understand the role of the various forms of media in politics. The "politics first" argument was given empirical support when looking at the role of the media in election campaigns, in violent conflicts and attempts at peace, in comparative political communication, and

Building Theory in Political Communication. Gadi Wolfsfeld, Tamir Sheafer, and Scott Althaus, Oxford University Press.
© Oxford University Press 2022. DOI: 10.1093/oso/9780197634998.003.0007

in the role of the media in historical change. It was also key in helping us dis-
entangle knotty normative questions that need to be sorted out for assessing
how communication ecosystems could support effective governance across a
range of regime types.

As discussed, there are certainly exceptions to this rule, and the most obvious one has to do with investigative journalism. Some might also argue that
as digital media become the more dominant form of political communication, user-generated content (e.g., the bystander video of George Floyd being
killed by a police officer in 2020) might also be considered as cases of "media
first." Our take on this is that when an individual or a group records such acts
in order to hold the police accountable, it is a political act in every sense of
the word. As we have written, when either individuals or groups carry out
some form of action with the goal of having political impact, it should, if they
achieve a certain amount of success, be understood as occurring in the political ecosystem.

In addition, how much user-generated content resonates with various elites, journalists, and publics also depends on political context.
The massive eruption of protests in the United States that broke out after
Floyd's death and the subsequent changes in public opinion about the
Black Lives Matter movement all tell us that when that particular match
was lit, there was a significant amount of political kindling available for
the ensuing fire.

The second proposition was the "media selection and transformation"
proposition: *All forms of media do not merely reflect the nature of the political ecosystem; they can also have an independent effect on political processes by selecting and transforming political events and issues into stories.*
Here, too, we have attempted to demonstrate throughout the book the
utility of this idea as it is applied to the different topics in political communication. The key challenge here is one that is well-known to all who
work in the field: How does one determine when any media effects on political processes should be considered independent, dependent, and conditional? While it is admittedly very difficult to make those distinctions, it
is worth the effort.

Consider, for example, the way in which communication technology
can have a major impact on many of the political processes that have been
discussed. Clearly, there are some cases in which political leadership can
have a major influence on people's access to the internet. North Korea is the
most notable example of this situation, and thus any influence the media

have on the public would be a dependent effect. On the other hand, the very fact that the internet exists has made a huge difference in the ability of social movements and oppositional forces around the world to mobilize support and tell their own stories. In addition, it is hard not to be impressed with how these major changes in communication ecosystems have also had an independent effect on people's ability to get actively involved in election campaigns in Western democracies. In most cases, these would probably be considered independent effects. Finally, there are also places where the importance of digital media becomes more significant for oppositional groups because those in power dominate the traditional media. This would be a good example of a conditional effect.

The three analytical dimensions of analysis were the structural, the cultural, and the situational. The basic idea is that employing these three dimensions makes it easier to come up with a list of hypotheses about how variations in the political and communication ecosystems might affect different political processes. The orientation tables that were presented in the various chapters were only suggestive and obviously incomplete, designed with the hope that other researchers would take up the important task of properly filling in the cells with their own work. This would contribute to advancing our goal of cumulating knowledge in the field.

As noted, another important goal of this volume has been to increase the level of dialogue among political communication researchers working in different fields. Among the best candidates for such a dialogue would be those who deal with the role of media in war and peace. It is worth again pointing to the fact that this was one of the first works that attempted to connect (in the same chapter) scholarly work carried out about the role of the media in wars with the studies of media and peace. We also see promise in employing the PMP approach as a bridge for integrating the enormous sets of literature in comparative political communication. Yet another good example would be those who deal with the role of the various forms of media in election campaigns to consider the work we discussed concerning the role of the media in historical change. Finally, the PMP approach also provides useful leverage for clarifying normative dimensions of media performance, as well as clarifying where and how normative criteria might usefully be operationalized to critically assess how well the political informational needs of citizens are being served by their communication ecosystems.

The PMP approach certainly has weaknesses that need to be addressed in the future. One obvious weakness of this work is that we tended to gloss over the significant conceptual issues that arise when researchers are studying issues using different "levels of analysis." This well-known problem refers to the difficulties scholars face as they move from thinking about research questions that focus on micro (individuals), meso (groups), and macro (e.g., markets, systems, or countries) forms of analysis. This difficulty is perhaps best understood by thinking about the different examples of the "second P" we have provided throughout the volume. An analysis concerned with the role of media in policy changes carried out by governments will be very different from one that looks at changes in public opinion, or possible effects on social movements. Hopefully we and others will be able to grapple with these complexities in future work. We do believe that the PMP approach can be usefully applied to all three levels of analysis.

Another important challenge is to better understand the enormous changes that have taken place in communication technology in recent years. The PMP approach was originally developed at a time when traditional media like newspapers and television broadcasters were still dominant and our major concerns had to do with the notion of "news." An effort was made throughout this volume to grapple with this issue, but it is clear that much more work is needed to deal with the complexities of today's "hybrid media system" (Chadwick, 2017). The good news is that an enormous number of political communication scholars are attempting to study this issue. The bad news is that too few of them are using a comparative approach. Here, too, we think the PMP approach can make a contribution.

There are three other areas where more conceptual and empirical work is required. The first has to do with what we have labeled the cultural dimension of analysis. Any scholar who attempts to use the problematic term "culture" is looking for trouble. It is a concept that has been used and misused in a thousand different ways and is now a sort of Rorschach test for those working in both social sciences and in the humanities. Nevertheless, it is far too important an analytical dimension to be left out of the PMP approach. Hopefully, by attempting to make specific claims about norms and routines within each chapter, we have made at least a bit of progress in this area. Our hope is that others will also try to better define this analytical tool as it relates to the various research questions raised in political communication scholarship.

It is also very apparent that much more work needs to be done with regard to the situational dimension of analysis. It is always tricky and sometimes even random how researchers decide what constitutes the set of critical events that can have a significant impact on the political and communication ecosystem. This challenge is one reason why we left this dimension out of the chapter on comparative political communication entirely. A particular lacuna is the paucity of research on how the role of the media can vary when dealing with a major event that affects either a specific region of the world or the entire world.

Nevertheless, as these words are being written, the world is being devastated by a coronavirus pandemic. There is little doubt that many political communication scholars will be exploring how various forms of media contributed to the different ways that various countries (and states) have responded to the virus. An argument could certainly be made that a large comparative study on this issue might provide invaluable insights as to how critical events can have a major impact on political and communication ecosystems and on the ultimate impact on the many political processes that are taking place.

Finally, there is an enormous amount of work that needs to be done with regard to non-WEIRD countries. We also have tried to make some progress in this area, but by any measure we have only scratched the surface. Further progress will require involvement of researchers who are experts in these areas of the world and who work in the field of political communication.

Here are a few examples of research that would be helpful in this regard. How does the role of digital media vary among countries with more or less democratic political systems? What are the roles of various forms of media in non-democratic elections? What is the relationship between the level of democracy, the nature of the media system, and the ability of dissident groups to be heard? What are the similarities and the differences between how more and less democratic regimes exploit various forms of media to promote wars? If any researchers would find the PMP approach useful in carrying out such studies, we would be more than happy to be consulted.

So that's the story we wanted to tell. It was clear from the beginning that a good number of our insights were built on the work of our colleagues in the field. We make no apologies for this. Ours may be just one addition to a vast and vibrant conversation involving generations of scholars, but by aligning this conversation to a smaller set of orienting points of interest, we hope our contribution is a useful and potentially an important one. By organizing this large body of work within a new conceptual space, we believe that the larger horizons marked out by our effort will orient other researchers to locate (and appreciate) one another's work more easily. If this happens, then by increasing the visibility of theoretical common ground and by helping to channel the field's growing weight of empirical evidence into especially productive forms, we hope to propel the scholarly community into new and better vantage points for future conversations.

Notes

Chapter 1

1. Note that we do not characterize the political ecosystem as having an impact on the communication ecosystem. Although a case could be made for this phrasing, we see the political ecosystem as likely to affect particular parts of the communication ecosystem more than others, rather than affecting the ecosystem as a whole. How the communication ecosystem responds to those political effects includes aspects that are usually not themselves directly affected by politics in the near term, such as the degree of economic competition among rival news organizations and the communication technologies available for disseminating particular types of political messages.

2. While many scholars prefer the term "legacy media," we prefer the more easily understood term "traditional media." The online sites of the news organizations (e.g., CNN.com) are considered traditional media because, apart from a few exceptions, they conform to the norms and routines of traditional media. In addition, we have chosen to use the term "digital media," rather than "new" or "newer" media, because media that are heavily dependent on user-generated content are no longer new. We fully realize that the term "digital" can be misleading because so much of the traditional media (e.g., newspapers, radio, television) employ digital technology. For now, however, there are no great alternatives.

3. We want to thank Regina Lawrence for making this point when reading an earlier version of this chapter.

4. These interviews were conducted as part of an international research project on the role of the media in violent conflicts. The project was given the name INFOCORE (http://www.infocore.eu/).

5. See: https://www.bellingcat.com/.

6. https://en.wikipedia.org/wiki/Me_Too_(hashtag).

7. https://www.economist.com/news/business/21717107-making-americas-august-news-groups-great-again-traditional-media-firms-are-enjoying-trump-bump.

8. http://news.gallup.com/poll/195542/americans-trust-mass-media-sinks-new-low.aspx.

9. https://www.salon.com/2016/12/10/pizzagate-explained-everything-you-want-to-know-about-the-comet-ping-pong-pizzeria-conspiracy-theory-but-are-too-afraid-to-search-for-on-reddit/.

10. It is also worth noting that both indexing and cascading activation were mainly developed around narrow cases in which "foreign news" was filtered through domestic media systems. PMP, on the other hand, is more inclusive in that it deals with all types of news and all types of media.

11. Another class of exceptions includes cases in which media organizations decide to use their programing to get people involved in politics. An excellent example of this would be BBC Media Action (http://www.bbc.co.uk/mediaaction), which produces programs in a variety of countries to encourage citizens to hold political discussions and participate in the political process.

12. https://www.nytimes.com/2010/08/26/us/26gainesville.html.

13. https://web.archive.org/web/20170930020819/http://archive.defense.gov/news/newsarticle.aspx?id=60779/archive.defense.gov/news/newsarticle.aspx?id=60779.

14. A good example of the latter is the 2009 "Balloon Boy" hoax that is analyzed in Boydstun (2013).

Chapter 2

1. https://www.thegreenpapers.com/P16/.

2. https://foreignpolicy.com/2019/02/27/india-kashmir-airstrikes-jem-battling-for-re-election-modi-takes-the-fight-to-pakistan/.

3. We are fully aware that our suggestion to always begin any analysis by thinking about the issue of political context is difficult for those carrying out experiments in the field of communication. Perhaps because experiments were first used in the natural sciences, there is a certain unsaid assumption that political and cultural contexts are irrelevant. We would only ask that those employing this methodology acknowledge that their results might change among varying contexts.

4. https://www.statista.com/statistics/373814/cable-news-network-viewership-usa/.

5. https://billmoyers.com/story/donald-trump-the-emperor-of-social-media/.

6. Some would argue that in any case, political leaders find themselves in a permanent campaign (Needham, 2005; Vasko & Trilling, 2019), so any distinction between the normal competition and what happens when it becomes an election campaign is artificial.

7. Some will object to the term "evil" in an academic manuscript. We think, however, that when it comes to sabotaging elections it is appropriate.

8. We write these words in the midst of the COVID-19 coronavirus pandemic. It is possible that the use of the term "viral" by researchers in the field may become more controversial. For now, however, we have chosen to use the term as it has been used in recent years.

9. https://www.bbc.com/news/world-us-canada-47208909.

10. An interesting article by Van Aelst and Walgrave (2011) looked at four European parliamentary democracies (Belgium, Netherlands, Sweden, and Denmark) and found that most of the politicians believed the media to be much more powerful than they were in setting the public agenda. The research attempts to grapple with the inconsistency between the *objective* empirical findings (which are more consistent with a PMP approach) and the *subjective* beliefs of these leaders.

Chapter 3

1. While there are hundreds of studies on this topic, here are a few that provide fairly extensive references to the literature: Bennett, Lawrence, & Livingston, 2008; Carruthers, 2011; Cottles, 2006; Hoskins & O'Loughlin, 2007; Robinson, 2004; Robinson et. al., 2006; Warren, 2015; Wolfsfeld, 1997).
2. See, for example, research on the spread of hate crimes in social media: Müller & Schwarz (2020).
3. Researchers need to make a distinction between a single event (which would be considered part of the situational dimension of analysis) and the *overall course* of events during a war, a peace process, or (on a different topic) a pandemic.
4. While it is sometimes helpful analytically to distinguish between the amount of political and military success and taking control over the flow of information, we should bear in mind that the level of success can either raise or lower the importance of leaks. Put simply, one must start by asking how much damaging information exists.
5. Some might be interested to know that the PMP approach was first developed when Wolfsfeld (2004) carried out this comparative study of the role of the media in peace processes.
6. This was also an important time when another structural variable, which we do not deal with, came to dominate the news: the economic incentives for publishing as much fresh news from the front as possible. Knightley (2004) wrote, "A large New York newspaper could sell up to five times its normal circulation when it ran details of a big battle" (p. 23). It is as true today as it was then: war and conflict translate into huge profits for the news businesses.
7. http://articles.latimes.com/2012/jun/21/entertainment/la-et-cyberskeptic-20120621.
8. An important parallel to this discussion could be provided by the literature on the relationship between the growth of partisan media and political polarization in the United States and other countries (Prior, 2013). Here, too, the lack of shared media can reduce the chances for compromise and reconciliation.
9. Many of the details of what happened were shown in the movie *The Post*.

Chapter 4

1. Purdum (2014), p. 292.
2. As he himself admitted, Dirksen was paraphrasing Victor Hugo.
3. There are a surprisingly large number of historical incidents that are referred to as Bloody Sunday. They stretch from an 1887 demonstration in London against British policies in Ireland to a 1991 attack on civilians in Lithuania (see http://en.wikipedia.org/wiki/Bloody_Sunday).
4. An interesting footnote was that, although the depiction in the film suggested that the broadcasts were shown "live," this type of broadcast was not yet possible in 1965.

5. During the period under discussion, there was no significant increase in the percentage of Black journalists hired by the mainstream news media. This is another important structural change, but this was a much later development, and as late as 2012, the National Association of Black Journalists was reporting a significant *decline* in the number of Black journalists. See: http://www.nabj.org/news/88558/.

6. There was also another 15-year-old in this iconic picture: Hazel Bryan. She became infamous as the hate-filled white girl yelling at Elizabeth. The history of how her views changed in subsequent years and how the two women eventually came to a partial reconciliation has itself become part of this history (Margolick, 2011).

7. Here are a few additional sources for those interested better understanding the role of the media in the US debate over the death penalty: Bandes (2003); Dardis, Baumgartner, Boydstun, De Boef, & Shen (2008); Fan, Keltner, & Wyatt (2002); Godsey & Pulley (2003); Greer (2005); Lipschultz & Hilt (1999); and Niven (2002).

8. We want to thank Amber Boydstun, one of the authors of this important book, for her very helpful comments concerning how we could best exploit the study for demonstrating the utility of the PMP approach.

9. https://en.wikipedia.org/wiki/Violent_Crime_Control_and_Law_Enforcement_Act.

10. http://www.thirdworldtraveler.com/Justice/End_Executions.html.

11. Thanks again to Amber Boystun for emphasizing these points in a private correspondence.

Chapter 5

1. The World Bank lists several relevant governance culture factors in its "Worldwide Governance Indicators" project, http://info.worldbank.org/governance/wgi/pdf/govmatters5.pdf.

Chapter 6

1. Variants of this basic story have been fleshed out helpfully in several sources, including Baker (2002); Habermas (1996b); Althaus (2006, 2012); and Wessler (2018).

2. As a nod to institutionalists and political theorists, we admit that every word in these last two sentences is loaded with controversy and deserving of greater nuance, but it is good enough for our limited purpose.

3. Carey's masterful definition of communication encompasses what he called the transmission and ritual views. In Carey's (1988) formulation, the transmission view holds that "communication is a process whereby messages are transmitted and distributed in space for the control of distance and people" (p. 15), while the ritual view sees communication as supporting "the maintenance of society in time . . . [through] the representation of shared beliefs" (p. 18).

4. The section that follows is a highly stylized rendition of themes drawn from a wide range of normative theory sources. Readers interested in further details are encouraged to consult sophisticated expositions of recent innovations within normative political theory regarding the nature and meaning of representation in both democratic and non-democratic contexts. A good overview of the larger literature on political representation is provided by Urbinati and Warren (2008). Building on the formative work of Robert Dahl (1971), Hannah Pitkin (1967), and others, germinal exchanges between Jane Mansbridge (2003, 2009, 2011) and Andrew Rehfeld (2006, 2009, 2011) have produced an innovative expansion of conventional types of representation and the varied political contexts in which representation occurs. The concept of political representation in non-democratic regimes is being explored in fruitful ways (e.g., Rehfeld, 2006, 2009). The greatly simplified discussion of responsiveness and accountability as essential activities of political representation in the pages that follow rests on recent innovative work that brings information flows and communication processes more explicitly into the representational dynamic (e.g., Althaus, 2012; Baker, 2002; Blasi, 1977; Ferree, Gamson, Gerhards, & Rucht, 2002; Ferree & Hess, 2002; Habermas, 1996a, 1996b; Held, 2006; Jacobs & Shapiro, 2000; Mutz, 2006, 2008; Strömbäck, 2005; Wessler, 2018).

5. Jane Mansbridge's (2009) contrast between a sanctions model and a selection model of political representation captures the distinction between formal and informal accountability mechanisms: formal mechanisms involve selection of which political actors will govern, while informal mechanisms involve sanctions against those political actors who are already governing.

6. Examples of news reports detailing this unusual approach include coverage from *Newsweek* https://www.newsweek.com/flamethrower-execution-death-camps-and-famine-north-koreas-gruesome-rights-1344039, Fox News https://www.foxnews.com/world/north-korea-dictator-kim-jong-uns-executions-anti-aircraft-guns-flamethrowers-mortars, and the *Washington Post* https://www.washingtonpost.com/news/worldviews/wp/2015/05/01/does-north-korea-execute-people-with-anti-aircraft-guns-new-satellite-images-suggest-the-rumors-may-be-true/. Kim could have executed entire governmental bureaus, but that would have made it difficult to get things done.

7. For example, see https://www.nytimes.com/2016/05/10/world/europe/bbc-british-broadcasting-corporation-charter.html.

8. Such misalignment can take many forms and spring from many causes. Factors emerging in the structural dimensions for one or both ecosystems are probably the most foundational reasons for misalignment between the two sovereigns, but the cultural dimensions can add their share of warping as well.

References

Aalberg, T., de Vreese, C., & Strömbäck, J. (2017). Strategy and game framing. In C. de Vreese, F. Esser, & D. N. Hopmann (Eds.), *Comparing political communication* (pp. 33–49). New York: Routledge.

Aalberg, T., Esser, F., Reinemann, C., Strömbäck, J., & de Vreese, C. H. (Eds.) (2016). *Populist political communication in Europe.* New York: Routledge.

Aalberg, T., Van Aelst, P., & Curran, J. (2010). Media systems and the political information environment: A cross-national comparison. *International Journal of Press/Politics, 5,* 255–271.

Aarts, K., Fladmoe, A., & Strömbäck, J. (2012). Media, political trust, and political knowledge. In J. C. Toril Aalberg (Ed.), *How media inform democracy: A comparative approach* (pp. 98–118). New York: Routledge.

Abbott, J. (2012). Democracy@ internet. org revisited: Analyzing the socio-political impact of the internet and new social media in East Asia. *Third World Quarterly, 33*(2), 333–357.

Abromeit, J., Norman, Y., Marotta, G., & Chesterton, B. M. (2015). *Transformations of populism in Europe and the Americas: History and recent tendencies.* London: Bloomsbury.

Aday, S. (1996). *Invisible ink: Newspaper coverage of gays and lesbians, 1980–1994.* Paper presented at the International Communication Association, Chicago, IL.

Aday, S., Livingston, S., & Hebert, M. (2005). Embedding the truth: A cross-cultural analysis of objectivity and television coverage of the Iraq war. *Harvard International Journal of Press/Politics, 10*(1), 3–21.

Aday, S., & Livingston, S. (2008). Taking the state out of state–media relations theory: How transnational advocacy networks are changing the press–state dynamic. *Media, War & Conflict, 1*(1), 99–107.

Aalberg, T., Esser, F., Reinemann, C., Strömbäck, J., & de Vreese, C. H. (2017). *Populist Political Communication in Europe.* New York: Routledge.

Alikhah, F. (2008). The politics of satellite television in Iran. In M. Semeti (Ed.), *Living with globalization and the Islamic State* (pp. 94–110). New York: Routledge.

Alikhah, F. (2018). A brief history of the development of satellite channels in Iran. *Global Media and Communication, 14*(1), 3–29.

Allcott, H., & Gentzkow, B. (2017). Social media and fake news in the 2016 election. *National Bureau of Economic Research Working Paper Series* No. 23089. doi: 10.3386/w23089.

Althaus, S. L. (2003). When news norms collide, follow the lead: New evidence for press independence. *Political Communication, 20*(4), 381–414.

Althaus, S. L. (2006). False starts, dead ends, and new opportunities in public opinion research. *Critical Review, 18* (1–3), 75–104.

Althaus, S. L. (2012). What's good and bad in political communication research? Normative standards for evaluating media and citizen performance. In H. A. Semetko

& M. Scammell (Eds.), *Sage handbook of political communication* (pp. 97–112). London: Sage Publications.

Althaus, S. L., Bramlett, B., & Gimpel, J. G. (2012). When war hits home: The geography of military losses and support for war in time and space. *Journal of Conflict Resolution, 56*(3), 382–412.

Althaus, S. L., Cizmar, A. M., & Gimpel J. P. (2009). Media supply, audience demand, and the geography of news media consumption in the United States. *Political Communication, 26*(3), 249–277.

Althaus, S. L., & Coe, K. (2011). Priming patriots: Social identity processes and the dynamics of public support for war. *Public Opinion Quarterly, 75*(1), 65–88.

Althaus, S. L., Swigger, N., Chernykh, S., Hendry, D., Wals, S., & Tiwald, C. (2011). Assumed transmission in political science: A call for bringing description back in. *Journal of Politics, 73*(4), 1065–1080.

Amsalem, E., Sheafer, T., Walgrave, S., Lowen, P., & Soroka, S. (2017). Media motivation and elite rhetoric in comparative perspective. *Political Communication, 34*(3), 385–403.

Anderson, K. (2010). *Little Rock: Race and resistance at Central High School.* Princeton, NJ: Princeton University Press.

Andrews, K. T., & Biggs, M. (2006). The dynamics of protest diffusion: Movement organizations, social networks, and news media in the 1960 sit-ins. *American Sociological Review, 71*(5), 752–777.

Andrews, T. (2012). What is social constructionism. *Grounded Theory Review, 11*(1), 39–46.

Aouragh, M., & Alexander, A. (2011). The Arab spring the Egyptian experience: Sense and nonsense of the internet revolution. *International Journal of Communication, 5,* 1344–1358.

Arditi, B., Barros, S., Bowman, G., & Howarth, D. (2005). *Populism and the mirror of democracy.* London: Verso.

Ariely, G. (2015). Does commercialized political coverage undermine political trust?: Evidence across European countries. *Journal of Broadcasting & Electronic Media, 59*(3), 438–455.

Aucoin, J. (2007). *The evolution of American investigative journalism.* Columbia: University of Missouri Press.

Azhgikhina, N. (2007). The struggle for press freedom in Russia: Reflections of a Russian journalist. *Europe-Asia Studies, 59*(8), 1245–1262.

Baek, M. (2009). A comparative analysis of political communication systems and voter turnout. *American Journal of Political Science, 53*(2), 376–393.

Baker, C. E. (2002). *Media, markets, and democracy.* New York: Cambridge University Press.

Balmas, M. (2014). When fake news becomes real: Combined exposure to multiple news sources and political attitudes of inefficacy, alienation, and cynicism. *Communication Research, 41*(3), 430–454.

Balmas, M., Rahat, G., Sheafer, T., & Shenhav, S. R. (2014). Two routes to personalized politics: Centralized and decentralized personalization. *Party Politics, 20*(1), 37–51.

Balmas, M., & Sheafer, T. (2010). Candidate image in election campaigns: Attribute agenda setting, affective priming, and voting intentions. *International Journal of Public Opinion Research, 22*(2), 204–229.

Balmas, M., & Sheafer, T. (2013). Leaders first, countries after: Mediated political personalization in the international arena. *Journal of Communication, 63*(3), 454–475.

Balmas, M., & Sheafer, T. (2014). Charismatic leaders and mediated personalization in the international arena. *Communication Research, 41*(7), 991–1015.

Bandes, S. (2003). Fear factor: The role of media in covering and shaping the death penalty. *Ohio State Journal of Criminal Law, 1*, 585–597.

Banducci, S., & Hanretty, C. (2014). Comparative determinants of horse-race coverage. *European Political Science Review, 6*(04), 621–640.

Barbera, P., Casas, A., Nagler, J., Egan, P., Bonneau, R., Jost, J., & Tucker, J. (2019). Who leads? Who follows? Measuring issue attention and agenda setting by legislators and the mass public using social media data. *American Political Science Review, 113*(4), 883–901.

Baum, M. (2013). The Iraq coalition of the willing and (politically) able: Party systems, the press, and public influence on foreign policy. *American Journal of Political Science, 57*(2), 442–458.

Baum, M. A. (2002). Sex, lies, and war: How soft news brings foreign policy to the inattentive public. *American Political Science Review, 96*(1), 91–109.

Baum, M., & Groeling, T. (2010). *War stories: The causes and consequences of public views of wars*. Princeton, NJ: Princeton University Press.

Baumgartner, F. R., De Boef, S., & Boydstun, A. E. (2008). *The decline of the death penalty and the discovery of innocence*. New York: Cambridge Univ Press.

Baumgartner, J., & Morris, J. S. (2006). The Daily Show effect: Candidate evaluations, efficacy, and American youth. *American Politics Research, 34*(3), 341.

Bene, M. (2017). Go viral on the Facebook! Interactions between candidates and followers on Facebook during the Hungarian general election campaign of 2014. *Information, Communication & Society, 20*(4), 513–529.

Benkler, Y., Faris, R., & Roberts, H. (2018). *Network propaganda: Manipulation, disinformation, and radicalization in American politics* (2nd ed.). New York: Oxford University Press.

Bennett, W. L. (1990). Toward a theory of press-state relations in the United States. *Journal of Communication, 40*(2), 103–125.

Bennett, W. L. (2003). Operation perfect storm: The press and the Iraq War. *Political Communication Report, 13*(3).

Bennett, W. L., & Iyengar, S. (2008). A new era of minimal effects? The changing foundations of political communication. *Journal of Communication, 58*(4), 707–731.

Bennett, W. L., Lawrence, R. G., & Livingston, S. (2008). *When the press fails: Political power and the news media from Iraq to Katrina*. Chicago: University of Chicago Press.

Bennett, W. L., & Paletz, D. L. (Eds.). (1994). *Taken by storm: The media, public opinion, and U.S. foreign policy in the Gulf War*. Chicago: University of Chicago Press.

Bennett, W. L., & Pfetsch, B. (2018). Rethinking political communication in a time of disrupted public spheres. *Journal of Communication, 68*(2), 243–253.

Berinsky, A. J., & Druckman, J. N. (2007). The polls—Review: Public opinion research and support for the Iraq War. *Public Opinion Quarterly, 71*(1), 126–141.

Blasi, V. (1977). The checking value in first amendment theory. *American Bar Foundation Research Journal, 2*(3), 521–649.

Blumell, L. E., & Huemmer, J. (2017). Silencing survivors: How news coverage neglects the women accusing Donald Trump of sexual misconduct. *Feminist Media Studies, 17*(3), 506–509.

Blumler, J. C., McLeod, J. M., & Roengren, K. E. (1992). An introduction to comparative communication research. In J. G. Blumler, J. M. McLeod, & K. E. Rosengren (Eds.), *Comparatively speaking: Communication and culture across space and time* (pp. 3–18). Newbury Park, CA: Sage.

Boas, T. C., & Hidalgo, F. D. (2011). Controlling the airwaves: Incumbency advantage and community radio in Brazil. *American Journal of Political Science, 55*(4), 869–885.

Boczkowski, P. J. (2009). Technology, monitoring, and imitation in contemporary news work. *Communication, Culture & Critique, 2*(1), 39–59.

Bonafont, L. C., & Baumgartner, F. R. (2013). Newspaper attention and policy activities in Spain. *Journal of Public Policy, 33*(1), 65–88.

Boorstin, D. J. (2012). *The image: A guide to pseudo-events in America.* New York: Vintage.

Boydstun, A. E. (2013). *Making the news: Politics, the media, and agenda setting.* Chicago: University of Chicago Press.

Boydstun, A. E., Hardy, A., & Walgrave, S. (2014). Two faces of media attention: Media storm versus non-storm coverage. *Political Communication, 31*(4), 509–531.

Brettschneider, F., & Gabriel, O. W. (2002). The nonpersonalization of voting behavior in Germany. In A. King (Ed.), *Leaders' personalities and the outcomes of democratic elections* (pp. 127–157). Oxford, UK: Oxford University Press.

Bright, J. (2016). The social news gap: How news reading and news sharing diverge. *Journal of Communication, 66*(3), 343–365.

Buccoliero, L., Bellio, E., Crestini, G., & Arkoudas, A. (2020). Twitter and politics: Evidence from the US presidential elections 2016. *Journal of Marketing Communications, 26*(1), 88–114.

Bueno de Mesquita, B., Smith, A., Siverson, R. M., & Morrow, J. D. (2003). *The logic of political survival.* Cambridge, MA: MIT Press.

Burkhardt, J. M. (2017). *Combating fake news in the digital age* (Vol. 53). Chicago, IL: American Library Association.

Burr, V. (2015). *Social constructionism.* New York: Routledge.

Burstein, P. (1979). Public opinion, demonstrations, and the passage of antidiscrimination legislation. *Public Opinion Quarterly, 43*(2), 157–172.

Byman, D., & Lind, J. (2010). Pyongyang's survival strategy: Tools of authoritarian control in North Korea. *International Security, 35*(1), 44–74.

Carey, J. W. (1989). A cultural approach to communication. In *Communication as culture: Essays on media and society* (pp. 13–36). Boston: Unwin Hyman.

Carlson, M. (2010). Embodying deep throat: Mark Felt and the collective memory of Watergate. *Critical Studies in Media Communication, 27*(3), 235–250.

Carney, N. (2016). All lives matter, but so does race: Black lives matter and the evolving role of social media. *Humanity & Society, 40*(2), 180–199.

Carruthers, S. L. (2011). *The media at war.* New York: Macmillan International Higher Education.

Carson, C. (1995). *In struggle: SNCC and the Black awakening of the 1960s.* Cambridge, MA: Harvard University Press.

Chadwick, A. (2017). *The hybrid media system: Politics and power.* Oxford: Oxford University Press.

Chaffee, S. H., & Metzger, M. J. (2001). The end of mass communication? *Mass Communication & Society, 4*(4), 365–379.

Chowdhury, M. (2008). The role of the internet in Burma's Saffron Revolution. Berkman Center research publication (2008-8).

Christensen, C. (2011). Twitter revolutions? Addressing social media and dissent. *The Communication Review, 14*(3), 155–157.

Clendinen, D., & Nagourney, A. (2001). *Out for good: The struggle to build a gay rights movement in America.* New York: Simon & Schuster.

Coddington, M. (2015). Clarifying journalism's quantitative turn: A typology for evaluating data journalism, computational journalism, and computer-assisted reporting. *Digital Journalism, 3*(3), 331–348.

Comey, J. (2018). *A higher loyalty: Truth, lies, and leadership.* New York: Pan Macmillan.

Commission on the Freedom of the Press, The (1947). *A free and responsible press.* Chicago: University of Chicago Press.

Conway, B. A., Kenski, K., & Wang, D. (2015). The rise of Twitter in the political campaign: Searching for intermedia agenda-setting effects in the presidential primary. *Journal of Computer-Mediated Communication, 20*(4), 363–380.

Cook, T. E. (2006). The news media as a political institution: Looking backward and looking forward. *Political Communication, 23*(2), 159–171.

Cortell, A. P., Eisinger, R. M., & Althaus, S. L. (2009). Why embed? Explaining the Bush Administration's decision to embed reporters in the 2003 invasion of Iraq. *American Behavioral Scientist, 52*(5), 657–677.

Cox, K. E., & Schoppa, L. J. (2002). Interaction effects in mixed-member electoral systems: Theory and evidence from Germany, Japan, and Italy. *Comparative Political Studies, 35*(9), 1027–1053.

Cunningham, S., Flew, T., & Swift, A. (2015). *Media economics.* New York: Macmillan International Higher Education.

Curran, J., Iyengar, S., Lund, A. B., & Salovaara-Moring, I. (2009). Media system, public knowledge and democracy. *European Journal of Communication, 24*(1), 5–26.

D'Anieri, P. (2005). The last hurrah: The 2004 Ukrainian presidential elections and the limits of machine politics. *Communist and Post-Communist Studies, 38*(2), 231–249.

Dahl, R. A. (1971). *Polyarchy: Participation and opposition.* New Haven, CT: Yale University Press.

Daniel, A. (1995). US media coverage of the Intifada and American public opinion. In Y. Kamalipour (Ed.), *US media and the Middle East: Image and perception* (pp. 62–71). Westport, CT: Greenwood Press.

Dardis, F. E., Baumgartner, F. R., Boydstun, A. E., De Boef, S., & Shen, F. (2008). Media framing of capital punishment and its impact on individuals' cognitive responses. *Mass Communication & Society, 11*(2), 115–140.

Darwish, K., Magdy, W., & Zanouda, T. (2017). *Trump vs. Hillary: What went viral during the 2016 US presidential election.* Paper presented at the International conference on social informatics, Oxford, UK.

Day, A. (2011). *Satire and dissent: Interventions in contemporary political debate.* Bloomington: Indiana University Press.

De Burgh, H. (2008). *Investigative journalism.* New York: Routledge.

Decon, D., & Stanyer, J. (2014). Mediatization: Key concept or conceptual bandwagon? *Media Culture & Society, 36*(7), 1032–1044.

Denham, B. E. (2010). Toward conceptual consistency in studies of agenda-building processes: A scholarly review. *The Review of Communication, 10*(4), 306–323.

de Vreese, C. H. (2017). Comparative political communication research. In K. Kenski and K. H. Jamieson (Eds.), *The Oxford handbook of political communication* (pp. 287–300). New York: Oxford University Press.

de Vreese, C., Esser, F., Aalberg, T., Reinemann, R., & Stanyer, J. (2018). Populism as an expression of political communication content and style: A new perspective. *The International Journal of Press/Politics, 23*(4), 423–438.

de Vreese, C., Esser, F., & Hopmann, D. N. (Eds.). (2017a). *Comparing political journalism.* New York: Routledge.

de Vreese, C., Esser, F., & Hopmann, D. N. (2017b). Our goal: Comparing news performance. In C. De Vreese, F. Esser, & D. N. Hopmann (Eds). *Comparing political journalism* (pp. 1–9). New York: Routledge.

de Vreese, C., Reinemann, C., Esser, F., & Hopmann, D. N. (2017c). Conclusion: Assessing news performance. In C. de Vreese, F. Esser, & D. N. Hopmann (Eds.), *Comparing political journalism* (pp. 168–183). New York: Routledge.

de Vreese, C. H., & Semetko, H. A. (2002). Cynical and engaged strategic campaign coverage, public opinion, and mobilization in a referendum. *Communication Research, 29*(6), 615–641.

Dingley, J. (2001). The bombing of Omagh, 15 August 1998: The bombers, their tactics, strategy, and purpose behind the incident. *Studies in Conflict and Terrorism, 24*(6), 451–465.

Dukalskis, A. (2017). *The authoritarian public sphere: Legitimation and autocratic power in North Korea, Burma, and China.* New York: Taylor & Francis.

Dunaway, J. (2008). Markets, ownership, and the quality of campaign news coverage. *The Journal of Politics, 70*(4), 1193–1202.

Dunaway, J., & Lawrence, R. G. (2015). What predicts the game frame? Media ownership, electoral context, and campaign news. *Political Communication, 32*(1), 43–60.

Edwards, S. B. (2016). *Black lives matter.* Minneapolis, MN: ABDO.

Edwards, G. C., & Wood, B. D. (1999). Who influences whom? The president, Congress, and the media. *American Political Science Review, 93*(2), 327–344.

Elenbaas, M., & De Vreese, C. H. (2008). The effects of strategic news on political cynicism and vote choice among young voters. *Journal of Communication, 58*(3), 550–567.

Ellsberg, D. (2003). *Secrets: A memoir of Vietnam and the Pentagon Papers.* London: Penguin.

Engesser, S., Ernst, N., Esser, F., & Büchel, F. (2017). Populism and social media: How politicians spread a fragmented ideology. *Information, Communication & Society, 20*(8), 1109–1126.

Entman, R. M. (2003). *Projections of power: Framing news, public opinion, and US foreign policy.* Chicago: University of Chicago Press.

Entman, R. M., & Page, B. (1994). The news before the storm: The Iraq War debate and the limits to media independence. In L. Bennett & D. L. Paletz (Eds.), *Taken by storm: The media, public opinion, and US foreign policy in the Gulf War* (pp. 82–101). New York: Cambridge University Press.

Epstein, R. A. (2011). *Citizens United v. FEC:* The constitutional right that big corporations should have but do not want. *Harvard Journal of Law & Public Policy, 34*(11), 639–661.

Esarey, A. (2005). Cornering the market: State strategies for controlling China's commercial media. *Asian Perspective, 29*(4), 37–83.

Esarey, A. (2006). *Speak no evil: Mass media control in contemporary China.* New York: Freedom House.

Esarey, A. W. (2006). *Caught between state and society: The commercial news media in China.* PhD dissertation, Columbia University.

Esen, B., & Gumuscu, S. (2016). Rising competitive authoritarianism in Turkey. *Third World Quarterly, 37*(9), 1581–1606.

Esser, F., de Vreese, C. H., & Strömback, J. (2012). Political information opportunities in Europe: A longitudinal and comparative study of thirteen television systems. *The International Journal of Press/Politics, 17*(3), 247–274.

Esser, F., & Pfetch, B. (2004). *Comparing political communication: Theories, cases, and challenges.* New York: Cambridge University Press.

Esser, F., & Strömbäck, J. (2012). Comparing election campaign communication. In F. Esser and T. Hanitzsch (Eds.), *Handbook of comparative communication research* (pp. 289–307). New York: Routledge.

Esser, F., & Strömbäck, J. (2014). *Mediatization of Politics: Understanding the transformation of Western democracies.* New York: Palgrave Macmillan.

Fairclough, A. (2001). *To redeem the soul of America: The Southern Christian Leadership Conference and Martin Luther King, Jr.* Athens: University of Georgia Press.

Fan, D. P., Keltner, K. A., & Wyatt, R. O. (2002). A matter of guilt or innocence: How news reports affect support for the death penalty in the United States. *International Journal of Public Opinion Research, 14*(4), 439–452.

Ferree, M., Gamson, W., Gerhards, J., & Rucht, D. (2002). Four models of the public sphere in modern democracies. *Theory and Society, 31*(3), 289–324.

Ferree, M. M., & Hess, B. (2002). *Controversy and coalition: The new feminist movement across four decades of change.* New York: Routledge.

Fink, K., & Anderson, C. W. (2015). Data journalism in the United States: Beyond the "usual suspects." *Journalism Studies, 16*(4), 467–481.

Finkel, E. J., Bail, C. A., Cikara, M., Ditto, P. H., Iyengar, S., Klar, S., Mason, L., McGratah, M. C., Nyhan, B., Rand, D. G., Skita, L. J., Tucker, J. A. Van Bavel, J. J., Wang, C. S., & Druckman, J. N. (2020). "Political sectarianism in America." *Science, 370*(6516), 533–536.

Flaxman, S., Goel, S., & Rao, J. M. (2016). Filter bubbles, echo chambers, and online news consumption. *Public Opinion Quarterly, 80*(S1), 298–320.

Fox, J. R., Koloen, G., & Sahin, V. (2007). No joke: A comparison of substance in the Daily Show with presidential election campaign. *Journal of Broadcasting & Electronic Media, 51*(2), 213–227.

Frère, M.-S. (2010). *The media and elections in post-conflict Central African countries.* Paper presented at the Conference on Election Processes, Liberation Movements and Democratic Change in Africa, Maputo.

Friedman, B. G., & Richardson, J. D. (2008). "A national disgrace": Newspaper coverage of the 1963 Birmingham campaign in the South and beyond. *Journalism History, 33*(4), 224–232.

Frosh, P., & Wolfsfeld, G. (2007). ImagiNation: News discourse, nationhood and civil society. *Media Culture & Society, 29*(1), 105–129.

Gabler, N. (2016). Donald Trump, the emperor of social media. Moyers on Democracy. Retrieved from: https://billmoyers.com/story/donald-trump-the-emperor-of-social-media/.

Gabriel, S., Paravati, E., Green, M. C., & Flomsbee, J. (2018). From *Apprentice* to president: The role of parasocial connection in the election of Donald Trump. *Social Psychological and Personality Science, 9*(3), 299–307.

Gallagher, M. E., & Hanson, J. K. (2015). Power tool or dull blade? Selectorate theory for autocracies. *Annual Review of Political Science, 18*(1), 367–385.

Gallagher, R. J., Reagan, A. J., Danforth, C. M., & Dodds, P. S. (2018). Divergent discourse between protests and counter-protests: #BlackLivesMatter and #AllLivesMatter. *PloS One, 13*(4), e0195644.

Galnoor, I. (1982). *Steering the polity: Communication and politics in Israel.* Thousand Oaks, CA: Sage Publications.

Gamson, W. A., & Modigliani, A. (1989). Media discourse and public opinion on nuclear power: A constructionist approach. *American Journal of Sociology, 95*(1), 1–37.

Gandhi, J., & Przeworski, A. (2007). Authoritarian institutions and the survival of autocrats. *Comparative Political Studies, 40*(11), 1279–1301.

Garrett, R. K. (2009). Echo chambers online?: Politically motivated selective exposure among Internet news users. *Journal of Computer-Mediated Communication, 14*(2), 265–285.

Gitlin, T. (1980). *The whole world is watching: Mass media and making and unmaking of the new left.* Berkeley: University of California Press.

Godsey, M. A., & Pulley, T. (2003). The innocence revolution and our evolving standards of decency in death penalty jurisprudence. *University of Dayton Law Review, 29*, 265.

Gomez, E. T. (2012). Monetizing politics: Financing parties and elections in Malaysia. *Modern Asian Studies, 46*(5), 1370–1397.

Green-Pedersen, C., Mortensen, P. B., & Thesen, G. (2017). The incumbency bonus revisited: Causes and consequences of media dominance. *British Journal of Political Science, 47*(1), 131–148.

Greer, C. (2005). Delivering death: Capital punishment, botched executions and the American news media (pp. 84–104). In P. Mason (Ed.), *Captured by the Media.* New York: Routledge.

Griffin, R. A. (2017). The "morning/mourning" after: When becoming president trumps being a sexual predator. *Women's Studies in Communication, 40*(2), 140–144.

Groeling, T., & Baum, M. A. (2008). Crossing the water's edge: Elite rhetoric, media coverage, and the rally-round-the-flag phenomenon. *The Journal of Politics, 70*(4), 1065–1085.

Grynbaum, M. M., & Sullivan, E. (2019). Trump attacks the *Times*, in a week of unease for the American press. *New York Times.* Retrieved from https://www.nytimes.com/2019/02/20/us/politics/new-york-times-trump.html.

Guillén, M. F., & Suárez, S. L. (2005). Explaining the global digital divide: Economic, political and sociological drivers of cross-national Internet use. *Social Forces, 84*(2), 681–708.

Gurnow, M. (2014). *The Edward Snowden affair: Exposing the politics and media behind the NSA scandal.* Indianapolis, IN: Blue River Press.

Habermas, J. (1996a). *Between facts and norms: Contributions to a discourse theory of law and democracy* (W. Rehg, Trans.). Cambridge, MA: MIT Press.

Habermas, J. (1996b). *Three normative models of democracy.* In S. Benhabib (Ed.), *Democracy and difference: Contesting the boundaries of the political* (pp. 21–30). Princeton, NJ: Princeton University Press.

Hague, R., Harrop, M., & Breslin, S. (2001). *Comparative politics and government: An introduction*: New York: Palgrave Foundations.

Hallin, D. C. (1989). *The uncensored war: The media and Vietnam.* Berkeley: University of California Press.

Hallin, D. C., & Mancini, P. (2004). *Comparing media systems. Three models of media and politics.* New York: Cambridge University Press.

Hamilton, James T. (2004). *All the news that's fit to sell: How the market transforms information into news.* Princeton, NJ: Princeton University Press.

Hamilton, J. T. (2007). News that sells: Media competition and news content. *Japanese Journal of Political Science, 8*(1), 7–42.

Hanitzsch, T. (2007). Deconstructing journalism culture: Towards a universal theory. *Communication Theory, 17*(4), 367–385.

Hanitzsch, T., Hanusch, F., & Lauerer, C. (2016). Setting the agenda, influencing public opinion, and advocating for social change: Determinants of journalistic interventionism in 21 countries. *Journalism Studies, 17*(1), 1–20.

Hanitzsch, T., Hanusch, F., Mellado, C., Anikina, M., Berganza, R., Cangoz, I., ... Karadjov, C. D. (2011). Mapping journalism cultures across nations: A comparative study of 18 countries. *Journalism Studies, 12*(3), 273–293.

Hanitzsch, T., & Mellado, C. (2011). What shapes the news around the world? How journalists in eighteen countries perceive influences on their work. *The International Journal of Press/Politics, 16*(3), 404–426.

Harcup, T., & O'Neill, D. (2001). What is news? Galtung and Ruge revisited. *Journalism Studies, 2*(2), 261–280.

Harp, D. (2018). Misogyny in the 2016 US presidential election. In J. R. Vickery & T. Everbach (Eds.), *Mediating misogyny: Gender, technology, and harassment* (pp. 189–207). New York: Springer.

Hayat, T., & Samuel-Azran, T. (2017). "You too, Second Screeners?" Second screeners' echo chambers during the 2016 US elections primaries. *Journal of Broadcasting & Electronic Media, 61*(2), 291–308.

Hayes, D., & Guardino, M. (2013). *Influence from abroad: Foreign voices, the media, and U.S. public opinion.* New York: Cambridge University Press.

Held, D. (2006). *Models of democracy* (3rd ed.). Cambridge: Polity Press.

Henrich, J., Heine, S. J., & Norenzayan, A. (2010). The weirdest people in the world? *Behavioral and Brain Sciences, 33*(2–3):61–83.

Hindman, M. (2008). *The myth of digital democracy.* Princeton, NJ: Princeton University Press.

Hindman, M. (2018). *The Internet trap: How the digital economy builds monopolies and undermines democracy.* Princeton, NJ: Princeton University Press.

Holsti, O. R. (2011). *American public opinion on the Iraq War.* Ann Arbor: University of Michigan Press.

Hopmann, D. N., de Vreese, C. H., & Albæk, E. (2011). Incumbency bonus in election news coverage explained: The logics of political power and the media market. *Journal of Communication, 61*(2), 264–282.

Hopmann, D. N., Van Aelst, P., & Legnante, G. (2012). Political balance in the news: A review of concepts, operationalizations and key findings. *Journalism, 13*(2), 240–257.

Horten, G. (2011). The mediatization of war: A comparison of the American and German media coverage of the Vietnam and Iraq Wars. *American Journalism, 28*(4), 29–53.

Hoskins, C., McFadyen, S., & Finn, A. (2004). *Media economics: Applying economics to new and traditional media.* Thousand Oaks, CA: Sage.

Houston, B. (2010). The future of investigative journalism. *Daedalus, 139*(2), 45–56.

Howard, P. N., & and Hussain M. M. (2011). The role of digital media. *Journal of Democracy, 22*(3), 35–48.

Houston, B. (2010). The future of investigative journalism. *Daedalus, 139*(2), 45–56.

Hughes, S., Mellado, C., Arroyave, J., Benitez, J. L., de Beer, A., Garcés, M., . . . & Márquez-Ramírez, M. (2017). Expanding influences research to insecure democracies: How violence, public insecurity, economic inequality and uneven democratic performance shape journalists' perceived work environments. *Journalism Studies, 18*(5), 645–665.

Humprecht, E., Esser, F., & Van Aelst, P. (2020). Resilience to online disinformation: A framework for cross-national comparative research. *The International Journal of Press/Politics, 25*(3), 493–516.

Inglehart, R., & Welzel, C. (2005). *Modernization, cultural change, and democracy: The human development sequence.* New York: Cambridge University Press.

Iyengar, S. (2018). *Media politics: A citizen's guide* (4th ed.). New York: W. W. Norton.

Iyengar, S., Curran, J., Lund, A. B., Salovaara-Moring, I., Hahn, K. S., & Coen, S. (2010). Cross-national versus individual-level differences in political information: A media systems perspective. *Journal of Elections, Public Opinion & Parties, 20*(3), 291–309.

Iyengar, S., & Kinder, D. R. (1988). *News that matters: Television and American opinion.* Chicago: University of Chicago Press.

Iyengar, S., & Simon, A. (1993). News coverage of the Gulf crisis and public opinion: A study of agenda-setting, priming, and framing. *Communication Research, 20*(3), 365–383.

Jackman, S. (2005). Pooling the polls over an election campaign. *Australian Journal of Political Science, 40*(4), 499–517.

Jackson, D. (2011). Strategic media, cynical public? Examining the contingent effects of strategic news frames on political cynicism in the United Kingdom. *The International Journal of Press/Politics, 16*(1), 75–101.

Jackson, G. (2013). Sovereignty, state. In G. Claeys (Ed.), *Encyclopedia of modern political thought* (pp. 761). Thousand Oaks, CA: Sage.

Jacobs, L. (1992). The recoil effect: Public opinion and policymaking in the U.S. and Britain. *Comparative Politics, 24,* 199–217.

Jacobs, L. R., & Shapiro, R. Y. (2000). *Politicians don't pander: Political manipulation and the loss of democratic responsiveness.* Chicago: University of Chicago Press.

James, J. (2011). Sharing mobile phones in developing countries: Implications for the digital divide. *Technological Forecasting and Social Change, 78*(4), 729–735.

James, P. (2017). *The German electoral system.* New York: Routledge.

Jamieson, K. H., & Cappella, J. N. (2008). *Echo chamber: Rush Limbaugh and the conservative media establishment.* New York: Oxford University Press.

Jasny, L., Waggle, J., & Fisher, D. R. (2015). An empirical examination of echo chambers in US climate policy networks. *Nature Climate Change, 5*(8), 782–786.

Jungherr, A. (2016). Twitter use in election campaigns: A systematic literature review. *Journal of Information Technology & Politics, 13*(1), 72–91.

Kaase, M. (1994). Is there personalization in politics? Candidates and voting behavior in Germany. *International Political Science Review/Revue internationale de science politique, 15*(3), 211–230.

Kaid, L. L. (2004). Political advertising. In L. Kaid (Ed.), *Handbook of political communication research* (pp. 173–220). New York: Routledge.

Kalb, M. (2018). *Enemy of the people: Trump's war on the press, the new McCarthyism, and the threat to American democracy.* Washington, DC: Brookings Institution Press.

Karan, K., Gimeno, J. D., & Tandoc, E., Jr. (2009). The internet and mobile technologies in election campaigns: The GABRIELA Women's Party during the 2007 Philippine elections. *Journal of Information Technology & Politics, 6*(3–4), 326–339.

Katz, E. (1996). And deliver us from segmentation. *Annals of the American Academy of Political and Social Science, 546*(July), 22–33.

Katz, J. E., & Mays, K. K. (2019). *Journalism and truth in an age of social media.* New York: Oxford University Press.

King, G., Pan, J., & Roberts, M. (2013). How censorship in China allows government criticism but silences collective expression. *The American Political Science Review, 107*(2), 326–343.

King, G., Pan, J., & Roberts, M. E. (2014). Reverse-engineering censorship in China: Randomized experimentation and participant observation. *Science, 345*(6199), 1–10.

King, P. (1991). Sovereignty. In D. Miller, J. Coleman, W. Connolly, & A. Ryan (Eds.), *Blackwell encyclopedia of political thought* (pp. 492–495). Cambridge, MA: Basil Blackwell.

Kiriya, I., & Degtereva, E. (2010). Russian TV market: Between state supervision, commercial logic and simulacrum of public service. *Central European Journal of Communication, 3*(4), 37–51.

Lavrakas, P. J., Traugott, M., & Miller, P. V. (2019). *Presidential polls and the news media.* New York: Routledge.

Lawrence, R. G. (2000). *The politics of force: Media and the construction of police brutality.* Berkeley: University of California Press.

Lederman, J. (2019). *Battle lines: The American media and the Intifada.* New York: Routledge.

Leigh, D., & Harding, L. (2011). *Wikileaks: Inside Julian Assange's war on secrecy.* Jackson, TN: Public Affairs.

Leuprecht, C., Hataley, T., Moskalenko, S., & McCauley, C. (2009). Winning the battle but losing the war? Narrative and counter-narratives strategy. *Perspectives on Terrorism, 3*(2), 25–35.

Levitsky, S., & Way, L. A. (2002). Elections without democracy: The rise of competitive authoritarianism. *Journal of Democracy, 13*(2), 51–65. doi:10.1353/jod.2002.0026.

Levitsky, S., & Way, L. A. (2010). *Competitive authoritarianism: Hybrid regimes after the Cold War.* New York: Cambridge University Press.

Levitt, J. (2010). Confronting the impact of Citizens United. *Yale Law & Policy Review, 29,* 217–234.

Lewis, J. (2004). Television, public opinion and the war in Iraq: The case of Britain. *International Journal of Public Opinion Research, 16*(3), 295–310.

Lewis, S. C. (2015). *Journalism in an era of big data: Cases, concepts, and critiques.* New York: Taylor & Francis.

Ley, B. L., Jankowski, N., & Brewer, P. R. (2012). Investigating CSI: Portrayals of DNA testing on a forensic crime show and their potential effects. *Public Understanding of Science, 21*(1), 51–67.

Li, D. (2004). Echoes of violence: Considerations on radio and genocide in Rwanda. *Journal of Genocide Research, 6*(1), 9–27.

Lipschultz, J. H., & Hilt, M. L. (1999). Mass media and the death penalty: Social construction of three Nebraska executions. *Journal of Broadcasting & Electronic Media, 43*(2), 236–253.

Lissak, M., & Horowitz, D. (1989). *Trouble in utopia.* Albany: State University of New York Press.

Livingston, S., & Bennett, W. L. (2003). Gatekeeping, indexing, and live-event news: Is technology altering the construction of news? *Political Communication*, *20*(4), 363–380.

Lock, A., & Strong, T. (2010). *Social constructionism: Sources and stirrings in theory and practice*. New York: Cambridge University Press.

Kellner, D. (2004). *Bring 'em on: Media and politics in the Iraq War*. Lanham, MD: Rowman & Littlefield.

Kellow, C. L., & Steeves, H. L. (1998). The role of radio in the Rwandan genocide. *Journal of Communication*, *48*(3), 107–128.

King, G., Pan, J., & Roberts, M. E. (2014). Reverse-engineering censorship in China: Randomized experimentation and participant observation. *Science*, *345*(6199).

Klapper, J. T. (1960). *The effects of mass communication*. New York: Free Press.

Knightley, P. (2004). *The first casualty: The war correspondent as hero and myth-maker from the Crimea to Kosovo*. Baltimore, MD: Johns Hopkins University Press.

Kriesi, H. (2012). Personalization of national election campaigns. *Party Politics*, *18*(6), 825–844.

Kull, S., Ramsay, C., & Lewis, E. (2003). Misperceptions, the media, and the Iraq War. *Political Science Quarterly*, *118*(4), 569–598.

Lankov, A. (2014). *The real North Korea: Life and politics in the failed Stalinist utopia*. Oxford: Oxford University Press.

Lee, T. (2002). *Mobilizing public opinion: Black insurgency and racial attitudes in the civil rights era*. Chicago: University of Chicago Press.

Lei, Y.-W. (2017). *The contentious public sphere: Law, media, and authoritarian rule in China*. Princeton, NJ: Princeton University Press.

Li, D. (2004). Echoes of violence: Considerations on radio and genocide in Rwanda. *Journal of Genocide Research*, *6*(1), 9–27.

Lind, R. A., & Salo, C. (2002). The framing of feminists and feminism in news and public affairs programs in US electronic media. *Journal of Communication*, *52*(1), 211–228.

Lippmann, W. (1922). *Public opinion*. New York: Free Press.

Lutton, L. (2000). The end of executions? *In These Times*. Retrieved https://inthesetimes.com/issue/24/24/lutton2424.html.

Lynch, M. (2010). *Voices of the new Arab public: Iraq, Al-Jazeera, and Middle East politics today*. New York: Columbia University Press.

MacArthur, J. R. (2004). *Second front: Censorship and propaganda in the 1991 Gulf War*. Oakland: University of California Press.

Mamdani, M. (2020). *When victims become killers: Colonialism, nativism, and the genocide in Rwanda*. Princeton, NJ: Princeton University Press.

Mancini, P., & Hallin, D. C. (2012). Some caveats about comparative research in media studies. In H. A. Semetko & M. Scammell (Eds.), *Sage handbook of political communication* (pp. 509–517). Thousand Oaks, CA: Sage.

Mansbridge, J. (2009). A "selection model" of political representation. *Journal of Political Philosophy*, *17*(4), 369–398.

Mansbridge, J. (2011). Clarifying the concept of representation. *The American Political Science Review*, *105*(3), 621–630.

Mansbridge, J. J. (2003). Rethinking representation. *American Political Science Review*, *97*(4), 515–528.

Margolick, D. (2011). *Elizabeth and Hazel*. New Haven, CT: Yale University Press.

Matthes, J. (2012). Framing politics: An integrative approach. *American Behavioral Scientist*, *56*(3), 247–259.

Mazzoleni, G. (2008). Mediatization of politics. In W. Donsbagh (Ed.), *The international encyclopedia of communication* (pp. 1–5). New York: Wiley-Blackwell.

Mazzoleni, G., & Schulz, W. (1999). "Mediatization" of politics: A challenge for democracy? *Political Communication, 16*(3), 247–261.

McCarty, N., Poole, K. T., & Rosenthal, H. (2013). *Political bubbles: Financial crises and the failure of American democracy*. Princeton, NJ: Princeton University Press.

McCombs, M. E., & Shaw, D. L. (1972). The agenda-setting function of mass media. *Public Opinion Quarterly, 36*(2), 176–187.

McCombs, M. E., Shaw, D. L., & Weaver, D. H. (2014). New directions in agenda-setting theory and research. *Mass Communication and Society, 17*(6), 781–802.

McGhee, F. (2014). Journalistic news framing of white mainstream media during the civil rights movement: A content analysis of the Montgomery bus boycott. *Media Watch, 5*(3), 282–294.

McLuhan, M. (1964). *The medium is the message*: Cambridge, MA: MIT Press.

Mellado, C., Mothes, C., Hallin, D. C., Humanes, M. L., Lauber, M., Mick, J., Silke, H., Sparks, C., Amado, A., Davydov, S., & Oliver, D. (2020). Investigating the gap between newspaper journalists' role conceptions and role performance in nine European, Asian, and Latin American countries. *The International Journal of Press/Politics, 25*(4), 552–75.

Meyen, M., Thieroff, M., & Strenger, S. (2014). Mass media logic and the mediatization of politics. *Journalism Studies, 15*(3), 271–288.

Meyer, C. O., Sangar, E., & Michaels, E. (2017). How do non-governmental organizations influence media coverage of conflict? The case of the Syrian conflict, 2011–2014. *Media, War & Conflict, 11*(1): 149–171.

Miles, H. (2010). *Al Jazeera: How Arab TV news challenged the world*: New York: Hachette.

Mitchell, G. (2000). *Making peace: Updated with a new preface*. Oakland: University of California Press.

Morozov, E. (2011). *The net delusion: The dark side of internet freedom*. Jackson, TN: Public Affairs.

Mudde, C. (2004). The populist zeitgeist. *Government and Opposition, 39*(4), 541–563.

Mudde, C., & Kaltwasser, C. R. (2017). *Populism: A very short introduction*. New York: Oxford University Press.

Müller, J. W. (2017). *What is populism?* London: Penguin.

Müller, K., & Schwarz, C. (2018). Fanning the flames of hate: Social media and hate crime. *Journal of the European Economic Association, 19*(4), 2137–2167.

Mutz, D. C. (2006). *Hearing the other side: Deliberative versus participatory democracy*. New York: Cambridge University Press.

Mutz, D. C. (2008). Is deliberative democracy a falsifiable theory? *Annual Review of Political Science, 11*(1), 521–538.

Napoli, P. M. (2003). *Audience economics: Media institutions and the audience marketplace*. New York: Columbia University Press.

Nasaw, D. (2001). *The chief: The life of William Randolph Hearst*. Boston, MA: Mariner Books.

Neuman, R. W., Guggenheim, L., Mo Jang, S., & Bae, S. Y. (2014). The dynamics of public attention: Agenda-setting theory meets big data. *Journal of Communication, 64*(2), 193–214.

Nir, L. (2011). Motivated reasoning and public opinion perception. *Public Opinion Quarterly, 75*, 504–532.

Nir, L. (2012). Cross-national differences in political discussion: Can political systems narrow deliberation gaps? *Journal of Communication, 62*(3), 553–570.

Nisbet, E. C., & Myers, T. A. (2010). Challenging the state: Transnational TV and political identity in the Middle East. *Political Communication, 27*(4), 347–366.

Nisbet, E. C., & Stoycheff, E. (2013). Let the people speak: A multilevel model of supply and demand for press freedom. *Communication Research, 40*(5), 720–741.

Niven, D. (2002). *Tilt?: The search for media bias.* Westport, CT: Praeger.

Norris, P. (2011). *Democratic deficit: Critical citizens revisited.* Cambridge, UK: Cambridge University Press.

Norris, P., & Van Es, A. A. (2016). *Checkbook elections?: Political finance in comparative perspective.* New York: Oxford University Press.

Obermayer, B., & Obermaier, F. (2016). *The Panama papers: Breaking the story of how the rich and powerful hide their money.* London: Oneworld Publications.

Ott, B. L. (2017). The age of Twitter: Donald J. Trump and the politics of debasement. *Critical studies in media communication, 34*(1), 59–68.

Patterson, J. T. (2002). *Brown v. Board of Education: A civil rights milestone and its troubled legacy.* New York: Oxford University Press.

Patterson, T. E. (2017). *News coverage of Donald Trump's first 100 days.* Cambridge, MA: Shorenstein Center.

Persily, N. (2017). The 2016 US election: Can democracy survive the internet? *Journal of Democracy, 28*(2), 63–76.

Pfetch, B. (2004). From political culture to political communications culture: A theoretical approach to comparative analysis. In F. Esser & B. Pfetsch (Eds.), *Comparing political communication: Theories, cases, and challenges* (pp. 344–366). New York: Cambridge University Press.

Pfetch, B., & Esser, F. (2012). Comparing political communication. In F. Esser & T. Hanitzsch (Eds.), *The handbook of comparative communication research* (pp. 25–47). New York: Routledge.

Pfetch, B., Mayerhöffer, E., & Moring, T. (2014). National or professional? Types of political communication culture across Europe. In B. Pfetsch (Ed.), *Political communication cultures in Europe: Attitudes of political actors and journalists in nine countries* (pp. 76–102). New York: Palgrave Macmillan.

Pfetch, B. & Voltmer, K. (2012). Negotiating control: Political communication cultures in Bulgaria and Poland. *International Journal of Press/Politics, 17*(4), 388–406.

Picard, R. G. (1989). *Media economics: Concepts and issues.* Thousand Oaks, CA: Sage Publications.

Pierskalla, J. H., & Hollenbach, F. M. (2013). Technology and collective action: The effect of cell phone coverage on political violence in Africa. *American Political Science Review, 107*(02), 207–224.

Pitkin, H. (1967). *The concept of representation.* Berkeley: University of California Press.

Poch, R., & Martin, B. (2015). Effects of intrinsic and extrinsic motivation on user-generated content. *Journal of Strategic Marketing, 23*(4), 305–317.

Prior, M. (2006). The incumbent in the living room: The rise of television and the incumbency advantage in US House elections. *The Journal of Politics, 68*(3), 657–673.

Prior, M. (2007). *Post-broadcast democracy: How media choice increases inequality in political involvement and polarizes elections.* New York: Cambridge University Press.

Prior, M. (2013). Media and political polarization. *Annual Review of Political Science, 16*, 101–127.

Punathambekar, A. (2015). Satire, elections, and democratic politics in digital India. *Television & NewMedia, 16*(4), 394–400.

Purdum, T. S. (2014). *An idea whose time has come: Two presidents, two parties, and the battle for the Civil Rights Act of 1964*. New York: Henry Holt.

Rahat, G., & Hazan, R. Y. (2001). Candidate selection methods: An analytical framework. *Party Politics, 7*(3), 297–322.

Rahat, G., & Kenig, O. (2018). *From party politics to personalized politics? Party change and political personalization in democracies*. Oxford: Oxford University Press.

Rahat, G., & Sheafer, T. (2007). The personalization(s) of politics: Israel, 1949–2003. *Political Communication, 24*(1), 65–80.

Rapaport, A. (2010). *The IDF and the lessons of the second Lebanon War*. Tel Aviv: Begin-Sadat Center for Strategic Studies, Bar-Ilan University.

Rehfeld, A. (2006). Towards a general theory of political representation. *The Journal of Politics, 68*(1), 1–21.

Rehfeld, A. (2009). Representation rethought: On trustees, delegates, and gyroscopes in the study of political representation and democracy. *The American Political Science Review, 103*(2), 214–230.

Reinemann, C., Matthes, J., & Sheafer, T. (2017). Citizens and populist political communication: Cross-national findings and perspectives. In T. Aalberg, F. Esser, C. Reinemann, J. Strömbäck & C. H. de Vreese (Eds.), *Populist political communication in Europe* (pp. 381–94). New York: Routledge.

Reinemann, C., Scherr, S., Stanyer, J., with Aalberg, T., Aelst, P. V., Berganza, R., Esser, r., Hopmann, D. N., Legnante, , N. H. G., Matthes, J., Papathanassopoulos, S., Salgado, S., Sheafer, T., Strömbäck, J., & Vreese, C. de (2017). Cross-conceptual architecture of news. In C. de Vreese, F. Esser, & D. N. Hopmann (Eds.), *Comparing political journalism* (pp. 150–167). New York: Routledge.

Reuter, O. J., & Szakonyi, D. (2015). Online social media and political awareness in authoritarian regimes. *British Journal of Political Science, 45*(1), 29–51.

Roberts, G., & Klibanoff, H. (2008). *The race beat: The press, the civil rights struggle, and the awakening of a nation*. New York: Vintage.

Roberts, M. (2018). *Censored: Distraction and diversion inside China's great firewall*. Princeton, NJ: Princeton University Press.

Robinson, J. P., and Martin, S. (2009). Of time and television. *The Annals of the American Academy of Political and Social Science, 625*(1), 74–86.

Rosen, J. (2006). The people formerly known as the audience. *PressThink*, accessed December 19, 2021. http://archive.pressthink.org/2006/06/27/ppl_frmr.html.

Rothbart, D., & Bartlett, T. (2008). *Rwandan radio broadcasts and Hutu/Tutsi positioning Global conflict resolution through positioning analysis*. New York: Springer.

Sahoo, N. & Tiwari N. (2019). Financing elections in India: A scrutiny of corporate donation. Observer Research Foundation: New Deli, India. Retrieved from https://www.orfonline.org/expert-speak/financing-elections-india-scrutiny-corporate-donation-49750/.

Samuel-Azran, T. (2010). *Al-Jazeera and US war coverage*. San Antonio, TX: Peter Lang.

Samuel-Azran, T., Yarchi, M., & Wolfsfeld, G. (2015). Equalization versus normalization: Facebook and the 2013 Israeli elections. *Social Media + Society, 1*(2), 1–9.

Schemer, C., Wirth, W., & Matthes, J. (2012). Value resonance and value framing effects on voting intentions in direct-democratic campaigns. *American Behavioral Scientist, 56*(3), 334–352.

Schneier, B. (2011). *Secrets and lies: Digital security in a networked world.* Hoboken, NJ: John Wiley & Sons.

Schuck, A., Boomgaarden, H., & de Vreese, C. (2013). Cynics all around? The impact of election news on political cynicism in comparative perspective. *Journal of Communication, 63,* 287–311.

Scotto, T. J., Clarke, H. D., Kornberg, A., Reifler, J., Sanders, D., Stewart, M. C., & Whiteley, P. (2010). The dynamic political economy of support for Barack Obama during the 2008 presidential election campaign. *Electoral Studies, 29*(4), 545–556.

Sellers, C., & Terrell, R. L. (2018). *The river of no return: The autobiography of a Black militant and the life and death of SNCC.* New York: William Morrow Paperbacks.

Sheafer, T. (2001). Charismatic skill and media legitimacy: An actor-centered approach to understanding the political communication competition. *Communication Research, 28*(6), 711–736.

Sheafer, T., & Dvir-Gvirsman, S. (2010). The spoiler effect: Framing attitudes and expectations toward peace. *Journal of Peace Research, 47*(2), 205–215.

Sheafer, T., Shenhav, S., & Balmas, M. (2015). Politicians as communicator. In C. Reinemann (Ed.), *Political Communication* (pp. 211–230). Berlin: deGruyter Mouton.

Sheafer, T., Shenhav, S., Takens, J., & van Atteveldt, W. (2014). Relative political and value proximity in mediated public diplomacy: The effect of state-level homophily on international frame building. *Political Communication, 31*(1), 149–167.

Sheafer, T., & Wolfsfeld, G. (2009). Party systems and oppositional voices in the news media. *International Journal of Press/Politics, 14*(2), 146–165.

Sheafer, T., & Wolfsfeld, G. (2004). Production assests, news opportunities, and publicity for legislators: A study of Irsraeli Knesset members. *Legislative Studies Quarterly, 29*(4), 611–630.

Shu, K., Wang, S., & Liu, H. (2018). *Understanding user profiles on social media for fake news detection.* Paper presented at the 2018 IEEE Conference on Multimedia Information Processing and Retrieval (MIPR).

Sifry, M. L. (2011). *WikiLeaks and the age of transparency.* New York: OR Books.

Singer, M. (2011). When do voters actually think "It's the economy"? Evidence from the 2008 presidential campaign. *Electoral Studies, 30*(4), 621–632.

Slothuus, R., & De Vreese, C. H. (2010). Political parties, motivated reasoning, and issue framing effects. *The Journal of Politics, 72*(3), 630–645.

Smyth, T. N., & Best, M. L. (2013). *Tweet to trust: Social media and elections in West Africa.* Paper presented at the Proceedings of the Sixth International Conference on Information and Communication Technologies and Development. December 7, 2013, https://dl.acm.org/doi/abs/10.1145/2516604.2516617

Soroka, S., Andrews, B., Toril, A. Shanto, I., Curran, J., Coen, S. Saahsi, K., & Jones, P. (2013). Auntie knows best? Public broadcasters and current affairs knowledge. *British Journal of Political Science, 43*(4), 719–739.

Sreberny, A., & Khiabany, G. (2010). *Blogistan: The internet and politics in Iran.* New York: Bloomsbury.

Stockmann, D. (2013). *Media commercialization and authoritarian rule in China.* New York: Cambridge University Press.

Stockmann, D., & Gallagher, M. E. (2011). Remote control: How the media sustain authoritarian rule in China. *Comparative Political Studies, 44*(4), 436–467.

Strömbäck, J. (2005). In search of a standard: Four models of democracy and their normative implications for journalism. *Journalism Studies, 6*(3), 331–345.

Strömbäck, J., and Kaid, L. L. (2008). A framework for comparing election news coverage around the world. In J. Strömbäck and L. L. Kaid (Eds.), *The handbook of election news coverage around the world* (pp. 1–20). New York: Routledge.

Strömbäck, J., & Kaid, L. L. (2008). *The handbook of election news coverage around the world*. New York: Routledge.

Strömberg, D. (2004). Mass media competition, political competition, and public policy. *The Review of Economic Studies, 71*(1), 265–284.

Strömberg, J., & Esser, F. (2014). Mediatization and politics: Towards a theoretical framework. In F. Esser & J. Strömback (Eds.), *Mediatization of politics: Understanding the transformation of Western democracies* (pp. 3–28). New York: Palgrave McMillan.

Stroud, N. J. (2017). Attention as a valuable resource. *Political Communication, 34*(3), 479–489.

Su, Z., & Meng, T. (2016). Selective responsiveness: Online public demands and government responsiveness in authoritarian China. *Social Science Research, 59*, 52–67.

Sullivan, P. (2009). *Lift every voice: The NAACP and the making of the civil rights movement*. New York: The New Press.

Tandoc, E. C., Jr., Lim, Z. W., & Ling, R. (2018). Defining "fake news": A typology of scholarly definitions. *Digital Journalism, 6*(2), 137–153.

Tang, W., & Iyengar, S. (2011). The emerging media system in China: Implications for regime change. *Political Communication, 28*(3), 263–267.

Tak, J. (2006). Political advertising in Japan, South Korea, and Taiwan. In L.L. Kaid and C. Holtz-Bacha (Eds.), *The Sage handbook of political advertising* (pp. 285–305). Thousand Oaks, CA: Sage.

Taylor, K. Y. (2016). *From #BlackLivesMatter to black liberation*. Chicago: Haymarket Books.

Tesler, M. (2015). Priming predispositions and changing policy positions: An account of when mass opinion is primed or changed. *American Journal of Political Science, 59*(4), 806–824.

Tresch, A. (2009). Politicians in the media: Determinants of legislators' presence and prominence in Swiss newspapers. *The International Journal of Press/Politics, 14*(1), 67–90.

Tsfati Y., & Nir, L. (2017). Framing and argumentation: Two pathways from selective exposure to political polarization. *International Journal of Communication, 11*, 301–322.

Tumber, H., & Palmer, J. (2004). *Media at war: The Iraq crisis*. Thousand Oaks, CA: Sage.

Unger, A. L. (1965). The public opinion reports of the Nazi Party. *Public Opinion Quarterly, 29*(4), 565–582.

Urbinati, N., & Warren, M. E. (2008). The concept of representation in contemporary democratic theory. *Annual Review of Political Science, 11*(1), 387–412.

Vaccari, C. (2013). *Digital politics in Western democracies: A comparative study*. Baltimore, MD: John Hopkins University Press.

Van Aelst, P., Strömbäck, J., Aalberg, T., Esser, F., de Vreese, C., Matthes, J., . . . Stanyer, J. (2017). Political communication in a high-choice media environment: A challenge for democracy? *Annals of the International Communication Association, 41*(1), 3–27.

Van Dijk, J. A. (2017). Digital divide: Impact of access. In P. Rössler (Ed.), *The international encyclopedia of media effects* (pp. 1–11). New York: John Wiley & Sons.

Van Dijk, J. A. (2020). *The network society*. Thousand Oaks, CA: Sage.

Van Erkel, P. F., Van Aelst, P., & Thijssen, P. (2018). Does media attention lead to personal electoral success? Differences in long and short campaign media effects for top and ordinary political candidates. *Acta Politica, 55*(2), 1–19.

Vliegenthart, R., & Walgrave, S. (2011a). Content matters: The dynamics of parliamentary questioning in Belgium and Denmark. *Comparative Political Studies, 44*(8), 1031–1059.

Vliegenthart, R., & Walgrave, S. (2011b). When the media matter for politics: Partisan moderators of the mass media's agenda-setting influence on parliament in Belgium. *Party Politics, 17*(3), 321–342.

Vliegenthart, R., Walgrave, S., Baumgartner, F. R., Bevan, S., Breunig, C., Brouard, S., ... & Palau, A. M. (2016). Do the media set the parliamentary agenda? A comparative study in seven countries. *European Journal of Political Research, 55*(2), 283–301.

Vos, D., & Van Aelst, P. (2017). Does the political system determine media visibility of politicians? A comparative analysis of political functions in the news in sixteen countries. *Political Communication, 35*(3), 1–22.

Walgrave, S., Boydstun, A. E., Vliegenthart, R., & Hardy, A. (2017). The nonlinear effect of information on political attention: media storms and US congressional hearings. *Political Communication, 34*(4), 548–570.

Walgrave, S., Soroka, S., & Nuytemans, M. (2008). The mass media's political agenda-setting power: A longitudinal analysis of media, parliament, and government in Belgium (1993 to 2000). *Comparative Political Studies, 41*(6), 814–836.

Wasserman, H. (2011). Mobile phones, popular media, and everyday African democracy: Transmissions and transgressions. *Popular Communication, 9*(2), 146–158.

Watts, D. J., & Rothschild, D. M. (2017). Don't blame the election on fake news: Blame it on the media. *Columbia Journalism Review, 5.* Retrieved from https://www.cjr.org/analysis/fake-news-media-election-trump.php.

Weaver, D., & Elliott, S. N. (1985). Who sets the agenda for the media? A study of local agenda-building. *Journalism Quarterly, 62*(1), 87–94.

Wessler, H. (2018). *Habermas and the media.* London: Polity Press.

Whyte, K. (2009). *The uncrowned king: The sensational rise of William Randolph Hearst.* New York: Vintage.

Williams, B. A., & Delli Carpini, M. X. (2011). *After broadcast news: Media regimes, democracy, and the new information environment.* New York: Cambridge University Press.

Williams, C. (2011). How Egypt shut down the internet. *The Telegraph,* January 11, 2011. Retrieved from https://www.telegraph.co.uk/news/worldnews/africaandindianocean/egypt/8288163/How-Egypt-shut-down-the-internet.html.

Winter, J. P., & Eyal, C. H. (1981). Agenda setting for the civil rights issue. *Public Opinion Quarterly, 45*(3), 376–383.

Wolfsfeld, G. (1997). *Media and political conflict: News from the Middle East.* Cambridge, UK: Cambridge University Press.

Wolfsfeld, G. (2004). *Media and the path to peace.* Cambridge, UK: Cambridge University Press.

Wolfsfeld, G. (2017). The role of the media in violent conflicts in the digital age: Israeli and Palestinian leaders' perceptions. *Media, War & Conflict, 11*(1), 107–124.

Wolfsfeld, G. (2022). *Making sense of media and politics: Five principles in political communication* (Second Edition). New York: Routledge.

Wolfsfeld, G., Segev, E., & Sheafer, T. (2013). Social media and the Arab Spring: Politics comes first. *International Journal of Press/Politics, 18*(2), 115–137.

Wolfsfeld, G., & Sheafer, T. (2006). Competing actors and the construction of political news: The contest over waves in Israel. *Political Communication, 23*(3), 333–354.

Wolfsfeld, G., & Tsfroni, L. (2018). Political leaders, media and violent conflict in the digital age. In R. Fröhlich (Ed.), *Media in war and armed conflict: The dynamics of conflict news production and dissemination* (pp. 218–242). London; New York: Routledge.

Woodward, B. (2005). *The secret man: The story of Watergate's Deep Throat.* New York: Simon & Schuster.

Woodward, B., & Bernstein, C. (2012). *All the President's men.* New York: Simon & Schuster.

Xenos, M. A., & Becker, A. B. (2009). Moments of Zen: Effects of The Daily Show on information seeking and political learning. *Political Communication, 26*(3), 317–332.

Yarchi, M., Wolfsfeld, G., Samuel-Azran, T., & Segev, E. (2016). Invest, engage, and win: Online election campaigns and their outcomes in an Israeli election. In M. Brown (Ed.), *Social media performance evaluation and success measurements* (pp. 225–248). Hershey, PA: IGI Global.

Zimmerman, W. (2014). *Ruling Russia: Authoritarianism from the Revolution to Putin.* Princeton, NJ: Princeton University Press.

Zoizner, A., Sheafer T., & Walgrave, S. (2017). How politicians' attitudes and goals moderate political agenda-setting by the media. *International Journal of Press/Politics, 22*(4), 431–449.

Index